The Wooster Group
and Its Traditions

P.I.E.-Peter Lang

Bruxelles · Bern · Berlin · Frankfurt am Main · New York · Oxford · Wien

Dramaturgies

Texts, Cultures and Performances

Johan Callens (ed.)

The Wooster Group
and Its Traditions

Dramaturgies
No.13

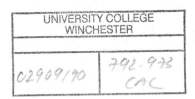
© P.I.E.-PETER LANG s.a.,
PRESSES INTERUNIVERSITAIRES EUROPÉENNES
Brussels, 2004
1 avenue Maurice, 1050 Brussels, Belgium
info@peterlang.com;   www.peterlang.net

Printed in Germany

ISSN 1376-3199
ISBN 90-5201-270-9
US ISBN 0-8204-6632-8
D/2004/5678/44

*CIP available from the British Library, GB
and the Library of Congress, USA.*

Bibliographic information published by "Die Deutsche Bibliothek"

"Die Deutsche Bibliothek" lists this publication in the "Deutsche Nationalbibliografie"; detailed bibliographic data is available in the Internet at <http://dnb.ddb.de>.

Table of Contents

Acknowledgements 9

List of Productions by the Wooster Group 11

Illustrations 13

Introduction. Of Rough Cuts, Voice Masks,
and Fugacious Bodies: The Wooster Group in Progress 45
Johan Callens

PART I. INSTITUTIONAL ATTEMPTS
AND COUNTER-ATTEMPTS

Obeying the Rules 63
David Savran

L.S.D. (Let's Say Deconstruction!): Narrating Emergence
in American Alternative Theatre History 71
Michael Vanden Heuvel

What Is This Dancing? The Pleasures of Performance
in the Wooster Group's Work 83
Greg Giesekam

Task and Vision Revisited: Two Conversations
with Willem Dafoe (1984/2002) 95
Philip Auslander

PART II. THE WORK

The Wooster Group: A Dictionary of Ideas 109
Bonnie Marranca

Theatre as an Allegory of Unreadability:
The Wooster Group's *The Road to Immortality Part Three,
Frank Dell's The Temptation of St. Antony* 129
Markus Wessendorf

Fugacity: Some Thoughts towards a New Naturalism in Recent Performance 141
Simon Jones

Brutus Jones 'n the Hood: The Wooster Group, the Provincetown Players, and *The Emperor Jones* (1993) 157
Roger Bechtel

Voice Masks: Subjectivity, America, and the Voice in the Theatre of the Wooster Group 167
Gerald Siegmund

South Pacific-North Atlantic: From Total War to Total Peace 179
Branislav Jakovljević

The Wooster Group's *House/Lights* 189
Ric Knowles

A Case of Belated Recognition: The Wooster Group in France 203
Frédéric Maurin

Framing the Fragments: The Wooster Group's Use of Technology 217
Jennifer Parker-Starbuck

PART III. SPIN-OFF

Double Take: Elevator Repair Service's *Highway to Tomorrow* and Euripides' *Bacchae* 231
Julie Bleha & Ehren Fordyce

The Builders Association: S/he Do the Police in Different Voices 247
Johan Callens

The Burden of Irony, the Onus of Cool: The Wooster Group's Influence on Cannon Company and Richard Maxwell 263
Daniel Mufson

Works Cited 275

Notes on Contributors 287

Acknowledgements

The essays in the present volume form a selection, in substantially different form, of contributions to the Brussels conference on the Wooster Group (Kaaitheater, 16-18 May 2002), of which Bonnie Marranca's "The Wooster Group, A Dictionary of Ideas" has been prepublished in *PAJ* 74 (2003): 1-18. Four additional essays cover areas, productions, or companies not dealt with at the time. Of these, Simon Jones's "Fugacity: Some Thoughts towards a New Naturalism in Recent Performance" makes available to a wider audience a shortened version of his contribution to a limited edition in box-form with artefacts, *Shattered Anatomies: Traces of the Body in Performance*, ed. Adrian Heathfield, Fiona Templeton, and Andrew Quick (Bristol: Arnolfini Live, 1997). Ric Knowles's essay on *House/Lights* is an excerpt of *Reading the Material Theatre* (Cambridge UP, 2004), reprinted with permission. Branislav Jakovljević's "South Pacific-North Atlantic: From Total War to Total Peace" has been reprinted with permission from *Theater* 31.1 (2001): 41-49. The organization of the Brussels conference and the publication of the present volume were generously supported by the Flemish Ministry of Education, the Fund for Scientific Research (Flanders), the Commission for Educational Exchange between the USA, Belgium and Luxembourg, and the Belgian Luxembourg American Studies Association. Sincere thanks go to the different photographers for granting permission to reproduce their work; to Clay Hapaz, Claire Hallereau, Christina Masciotti, Markus Wessendorf, Daniel Mufson, and Julie Bleha for their assistance in making the photographs available; and to Willem Dafoe and Philip Auslander for the interview. The preparation of the manuscript was taken excellent care of by Sandra Kuzniak and Kathleen Dassy. Catherine Closson, senior editor at P.I.E.-Peter Lang, and Marc Maufort, editor of the "Dramaturgies" series, wholeheartedly supported the book project. The result is dedicated to Hugo De Greef, Agna Smisdom, and Johan Reyniers, former and current artistic directors of the Kaaitheater, for helping us to enjoy the Wooster Group productions on the European continent.

Johan Callens
September 2004

List of Productions
by the Wooster Group

2003	*Poor Theater*
2001	*To You, The Birdie! (Phèdre)*
1999	*North Atlantic*
1998	*House/Lights*
1995	*The Hairy Ape*
1994	*Fish Story*
1993	*The Emperor Jones*
1991	*Brace Up!*

The Road to Immortality

1987	*Frank Dell's The Temptation of St. Antony*
1984	*North Atlantic*
	L.S.D. (...Just the High Points...)
1982	*For the Good Times* [dance]
1981	*Hula* [dance]
	Route 1 & 9 (The Last Act)

Three Places in Rhode Island

1979	*Point Judith (an epilog)*
1978	*Nayatt School*
1977	*Rumstick Road*
1975	Sakonnet Point

Fig. 1: *Frank Dell's The Temptation of St. Antony*
Directed by: Elizabeth LeCompte
Pictured (l-r): Kate Valk, Anna Kohler, Ron Vawter,
Michael Stumm and Peyton Smith
Photo: © Paula Court

Fig. 2: ***Frank Dell's The Temptation of St. Antony***
Directed by: Elizabeth LeCompte
Pictured: Kate Valk and Ron Vawter
Photo: © Paula Court

15

Fig. 3: *Frank Dell's The Temptation of St. Antony*
Directed by: Elizabeth LeCompte
Pictured: Ron Vawter
Photo: © Paula Court

Fig. 4: ***Frank Dell's The Temptation of St. Antony***
Directed by: Elizabeth LeCompte
Pictured: Ron Vawter
Photo: © Paula Court

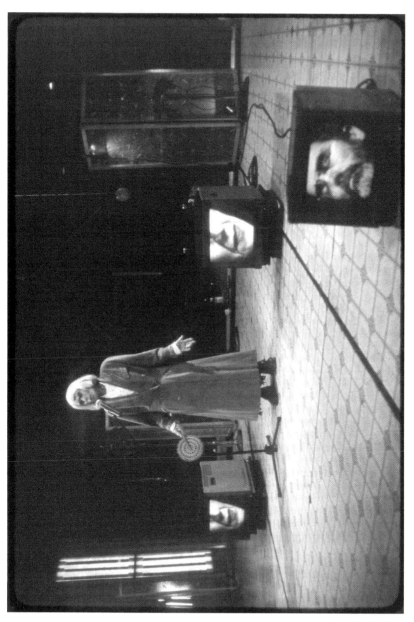

Fig. 5: *Brace Up!*
Directed by: Elizabeth LeCompte
Pictured (l-r): Peyton Smith (on large monitors), Beatrice Roth,
and Roy Faudree (on small monitor) – Photo: © Paula Court

Fig. 6: *Brace Up!*
Directed by: Elizabeth LeCompte
Pictured (l-r): Michael Stumm, Ron Vawter, Willem Dafoe, Roy Faudree,
Joan Jonas, Peyton Smith, Paul Schmidt, and Beatrice Roth
Photo: © Bob Van Dantzig

Fig. 7: *Brace Up!*
Directed by: Elizabeth LeCompte
Pictured (l-r): Beatrice Roth, Dave Shelley, Paul Schmidt (on monitor),
Karen Lashinsky, Kate Valk, and Paul Schmidt – Photo: © Paula Court

Fig. 8: ***Fish Story*** – Directed by: Elizabeth LeCompte
Pictured (l-r): Peyton Smith, Kate Valk, and Roy Faudree
Photo: © Mary Gearhart

Fig. 9: *Fish Story*
Directed by: Elizabeth LeCompte
Pictured (l-r): Jeff Webster, Kate Valk, and Scott Renderer
Photo: © Mary Gearhart

Fig. 10: *The Emperor Jones*
Directed by: Elizabeth LeCompte
Pictured (l-r): Kate Valk and Willem Dafoe
Photo: © Mary Gearhart

23

Fig. 11: *The Emperor Jones*
Directed by: Elizabeth LeCompte
Pictured (l-r): Kate Valk, David Linton, Dave Shelley, and Willem Dafoe
Photo: © Paula Court

Fig. 12: ***The Emperor Jones***
Directed by: Elizabeth LeCompte
Pictured: Kate Valk
Photo: © Paula Court

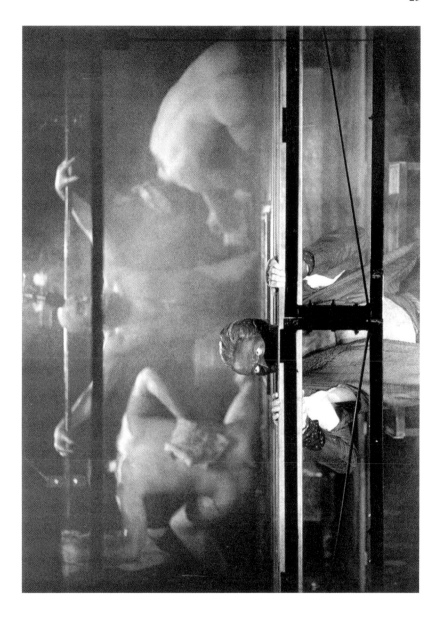

Fig. 13: *The Hairy Ape*
Directed by: Elizabeth LeCompte
Pictured (l-r): Roy Faudree, Willem Dafoe, Dave Shelley, and Paul Lazar
Photo: © Mary Gearhart

Fig. 14: *The Hairy Ape*
Directed by: Elizabeth LeCompte
Pictured (l-r): Willem Dafoe and Kate Valk
Photo: © Mary Gearhart

Fig. 15: *The Hairy Ape*
Directed by: Elizabeth LeCompte
Pictured (l-r): Willem Dafoe (on monitor), Roy Faudree, and Paul Lazar
Photo: © Paula Court

Fig. 16: ***The Hairy Ape***
Directed by: Elizabeth LeCompte
Pictured (l-r): Kate Valk (in ape mask) and Willem Dafoe
Photo: © Mary Gearhart

Fig. 17: *House/Lights*
Directed by: Elizabeth LeCompte
Pictured: Kate Valk
Photo: © Paula Court

Fig. 18: *House/Lights* – Directed by: Elizabeth LeCompte
Pictured (l-r): Kate Valk and Suzzy Roche
Photo: © Mary Gearhart

Fig. 19: *House/Lights*
Directed by: Elizabeth LeCompte
Pictured (l-r): Kate Valk and Roy Faudree
Photo: © Paula Court

Fig. 20: *House/Lights*
Directed by: Elizabeth LeCompte
Pictured (l-r): Sheena See, Helen Pickett, Kate Valk, Roy Faudree, Tanya
Selvaratnam, and Suzzy Roche – Photo: © Paula Court

Fig. 21: *North Atlantic* – Directed by: Elizabeth LeCompte
Pictured (l-r): Ari Fliakos, Steve Cuiffo, Willem Dafoe, Michelle Stern,
Kate Valk, and Helen Pickett – Photo: © Paula Court

Fig. 22: ***North Atlantic*** – Directed by: Elizabeth LeCompte
Pictured (l-r): top row – Helen Pickett, Michelle Stern, Kate Valk, Emily
McDonnell; middle row – Chad Coleman, Willem Dafoe, Steve Buscemi;
front – Ari Fliakos – Photo: © Mary Gearhart

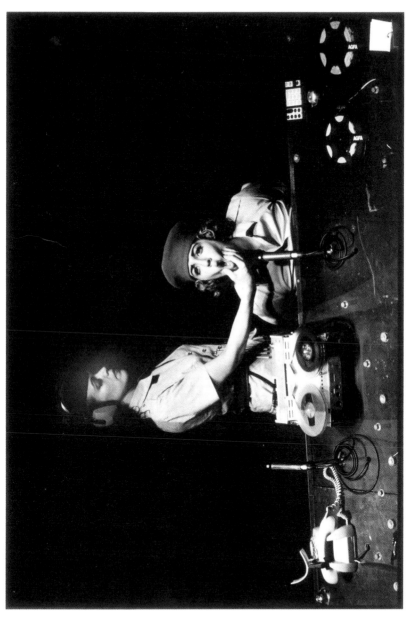

Fig. 23: *North Atlantic*
Directed by: Elizabeth LeCompte
Pictured (l-r): Kate Valk and Helen Pickett
Photo: © Paula Court

Fig. 24: *To You, The Birdie! (Phèdre)*
Directed by: Elizabeth LeCompte
Pictured (l-r): Scott Shepherd, Frances McDormand, Kate Valk,
and Suzzy Roche (on monitor) – Photo: © Paula Court

Fig. 25: *To You, The Birdie! (Phèdre)*
Directed by: Elizabeth LeCompte
Pictured (l-r): Frances McDormand, Kate Valk, and Ari Fliakos
Photo: © Paula Court

Fig. 26: ***To You, The Birdie! (Phèdre)*** – Directed by: Elizabeth LeCompte
Pictured (l-r): Dominique Bousquet and Ari Fliakos
Photo: © Mary Gearhart

Fig. 27: *Highway to Tomorrow*
Directed by: John Collins and Steve Bodow
Pictured: Randall Curtis Rand
Photo: © John Collins

Fig. 28: ***Highway to Tomorrow***
Directed by: John Collins and Steve Bodow
Pictured: Susie Sokol
Photo: © John Collins

Fig. 29: *Jump Cut (Faust)*
Directed by: Marianne Weems
Pictured: Heaven Phillips and David Pence
Photo: © Peter Norrman

42

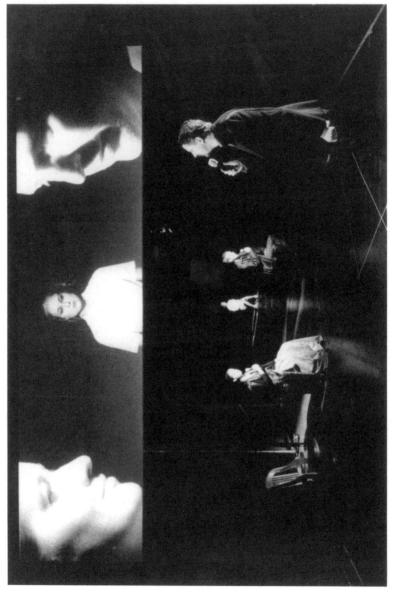

Fig. 30: *Jump Cut (Faust)*
Directed by: Marianne Weems
Pictured: (on screen) Moira Driscoll, Heaven Phillips, Jeff Webster
(on stage) Moira Driscoll, Heaven Phillips, Jeff Webster, David Pence
Photo: © Peter Norrrman

Fig. 31: *House*
Directed by: Richard Maxwell
Pictured (l-r): Laurena Allan, Yehuda Duenyas,
John Becker, Gary Wilmes (lying down)
Photo: © David Quantic

Fig. 32: ***Boxing 2000***
Directed by: Richard Maxwell
Pictured (l-r): Jim Fletcher, Robert Torres, Lakpa Bhutia
Photo: © Michael Schmelling

Of Rough Cuts, Voice Masks, and Fugacious Bodies

The Wooster Group in Progress

Johan CALLENS

Vrije Universiteit Brussel

In 1975 a group of New York artists, led by Elizabeth LeCompte, began working in the margins of Richard Schechner's Performance Group. Five years later they officially assumed the name of the Wooster Group, after the street in SoHo from which they had been operating. By then, the company – whose core members have included Willem Dafoe, Kate Valk, Peyton Smith, and Jim Clayburgh, beside Spalding Gray (1941-2004) and Ron Vawter (1948-1994) – had acquired a devoted following on the downtown scene, impressed by the innovatory character of *The Rhode Island Trilogy* (1975-1979). More than twenty years later, the continuous output of high quality work and worldwide show-ings (including several revivals) have enhanced the Wooster Group's reputation, so much so that the company began to be perceived by critics and spectators alike as exemplary within the theatrical avant-garde. Strangely enough the significance of the Wooster Group is insufficiently reflected in book-length critical studies, granted that the relative absence of primary written and audio-visual records forms a major handicap and that the complexity of LeCompte's stage productions defies the con-straints of linear critical prose. Apart from a substantial number of articles and book chapters, at the time of writing only one monograph was available, David Savran's indispensable *Breaking the Rules: The Wooster Group 1975-1985* (1986). By offering a survey of the stage work subsequently produced (minus the latest show, *Poor Theater*, the choreographies, and the collaborations with Richard Foreman), the essays here presented should resume the debate about the Wooster Group's place in theatre history.

The "traditions" meant in the title of this volume extend into the past (the 1960s counterculture, the historical avant-garde, vaudeville, even the naturalist theatre and Tieck's romantic drama), as well as into the future (through the impact on the next generation of performance artists). If this contextualizing doubly guarantees the company's longevity, it also threatens it with an increasing institutionalization. Hence, Part I of this volume, "Institutional Attempts and Counter-Attempts," advances the canonization of the Wooster Group as a thesis requiring further exploration in print and on stage. The essays included in this section deal not just with the academic appropriations (in the guise of poststructuralism and politics, the need for accountability, or the inscription within art history), but also with the at times paradoxical resistances to them (by way of a lingering utopianism, some input from the sciences of complexity, and a performative, anti-pedagogical emphasis). The canon, into which the Wooster Group so perceptively has intervened, is similarly divided into heirs apparent (Racine, Chekhov, O'Neill, Wilder, T.S. Eliot, Miller) and contestants (Flaubert, Stein). The essays in Part II, "The Works," chronicle the productions enlivened by these antagonistic forces, from *Frank Dell's The Temptation of St. Antony* (1987) up to *To You, The Birdie! (Phèdre)* (2000), shifting the critical perspective as the need arises: from the focus on the attenuated relationship between text and performance, author and director, to the identity and gender implications of the seemingly more formalist experimentation with scenography and technology, from the enlightening dynamics of Cold War politics in a post-Iron Curtain era and the evolving racial politics of casting practices among the Provincetown Players and the Wooster Group, to the politics of spatial reception within and across countries. The changes to which such spatial and temporal shifts subject productions are dealt with, too, whether the Wooster Group's *North Atlantic* or the adaptations of *The Bacchae* and the Faust myth by Elevator Repair Service and the Builders Association. The latter two are discussed in Part III, "Spin-Off," which demonstrates how other artists have come to terms with LeCompte's influence – with regard to techniques used and stances taken (adoption, parody, revision, etc.) – in the process proving or disproving Savran's provocative pun on his earlier title.

If Savran posits the Wooster Group's recuperation as a thesis tested and contested by the here assembled critics, this is because of the company's growing appreciation by the *New York Times* and scholars alike, the increased funding opportunities and impact on the burgeoning New York scene, less by the enhanced technological sophistication or changed methods and personnel. Accordingly the Wooster Group may well be the last representative of the twentieth-century avant-garde, as Richard Schechner (1981) and Arnold Aronson (2000) have argued. One central explanation for this turn of events, Savran claims, is the

Wooster Group's reliance on the avant-garde's aesthetic strategies, which tend to preserve the very structures and principles they subvert. Thus, LeCompte's early radical deconstructions and later reframings of canonical texts very much confirm their cultural capital, as well as make her work eminently attractive to academia in which the cultural studies approach now holds sway. Given the remarkable consistency of LeCompte's methods and ideological stance (a curiously aestheticized form of radical politics), the major reason, according to Savran, for the Wooster Group's institutionalization would seem to be the appropriation of the avant-garde's subversive strategies by neoliberalism and post-structuralism, in the service of a consumerist entertainment industry or what John Seabrook has called the "Nobrow" dissolution of cultural hierarchies. In this sense the Wooster Group have proven prescient. Beyond that, their interest resides not in any misplaced nostalgia but in their lingering apocalyptic utopianism shared with the 1960s counter-culture out of which they emerged.

In "L.S.D. (Let's Say Deconstruction): Narrating Emergence in American Alternative Theatre History" Michael Vanden Heuvel com-plements Savran's analysis, by demonstrating how the reception of the Wooster Group in the U.S. became imbricated in that of poststructuralist theory. Hardly known beyond universities at the time LeCompte dis-tanced herself from Schechner's environmental yet ritualistic theatre and became a staple of the local New York scene, poststructuralism, and more particularly its deconstructive method, only began to leave its imprint on theatre criticism when the Wooster Group achieved wider notoriety through the withdrawal of funds by the New York State Coun-cil on the Arts on account of the blackface in *Route 1 & 9 (The Last Act)* (1981). By the time *Breaking the Rules* was released deconstruction had become an ingrained practice, implied yet consolidated among still wider audiences by Savran's casual but expert approach and the method's consequent productivity. When the reaction against poststruc-turalism set in to the benefit of a more empiricist, materialist criticism (of the kind practiced in this volume by Ric Knowles), *Brace Up!* (1991) went into production, marking the Wooster Group's apparent return to a less iconoclastic treatment of canonical drama and textual authority. Consequently, the demise of poststructuralism was interpreted as evidence of the company's outdated critical approach and the death of the avant-garde, whose last representative it allegedly is. Presumably, the dearth of critical monographs on the Wooster Group can also be accounted for, at least partly, by the widespread belief in this narrative among publishers, acquisitions' and series' editors.

Despite LeCompte's occasional reliance on poststructuralist theory (e.g. Barthes's *Empire of Signs* for *Brace Up!*) and deconstruction's "natural" concurrence with readerly and performative interventions in dramatic texts as such, this double narrative (conjoining the fates of the avant-garde and poststructuralism) provides a dead end from which Vanden Heuvel proposes an outcome by advancing, as he and others (William Demastes, Simon Jones,etc.) have done elsewhere, the sciences of complexity. In contrast to French poststructuralism's more exclusive insistence on textual play, imagination, and irrationality, this counter-tradition tries to reconcile the forces of instability to which complex systems are subject with the temporary orders they develop and approach in a state of optimum distribution. Vanden Heuvel speculates that the Wooster Group's later, apparently more conservative productions constitute such volatile stage of "self-organized criticality" – a juncture or node from which it may develop, at the least occasion, in any new direction, restructuring itself along the way. The increased institutionalization of the Wooster Group, then, a corollary of the dissemination, banalization, and formalist reduction of its deconstructive method in academia and the popular media, need not have augured the company's recuperation by the culture industry.

Greg Giesekam's "What Is This Dancing? The Pleasures of Performance in the Wooster Group's Work" offers still another way out of the critical impasse, following his and his students' divided reactions to the company's work over an almost twenty year period. Early on Giesekam's involvement with community theatre in and around Glasgow made him suspicious of the alleged elitism of the Wooster Group as an avant-garde company (whether of a formal or political nature). He nonetheless had to grant his visceral enjoyment of their performative "pyrotechnics" in the kind of immersive experience that obviates traditional distinctions between form and content. To the extent, however, that these pyrotechnics, the bravura shapeshifting between styles and modes, resist instant conceptualizations and a clearcut political positioning (apart from partaking of postmodern irony and the entertainment industry's spectacularity), critics like Savran and Vanden Heuvel have felt increasingly uneasy with them. The debate over this issue goes back to 1980s' critical interventions by Philip Auslander and Johannes Birringer, besides LeCompte's prior emergence out of Schechner's more explicitly politicized Performance Group. Yet it also pertains to the need within academia and theatre studies for what Giesekam calls "accountability," a need ethical and American (if we go by Max Weber's link between Protestantism and capitalism). By this need Giesekam means a productivity or usefulness in terms of a coherent story or argument, conducive to the social change which Marxist critics like Fredric Jameson have been committed to, and which, in Jon McKenzie's view, survives in the "performative" imperative now displacing Foucault's disciplinarian one. To this accountability Giesekam opposes Lyotard's libidinal art or "jouissance," involving what Barthes has called a textual "pleasure" and "obtuseness," a play whose waste and excess, its very supplementarity permits a less easily defined and recuperated resistance. True, in the light of this need for productivity the Wooster Group's performative virtuosity may again acquire negative overtones, further darkened by their protracted search for subsidies and the struggle to survive in an inimical artistic context. But to abide with Giesekam, it is the Wooster Group's performative play, whether situated in the cultural margins or at the interface of traditional, hierarchical polarities (form/content, ethics/aesthetics, relevant/irrelevant, mature/ childish, guilt/pleasure, text/performance, etc.) which constitutes the continuing attraction and longevity of their shows, beyond any short-lived political and social programs, or eventual critical and institutional attempts on them.

Auslander's interview with Willem Dafoe, "Task and Vision Revisited" prolongs Giesekam's emphasis on performance, without necessarily resolving the tensions between accountability and play, even if the critic and performer already discussed these and related issues in 1984. While the intervening years have seen the flowering of Dafoe's film career and the emergence of new companies from the Wooster Group's interning system, experience has put to the test his views on the screen and stage persona, the Wooster Group's much vaunted uses of technology, and the threat of institutionalization. Dafoe dispels any suggestions of routine and control by the renewed challenge of each new production and the continuing, dance-like pleasure generated by his task- (rather than psychology-) based acting. Such acting makes for a physical and mental sensation approximating at best a "kind of grace," a paradoxical self-discovery through self-abandonment, which emotionally and intellectually frees the performer as well as the spectator from any preset agenda or significations. If this emancipation may have helped Wooster Group audiences to grow exponentially over the years, Dafoe's performative dynamics nonetheless prove very much an internal one, geared towards finding the right mix between his fellow performers, the frame, and the technology amidst the company's collective attempts to shape their relationship to certain material into powerful stage images. Despite the Woosters' hard-won longevity, their endeavour's success is very much a fleeting thing, in part because of the diversity and welter of the sources relied on.

Marranca's alphabetical repertory of subjects, introducing Part II devoted to the Wooster Group productions staged between 1987 and 2000, gives an idea of the company's breadth of interest, without, however, aiming for your common dictionary's pretense at a false (because tautological) exhaustiveness. After all, LeCompte resists the modernist striving for artistic containment, despite displaying the modernist belief in the significance of art, and the systematic, self-conscious evaluation of that art in the very process of making it, as evidenced by the Wooster Group's reconceptualizations of dramaturgy, scenography, acting, and directing. In Marranca's argument, these reconceptualizations were fed by the wider art scene, notably phenomena like John Cage's sound experiments, Robert Rauschenberg's mixed media collages, Joan Jonas's self-monitored shows, Carolee Schneemann's installation-like and Foreman's personally-invested performances, Jack Smith's "rehearsal" aesthetics of failure, and Gordon Matta-Clark's "rough cuts" through houses slated for demolition. By the same token, Marranca distinguishes LeCompte's work from theatre artists like Robert Wilson, for being intertextual but neither decorous nor symbolic. Her deconstructive method, too, is said to derive from the art scene, less from poststructuralist theory, considering also how e.g. Gustave Flaubert's *Temptation of St. Antony* and Gertrude Stein's *Doctor Faustus Lights the Lights*, texts the company tackled, already constitute authorial deconstructions of sorts. LeCompte's deconstructions still implicate the humanist Enlightenment tradition yet set up an alternative anti-pedagogical project of re-educating the audience in the contemporary multimedia experience, geared towards perception and image processing, towards the destabilizing rather than the orderly transmitting of fixed, authoritative knowledge, towards the multiplication of meanings rather than encyclopedia's fixing them. Here Marranca's analysis rejoins Giesekam's. For if the informational and mediatic overkill or the persistent autobiographical grounding of the material and its continual repro--cessing pose the problem of narcissism and impenetrability (i.e. the elitism Giesekam touched upon), the productions also resist the legitimizing process underlying the critics' politicizing and theorizing, by insisting instead on the theatrical opportunities for enjoyment. Ironically, such enjoyment may be undermined by the American antitheatrical prejudice, as much as by the Wooster Group's own moral qualms, even if the death of Ron Vawter may have diminished the later works' emotional investment in human transcendence.

Vawter still featured in *Frank Dell's The Temptation of St. Antony* (1987). To Markus Wessendorf the final instalment of *The Road to Immortality* trilogy offers an extreme case of the twentieth-century directors' problematization of the relationship between text and performance. It also represents the hinge between the Wooster Group's early deconstructions and subsequent reframings (Aronson 2000: 191-2). Ostensibly dramatizing a theatre troupe's rehearsals for a magic show in a Washington hotel room, *Frank Dell*, true to its full title, is also based on Flaubert's highly theatrical yet practically unstageable epic drama, notwithstanding recent "gospel" attempts by Robert Wilson (shown e.g. at the 2003 Ruhr Triennale). Short of abandoning textuality and severing the referential tie altogether, *Frank Dell* is shown to substitute a post-literary (performative and intermedial) textuality for Flaubert's nineteenth century literary one. It does this by stretching to the limit the participatory and ultimately undecidable play made possible by the gap between signifiers and signifieds. Short, too, of pre-empting this play by collapsing signifier and signified in audiovisual literalizations of St. Antony's dramatic fantasies, triggered by his readings of the Bible, the Wooster Group fully exploitf the dynamic principle at the heart of Flaubert's text. The enhanced intertextuality (by references to Albert Goldman's biography of Lenny Bruce, Geraldine Cummins's *The Road to Immortality*, Ingmar Bergman's *The Magician*, a video by Ken Kobland, etc.) and the analogical relationship which the program posits between the Wooster Group production and *La tentation de saint Antoine* ultimately give away *Frank Dell*'s character as an "allegory of unreadability." This means that the figural and literal coexist as proper meanings, like the different layers of a palimpsest, without ever fusing into a unified and totalized symbolic reading.

Reading *Frank Dell* as "an allegory of unreadability" neatly brings out its "fugacity," the concept developed in Simon Jones's wide-ranging analysis, anchored by *Brace Up!*. Begging to differ from those who see in the Wooster Group's deconstructions of classic realist texts a total break with the naturalist tradition, Jones builds a case for seeing their work, up to and including *Brace Up!*, as an inflection of that tradition, in keeping with the "new naturalism" of the sciences of complexity, thermodynamics, and quantum physics. As intimated above, Jones pursues a project already broached by Vanden Heuvel (1991, 1993, 1995), by drawing on the likes of Prigogine (instability, the irreversibility of time) and Deleuze (the fold or cleavage that cuts and joins; the differentiator), and by distancing himself from the pessimism of Paul Virilio and others. The latter sees in the temporal acceleration and consequent virtualization of spatial reality an objectification or de-naturing of the subject (its disappearance into the screen of the fourth wall or the traditional stage's dead center, driven along the viewer's Subject/Object axis). By contrast, Jones himself construes the Wooster Group project as a re-naturing that transcends the false I/Not-I dichotomy of Zola's experimental method, by intensifying and refracting, as in a musical fugue, the proscenium arch's divisionary line (rail, ramp, lower fore-stage).

Insofar as the ensuing complexity is full of potential for new visions, Jones disagrees with those critics who have criticized the Wooster Group's wavering as a failure of commitment. In their apparent longing for a stable, political interpretation Jones sees a prolongation of the (neo)classical theatre's idealized linear perspective, which the naturalist theatre democratized rather than abolished. Just so, the participatory aims of Schechner's environmental theatre, out of which the Wooster Group grew, may be said to further the naturalist goal of identification (supported e.g. by his performers' daily "psychotherapy"). Still, the environmental theatre, in Jones's "perspectival genealogy" constituted by the stages' organizing geometries, also destabilized the classically centered viewing lines. It is a destabilization which LeCompte's centrifugal theatre further intensifies, notwithstanding her political differences with Schechner. True, like Marranca, Jones is also aware of LeCompte's visual arts pedigree, from Giotto (*Rumstick Road*) to Cézanne (*Nayatt School*), even if her project of refracting the singular, deep perspective is carried out architecturally and bodily, rather than on the flat canvas. But then one way of viewing twentieth-century painterly developments is as a concerted effort to escape the limits of the frame and two-dimensionality (through collage, montage, installation, etc.). In a similar way, hurrying the realistic drawing room through different incarnations – from skeletal walls to plain platform, raised, folded, overturned (even inundated as in Ken Kobland's 1979 video, *By the Sea*) – the Wooster Group's scenographies prove "ec-centric." The acting, too, whether peripheral, excessively central, or cross-cutting the dramatic action, ultimately weakens our relation to ourselves yet re-implicates Subject and Object, Self and Other into a fleeting (superhuman) third person, ever becoming (no longer re-presented), much as space becomes a space-event, is turned inside-out in what should prove an exhilarating and liberating projection.

Simon Jones's inscription of *Brace Up!* into the naturalist tradition is supported by the Wooster Group's deliberate self-inscription into the American avant-garde of the early twentieth century with their 1994 production of *The Emperor Jones* (1920). Far from resubmitting to textual authority by presenting the canonical play largely uncut, unaltered, and under its original title, LeCompte still questions it in its discursive and personalized manifestations. As pointed out by Roger Bechtel, she indeed decided to include in the program to the production a section of W.E.B. DuBois's "The Negro and Our Stage," an essay originally reprinted in the program for the Provincetown Players' 1923 revival so as to exonerate the playwright of racism. Echoing Wessendorf's revelatory reading of the program notes for *Frank Dell*, Bechtel spots in LeCompte's decision not just a wish to historicize the play, but a wish to expose "O'Neill" as a historically and socially determined author function along Foucauldian lines, reified in the production by Smithers's O'Neillian mustache. In this manner the Wooster Group historicized their own repeated use of blackface within its shifting social contexts. If indeed "O'Neill," when casting the African-American actor, Charles Gilpin, caused an uproar by violating the former blackface code, the Wooster Group provoked censure (and censorship) by respecting that code in *Route 1 & 9 (The Last Act)*. Yet, that censure had largely abated for Kate Valk's cross-gender, blackface performance in *The*

Emperor Jones, protected as the company were by their increased reputation and an evolved cultural discourse, no matter that these tended to occlude the lingering discrimination of O'Neill's text and the Wooster Group's audience. The result of O'Neill's and LeCompte's explicit historical positionings, says Bechtel, is a dialectical "constellation" of historical moments in which the inherent doubleness of irony is multiplied and activated in a complex circulation, generating an increased self-awareness.

Echoing both *Frank Dell's* allegory of unreadability and the dialectical constellation of *The Emperor Jones*, Gerald Siegmund construes O'Neill's *The Hairy Ape*, and by extension the Wooster Group's entire work-in-progress, as the allegory of a (Hegelian) consciousness knowingly on the way to itself. This is what truly warrants the play's subtitle, a "Comedy of Ancient and Modern Life." From being objectively given without any self-recognition (like the naturalist homogenizing stage or the epic subject), Yank's consciousness is sundered and set in motion by Mildred's gaze and Paddy's misnaming, optic and acoustic forces of a false subjectivation. Yet instead of tragically rebelling, the comic subject playfully accepts that it can never achieve full recognition, except by embracing its false identity in death. That false identity, Siegmund agrees with Bechtel, is both individual and cultural, a distortion fixed by gender, race, class, and history. In the Wooster Group's self-conscious stagings, this false identity substitutes for realism's psychologically rounded characters and, as Siegmund shows, becomes a theatrical *prosopopoeia*. Temporary disfigurations or reconfigurations function as voice masks cut loose from a proper body and set adrift, echoing, yet liberating in the opened up space the silenced voices or psychic bodies of the (unkn)own, past and present: the African-American and immigrant working populations evoked in Dafoe's blackface and rap-like delivery, the homosexual in Peyton Smith's electronically mediated voice. To the extent that the liberated voices also reactivate vaudeville and popular entertainment (soaps, boxing, cartoons, with their all too physical, deindividualized farcical, dancing bodies), the Wooster Group jog the memory of the theatre, turning it into an echo chamber of diffuse traditions, including those repressed by the dominant culture.

Revivals, too, jog theatrical memory, like the 1999 version of *North Atlantic*, a production based on a script by Jim Strahs and originally intended to be part of *L.S.D. (...Just the High Points...)*, which premiered in 1984, five years before the Iron Curtain came down and freed the repressed voices of Eastern Europe. If *L.S.D.*'s point had been to explore the paranoia provoked by the House Un-American Activities Committee (an analogue to that triggered by the Salem witch trials in Arthur Miller's *The Crucible*), *North Atlantic* shifted the focus to the production of that paranoia by the military bureaucracy. In Branislav

Jakovljević's interpretation, *North Atlantic* illustrates the state apparatus's appropriation and "purification" of war as a high-tech, deterritori-
alized and invisible, allegedly impersonal and amoral venture. As such it
renews the question of political resistance in the current (post-)Cold
War era, in which the 1960s radical and transgressive activism is no
longer feasible, since the performance standards of the military have
infused culture at large. That the mechanized movements of military
drill and the routine gestures of efficiency in *North Atlantic* acquired a
dance-like character misled some critics, in 1984 as well as in 1999, into
dismissing the production as a poor take on Rodgers and Hammerstein's
South Pacific, rather than a postmodern critique on Cold War politics
under the rule of NATO, from its inception in 1949 onto the 1989
collapse of the Iron Curtain and beyond. Instead of abandoning its
original historical context (massive European protest against the 1983
deployment of midrange nuclear missiles by the U.S.), the revision of
North Atlantic underscored that context, polemically "quoting" it, like
the military and bureaucratic gestures recycled. By insisting on the
outdated technology (once again drawn attention to in the discursive
margin of the program) the Wooster Group deprived the military of one
of its sources of appeal. Simultaneously the resulting defamiliarization
brought out the mutation of the Cold War into Total Peace: ever so
insidious and intrusive, its illusory sanctuaries (whether South Pacific
islands or aircraft carriers leagues removed from frontlines off the Dutch
coast or the Gulf) only confirming the Pax Americana's oppressive
pervasiveness.

The following two contributions shift Bechtel's and Jakovljević's
comparative historical focus to the politics of spatial reception. Though
still historicized, it is a reception prolonging Giesekam's geographical
alignment of the rift between more formalist and political assessments
of the Wooster Group. To him, especially North American theatre critics
have felt uneasy at the productions' unclear political allegiance or
progressiveness, their postmodern ironies, not to say political incorrect-
ness. It is an unease here confirmed by Ric Knowles's speaking of
LeCompte's "sentimental" liberal individualism and pluralism or by
Bechtel's recalling that this liberalism proved no excuse for the blackface in *Route 1 & 9 (The Last Act)*. European critics, by contrast, seem
more prone to enjoying the different pleasures the Wooster Group offer,
without denying them the political relevance which New Yorkers, in the
eyes of Knowles, would no longer grant them. The Canadian critic
indeed believes that locals tend to relegate the company to Off-Off
Broadway, whereas on the continent they are granted the exemplariness
of an "American" avant-garde.

In Knowles's materialist assessment, however, the American/ European divide still proves too broad a distinction. Hence his reception

study of *House/Lights* traces the vicissitudes of audience reactions in New York, Columbus (Ohio), Chicago, Montréal, Paris, and Glasgow, over a three-year period (1997-2000). Even Off-Off Broadway requires further specification into neighborhoods and theatrical spaces, notably the "urban pastoral" position now occupied by the Performing Garage in a gentrified SoHo, sandwiched between the downtown financial markets and midtown skyscrapers, a zone artificially managed for residents from the professional-managerial class and non-residential tourists. Within this context a treatment of *Doctor Faustus Lights the Lights* is more than apt, Knowles suggests, given Stein's portraying technological progress as a loss of innocence, apart from contemplating typical concerns of the "classical pastoral" (time, art, and nature). Far from being at odds with the avant-garde reputation of the performance company, this urban pastoralism, in Knowles's argument, underscores the company's already mentioned belatedness in the history of the avant-garde. It also makes for a recuperative nostalgia weakening their deconstructions of the "compulsory normativity" in American drama classics such as *Our Town*. (Maybe this explains Savran's weeping during the Woosters' last act of *Our Town*, despite *Route 1 & 9*'s earlier hard core pornography and the title's and the video footage's invocation of the industrialized New Jersey landscape.) At the same time, an idealized American avant-garde is reconstructed, one that allegedly could or did infuse and uplift the mainstream, without being either marginal and oppositional or downgraded by serving the capitalist culture industry, the way it now does.

Heeding the call for ever more finely meshed reception studies, Fré-déric Maurin qualifies Knowles's impression of French unanimity ("the familiar in-Europe welcome"). Unlike many avant-garde American artists who found a welcoming home in Paris (e.g. Robert Wilson, Peter Sellars, and Foreman to a lesser degree), the Wooster Group were late being acknowledged in France. Seven years separated *Route 1 & 9 (The Last Act)* (Paris, 1985), the company's first showcasing, from the next one, *Brace Up!* (Bordeaux, 1992). These were followed by *Fish Story* (1994) and the passage of Wooster Group associates Marianne Weems (the Builders Association) and Roy Faudree (No Theater) (1998), both at Créteil. Yet, it was not until the efforts of a major institution like the Festival d'Automne that the company was given wider exposure, first in 1999 with *House/Lights*, and again in 2001 with the retrospective of *North Atlantic*, *The Hairy Ape*, and *To You, The Birdie! (Phèdre)*. Only then the Woosters' innovating intermedial vocabulary seemed to catch on, helped by a younger generation of artists relieving Robert Wilson's increasingly vapid international style, and in the face of the Parisian vogue for non-Western and Eastern European directors. The price to pay for this wider coverage was a certain canonization – the double bind tying up the present collection of essays – next to the producers' and media's marketing ploy of highlighting the presence of movie stars like Willem Dafoe and Frances McDormand at the expense of the theatre collective. Notwithstanding these drawbacks, retrospectives like the one in Paris allow audiences within a few weeks to assess the nature and development of an aesthetics spanning several decades. Because of the language barrier, the Parisian audiences even more than native New Yorkers were challenged to loosen their cognitive grasp (despite the French supertitles for *The Hairy Ape* and the program's three synopses, somewhat superfluous for Racine, a French national treasure). Whether convinced or not by Giesekam's plea for pleasurable enjoyment, the French were forcefully immersed into the Woosters' controlled anarchy delivered with a casual virtuosity. Maurin consequently grants the danger that in Paris the entertainment value may have obscured the well-foundedness of LeCompte's theatrical deconstructions and the paradoxical critique of America, couched as it was in a most infectious yet very American material language: energetic, physical, and technological.

In "Framing the Fragments: The Wooster Group's Use of Technology" Jennifer Parker-Starbuck pays closer attention to this material language. Using *To You, The Birdie! (Phèdre)* (2001) as a case study, she demonstrates how LeCompte develops a posthuman, cyborgian theatre which foregrounds the technologies of the self in order to reconfigure them. The production's mediated narration and the prosthetic use of the flat screen monitors fracture and displace the traditional identity of the speaking subject (see also Callens, 2001). Yet, as in Siegmund's conceptualization of the Wooster Group's *Hairy Ape*, the resulting gaps and mirrorings make room for questions about the relationship between Self and Other. Such questioning is necessary to counter the objectifying surveillance technologies inscribing the female desiring subject with normative meanings, whether that of the neoclassical theatre in Racine's absolutist era or the postmodern media headed by an omnipresent screen goddess, substituting for Racine's hidden god. The Wooster Group do not for that matter adopt the outdated technophobic stance of culture critics like Virilio and Baudrillard who deplore the pervasiveness of the technologies constituting our televisual culture and what Margaret Morse dubs our "automated" cultural exchanges. Instead the company is said to take a more positive, truly postmodern approach when framing and exposing these regulatory technologies, in order to re-embody the screened self as the subject of a video-installation-like performance interacting with its viewers/participants, as a desiring subject thriving on its integration of technology and the human body.

Part III shifts the emphasis of this volume to the "Spin-Off": performance companies and artists like Elevator Repair Service, the Builders Association, Cannon Company, and Richard Maxwell, who have been associated with the Wooster Group and show their impact in diverse forms. Emulating ERS's theatrical strategy with regard to Euripides' *Bacchae*, Julie Bleha and Ehren Fordyce in their collaboratively written essay provide a double take on *Highway to Tomorrow*, which during its development from May to October 2000 went through several incarnations before premiering in New York. Their careful critique of this developmental process repeatedly lays bare practices like the belated casting, the reliance on rehearsal tapes, found material, spatial constraints, non-realistic movement patterns, and structuring choreographies – all typical of the Wooster Group, for whom John Collins, founder of ERS, has been doing the sound design. As exemplified in *Highway to Tomorrow*, ERS also share with the Wooster Group a provisional, non-authoritative, and perspectival stance towards dramatic texts, which manifests itself in the doubling or incremental layering rather than theatrical substitution of these texts, especially those resisting simple stagings, like Euripides' generically unstable *Bacchae*, or Flaubert's *Tentation* and Stein's *Doctor Faustus* for that matter. Since any stage translation necessarily is a betrayal (*traduttori, traditori*), Dionysus' and Teiresias' lessons about the divided and ironic nature of identity, together with Pentheus' and Agave's misrecognitions, possess a metatheatrical quality, which ERS mined for its confusing tragicomic effect, much as Siegmund did in his generic approach to Yank's self-consciousness in *The Hairy Ape*. Starting from minimal means, yet touching upon the fundamentals of theatre, *Highway to Tomorrow* thus is said to move from the double-takes of absurdly anachronistic updatings, linguistic puns, puppetry, physical comedy, cross-dressing and twice-told tales to a deeper emotionality, stopping short, however, of any redemptive catharsis, aided by the audience's final, ambiguous laughter. By way of its comic unruliness ERS's production brings into play the emotional and pleasurable audience reception discussed by Giesekam. As an embodied experience such reception would seem to require a minimum degree of (Dionysian) faith, the suspension of disbelief which sophisticated urbanites (whether in classical Athens or postmodern New York) resist, no matter how much they may be interpellated.

As if to warn against the potential danger of interpellations, Marianne Weems in *Jump Cut (Faust)* tackled a staple of German nationalism. Her company's name, the Builders Association, and an early production of Ibsen's *Master Builder* go some distance towards demonstrating the relative emphasis of Weems's work, from which my analysis departs, before turning to *Jump Cut (Faust)*. Developed over several years (1995-98) in New York, Zürich, and München, this production profited along the way from the writerly talents of John Jesurun. The result of this protracted confrontation with various Faustian voices and their ideological policings (the Nazi appropriations of productions by Reinhardt and Gründgens) is a perhaps more explicitly political interpretation than what the Wooster Group, shying away from the tendentiousness of much 1960s activist theatre, would allow. Yet LeCompte's outspoken intermedial concerns (as manifested in the image and movement copping or the mixing of live and prerecorded material), together with their consequent perspectival dislocations (also characterizing ERS's *Highway to Tomorrow*), again transpire in Weems's explorations, notably in the interdisciplinary crossings of the Faust material by way of Gorski and Murnau. In the latter case, these involve not just theatre and film but also Renaissance and Romantic painting. Just so, the encyclopedic intertextuality, the reliance on silent film intertitles, and the epistolary frame ground *Jump Cut (Faust)* in discourse, in a manner inviting comparison with *Frank Dell's The Temptation of St. Antony*, as analyzed by Wessendorf.

Among the New York performance artists associated with the Wooster Group, Richard Kimmel of the Cannon Company and Richard Maxwell have perhaps taken the most revisionist approach (albeit in opposite directions). Continuing Giesekam's problematization of the apparent critical ban on a pleasurable enjoyment of LeCompte's work and Siegmund's foregrounding of its self-reflexivity (always involving a doubleness of sorts), Daniel Mufson centers Kimmel's and Maxwell's critical stance on their attempts to wed postmodern irony with an emotional response, both equally indispensable to authentic performances.

Kimmel retraces the Wooster Group lineage even further than the 1960s' counterculture and the historical avant-garde. In his 1999 adaptation of Ludwig Tieck's *Puss in Boots* (1796) he turns the romantic irony against those contemporary artists abiding with the canonical influence of the contemporary avant-garde, represented by Anne Bogart, Foreman, Wilson, and LeCompte, much as Tieck turned that irony against the bourgeois illusionary theatre of his day. In Mufson's analysis, the Cannon Company blatantly parodied the Wooster Group vocabulary (e.g. blackface and video stand-ins for absent performers), to provoke the vociferous emotional reaction he so much misses in the wake of the increasingly sanctioned works of the established avant-garde. As such, Kimmel reconstructs and deploys Tieck's destructive metatheatricality against the avant-garde's own deconstructions of canonical drama in order to short-circuit their beloved irony.

Maxwell, by contrast, in his earliest productions (*House, Showy Lady Slipper*, etc.) appears to forego any emotion whatsoever, together with the cool perfection of the sophisticated scenographic and audiovisual technology by now associated with the Wooster Group. And yet, Mufson believes Maxwell's early minimalist style may well free a more compassionate humor than the at times intellectually superior mockery of the established avant-garde, aimed, detractors argue, as much at the audience as the characters of the dramas deconstructed (whether in collusion or derision). To the extent that more recent shows (*Boxing 2000, Drummer Wanted*, etc.) seem to allow for gestural and verbal outbursts, Maxwell may well have moved from Kimmel's excessive parodistic critique to a more creative balance of irony and emotionality, even if parody should already be construed as a creative force. Thus Maxwell leaves room for audience involvement while forestalling the disengaged multiplication or endless deferral of meanings, which Siegmund here dubs the Wooster Group's echo chamber and Marvin Carlson elsewhere the memory machine of its haunted stage.

Regardless of the manner in which contemporary performance artists come to terms with the influence of the Wooster Group, its ineluctability attests to the power and quality of their work, if also to its institutional impact. Much as in the classic assessment of T.S. Eliot, whose *The Cocktail Party* the Wooster Group dismantled in *Nayatt School*, Elizabeth LeCompte's individual talents and her company's collective artistry have succeeded, not just in making history, but in rewriting it, even if this meant, in Eliot's words, neither "blind" nor "timid adherence" but "great labour" as well as fun. For Eliot as for the Wooster Group the historical sense that infuses authentic work in most original ways, should guarantee its present and future vitality, besides the lingering need to reassess its place in theatre history.

PART I

INSTITUTIONAL ATTEMPTS AND COUNTER-ATTEMPTS

Obeying the Rules

David SAVRAN

City University of New York, Graduate Centre

Hunched over a typewriter in a sweltering SoHo loft, writing what would become the first chapter of *Breaking the Rules*, I never imagined I would find myself some two decades later contributing an essay for a collection dedicated to probing and canonizing (whether it wants to or not) the work of the Wooster Group. Twenty years ago their work seemed anything but the stuff of canons. Because of their brilliance and recklessness (two qualities ill-appreciated by the press and upper-middlebrow theatre aficionados alike), I feared for their longevity. Not that they were a fly-by-night affair – they owned the Performing Garage, after all – but they seemed almost like squatters in a rapidly gentrifying SoHo. Their office, which doubled as a dressing room, was a tiny, cold retreat laden with file cabinets and an ancient desk while the performance space had a distinctly improvised quality to it. During the winter, it was heated by one large gas heater in the rear of the building which had a long, elephant trunk-like tube attached to it to transport the hot air to other parts of the Garage. There was no shower. Spalding Gray was no household name, Willem Dafoe no movie star. The Group had been defunded, battered, and demoralized by the controversy over *Route 1 & 9* (1981) and managed to survive only because of extensive European touring. Even their stage technologies, which included 16mm films, old victrolas, and color slides, seemed deliberately archaic and makeshift. Here, I thought, was a poor theatre dedicated not to sacralization but blasphemy.

When I started writing about *Route 1 & 9* and realized that the essay was destined to become only a chapter of what had to be an entire book, my New York friends thought I had gone over the edge. And even I suspected it was an insane project for an assistant professor to take on. The Wooster Group, after all, was known only to a small group of devotees and was merely one player among many in what was then – unlike now – a thriving, dynamic, and edgy downtown theatre and performance scene. The press had it out for them. The *New York Times* called their work "pointless," ridiculed them for their desecration of the modernist classics, and wished they "would sweep" the stage of all their "avant-garde detritus" (Gussow, 1981). The *Village Voice*, meanwhile, took them more seriously but complained repeatedly about their alleged self-indulgence and racism. When Arthur Miller threatened to sue them in 1984 for what was unquestionably the best imaginable production of *The Crucible*, their fate was sealed – or so it seemed. But then *Platoon* came out and Willem was nominated for an Academy Award. Then the Group began a collaboration with Peter Sellars, *enfant terrible du jour*. And Spalding's monologues were helping to turn him into a household name – at least in certain hip households south of Fourteenth Street.

Today, as this collection of essays demonstrates, the Wooster Group collects massive amounts of cultural and symbolic capital. Elizabeth LeCompte has won the most prestigious awards and grants, and the Group is hailed wherever the word avant-garde is still mumbled. *To You, The Birdie! (Phèdre)*, one of the hottest tickets in New York during the 2001-02 season, was pronounced an "exhilarating dissection" of *Phèdre* by Ben Brantley in the *New York Times* and Kate Valk judged (correctly!) a "dazzlingly accomplished leading lady" (2002). Even *Entertainment Weekly* weighed in on the piece, awarding it a quite respectable B+.

I am gratified that the Wooster Group is finally getting its due – and curious as to how it all came to pass. In the remainder of this essay, I want to consider how and why this transformation occurred, and what it suggests about the politics of cultural production in the U.S. For it seems to me that the Group's success attests to the inexorable workings of a certain and persistent cultural logic. Having seen and studied their work for twenty years, I am convinced that this transformation has at least as much to do with the culture surrounding the Wooster Group as with the content of their performances. This is not to say that their work hasn't changed. As I and others have often noted, Liz LeCompte has always used an extraordinary range of texts as well as the members of the Group as "found objects" out of which she constructs a piece. And while the objects may have changed, the method remains much the same. Like Richard Foreman, whose disembodied voice dominates so many of his plays, Liz has always been curiously absent yet ubiquitous, the hidden god whose invisible hand – rather than voice – can be felt both everywhere and nowhere. Although the Group's technologies have become far more sophisticated and their personnel has changed – with Spalding's exit and later suicide, Ron Vawter's death, and Willem's sojourns in Hollywood – their pieces remain deconstructionist readings of classic plays. The plays may have become larger and larger parts of the finished pieces, but the Group's compositional strategies remain consistent. They still interweave and often violently juxtapose dissimilar visual, verbal, gestural, and musical texts. They still delight in the collision of different orders of representation, high culture and kitsch, the prerecorded and live, Racine's immortal tragedy and a real game of badminton. Even without Ron Vawter and Peyton Smith, the imagined community of performers remains surprisingly stable. Substitute Scott Shepherd for Ron and Frances McDormand for Peyton in *To You, The Birdie! (Phèdre)*, and you have the traditional Wooster Group *dramatis personae*.

The ideological force of the Group's work also remains, I believe, curiously consistent. In a 1991 analysis of *Frank Dell's The Temptation of St. Antony* I argued that the piece bore witness to the growing aestheticization of the Group's work in the wake of the controversies over funding practices of the National Endowment for the Arts. This critique was rooted in my conviction, as I argued in *Breaking the Rules*, that the Group's earlier work had been motivated and buttressed by what I then called a radical politics. Although Liz denied radical motivations and styled herself relatively apolitical, I assumed that she was understandably reluctant to lay claim to a radical political agenda during the Reagan years. But I think I was wrong and, in fact, I now take her at her word when she asserts that the work is dictated not by politics but, in effect, by what Brecht called culinary principles: an aesthetics of pleasure and consumption. Looking back on my many interactions with the Group and their work, I now believe that only Ron Vawter was unambiguously political.

The Wooster Group's continuing place among the avant-garde is a more complicated affair. Although Richard Schechner decreed the American avant-garde dead in 1981, Arnold Aronson insists that the obsequies were not pronounced for another ten years or so (2000: 181). If one accepts his argument, the avant-garde can be seen to have expired as a result of a multitude of complaints, among them the rapidly escalating cost of Manhattan real estate, changes in governmental and nongovernmental funding for the arts, the aging of the 1960s' generation, the AIDS crisis, the decline of mass-movement politics, the triumph and normalization of poststructuralism, the increasing need of the commercial theatre to replenish itself with the blood of the nonprofits, and the growing obsolescence of an Adornian disdain for mass culture. I am most intrigued by Aronson's contention that "[i]n many respects, the Wooster Group was the last major exponent of the postwar American avant-garde movement" (2000: 185). For the Group's work certainly embodies those characteristics that Peter Bürger famously identifies with the historical avant-garde: revolt against the purported autonomy of the aesthetic, desacralization of art, delight in provoking shock, criticism of theatre as an institution, undoing of the opposition between producer and spectator, "radical negation of the [...] individual creation," "liquidation of the category 'work'," and a fondness for "killing the 'life' of the material" they licitly or illicitly appropriate (51, 56, 70).

I want to argue that the Group's positioning at the end of a tradition dedicated to ending all traditions is the sign less of Liz LeCompte's dogged persistence in the face of cultural change than of the Group's prescience. For more than any other American theatre company, the Group emblematized even twenty-five years ago the figuration that finally would triumph in the 1990s: John Seabrook's Nobrow, in which the old cultural hierarchy is overthrown and the distinctions between high and low, art and commerce, sacred and profane, avant-garde and kitsch become virtually meaningless. Representing an unprecedented diversification of cultural offerings, Nobrow also attests to an equally unprecedented commercialization of the public sphere and concentration of the mass media. It is the moment emblematized by Allen Ginsberg peddling for the Gap and William Burroughs hawking for Nike, the moment when "hip" became "the orthodoxy of Information Age capital-ism" (Frank). The Group's celebration of Nobrow *avant la lettre* ac-counts in part for the critical opprobrium heaped on them during the 1970s and 1980s, when they were breaking the unspoken bylaws of both cultural orthodoxy and the avant-garde. To this day, they represent the last stand of the avant-garde because of their instrumentality in both destroying and preserving the very meaning of the word.

The change in the Wooster Group's cultural status that began in the late 1980s can be charted with remarkable precision by examining the coverage of them in the *New York Times*, that imperious arbiter of upper-middlebrow taste, style, and culture. The two lead theatre critics for the *Times* in the eighties, Frank Rich and Mel Gussow, loathed and ridiculed the Group for their "vapid" and "stale" "assaults on classics" (Rich; Gussow, 1984). In 1987, however, Stephen Holden took over the avant-garde beat and penned somewhat more thoughtful critiques of the work directed by a now – "intrepid [...] Elizabeth LeCompte." And by 1994 the coverage had been completely transformed. Then-second-stringer Ben Brantley wrote an appreciative review of *Fish Story* in which he praised the piece's "authority and precision" and its "deeply felt emotional core." Since then, Brantley has been promoted to chief critic for the *Times* and his reviews of the Group's work now read more like hagiography than criticism. Terrified of being uncool, he persis-tently champions the dwindling survivors of the avant-garde of yore, especially Foreman and the Wooster Group, along with more literary-minded young Turks like Richard Maxwell.

The critical rehabilitation and popularization of the Wooster Group is symptomatic of the wholesale cultural transformation that Seabrook calls Nobrow. Yet the Group's distinctive position suggests that their

work has particular features that make it uniquely capable of recuperation. I would like to argue here that its uniqueness is in part the result of
its reinvigoration of a classic strategy that dates back to the emergence
of the first avant-garde at the end of the 19th century. As Pierre Bourdieu
reminds us, the small-scale producers of avant-gardist art invariably
rehearsed what he calls a "more or less disavowed relation to the commercial enterprise," "renouncing economic profit," at least in the short
term, in favor of massive accumulations of cultural capital. Since the
late nineteenth century, the most effective way for young insurgents to
accrue cultural capital has been to practice heresy, to "break the silence
of the *doxa* and call into question the unproblematic, taken-for-granted
world of the dominant groups." In order to accomplish this mission, "to
gain a foothold in the market," these insurgents – who represent, after
all, a dominated fraction of the dominant class (the bourgeoisie) – have
"to resort to subversive strategies." And their success depends strictly on
their ability to "overturn [...] the hierarchy of the field *without disturbing the principles on which the field is based.*" "Thus," Bourdieu notes,
their "revolutions are only ever partial ones, which [...] transgress the
conventions but do so in the name of the same underlying principles."
(82-84)

The very phrases that Brantley uses to praise the Group's work bear
out Bourdieu's observations. For they reinforce the idea that not despite,
but because of its heresies, the Group ends up ironically respecting the
rules of art and performance established by the pioneers of theatrical
modernism. After all, Brantley writes, its method isn't "just postmodern
riffing" but the "tak[ing ...] apart" of a classic text "the better to see it as
a whole" (2002). The Group's habit, moreover, of returning to classic
texts also serves as an example of what Bourdieu calls "the strategy *par
excellence*" of "all aesthetic revolutions," "the 'return to the sources,'
[...] because it enables the insurgents to turn against the establishment
the arms which they use to justify their domination." Thus the Group
uses *Our Town* to problematize Wilder's own racist notions of community and nation, or *The Emperor Jones* to interrogate O'Neill's depen-
dence on the very stereotypes of minstrelsy he attempts to displace, or
Phèdre to demonstrate the patterns of surrogacy and psychic ventrilo-
quism that naturalize absolutism and neoclassical tragedy alike and that
mask class relations. And it is no coincidence that Bourdieu's list of the
weapons used by the insurgents to "beat the dominant groups at their
own game" describes precisely many of the hallmarks of the Wooster
Group's classical aesthetic: "asceticism, daring, ardour, rigour and
disinterestedness" (84).

I do not mean to suggest here that the Wooster Group has sold out –
a meaningless phrase these days – or carefully premeditated its ascen-
sion to the cultural pantheon, but that the field of what used to be called

avant-gardist theatre is defined precisely by the partial revolution they
so brilliantly enact. This "return to the sources" also accounts, I believe,
for the Group's allure for academics and its influence on auteurs like
Richard Maxwell and Richard Kimmel as well as downtown theatre
collectives like Elevator Repair Service and the Builders Association.
Neither Foreman nor Wilson can be said exactly to have acolytes, but
Liz LeCompte has drawn a devoted band of disciples in New York (and
elsewhere) who honor her work by appropriating and refurbishing her
now-classic reading and performance strategies. I can see, moreover,
that my own attraction to her work was – and is – determined in part by
my abiding yet furtive veneration for the classic plays the Group vandal-
izes, reinvents, and thereby recanonizes. (I never allowed myself to
weep during the last act of *Our Town* until I saw *Route 1 & 9*.) And I
know that the contextualizing strategies I employ in my own scholarship
owe everything to their work, and to *L.S.D.* in particular. For more than
anyone else, Liz LeCompte pioneered what has since become the *modus
operandi* of what is now called cultural studies: reading against the
grain. And the widespread veneration for, co-optation, and domestica-
tion of the transgressive strategies she employs prove the veracity of
Derrida's observation about the inadvertent and "fatal complicity" of
"all destructive discourses: they must inhabit the structures they demol-
ish" (1978: 194). Given Derrida's use of an architectural metaphor, it is
perhaps not surprising that the settings for the Wooster Group's early
pieces all included a house (in its many permutations) or that all of their
pieces can be regarded as architectonic projects, houses in which to
recollect, play, and live among the debris.

The hours I spent among celebrity-packed crowds at St. Ann's Warehouse for sold-out performances of *To You, The Birdie! (Phèdre)* seem
light-years away from the evenings almost twenty years ago when I
huddled with two or three other spectators in a very cold Performing
Garage watching early incarnations of *L.S.D.* And if I experience this
change of status as a loss, it is in part because I can no longer stake a
proprietary claim to the Wooster Group. I suspect, however, that it is the
result of more than my own selfish regret. For books like this one, it
seems to me, attest to the fact not only that the American avant-garde is
dead and buried but also that an oppositional theatre is now an oxymo-
ron. Perhaps the widespread veneration for the Wooster Group partly
represents nostalgia for a time (in the U.S. at least) when oppositional
social formations had a precise meaning and when theatre, so it seemed,
could make a difference, when a piece like *Route 1 & 9* was truly dangerous and could shock and scandalize even jaded New Yorkers. But
with the triumph of neoliberalism, on the one hand, and a poststructuralism, on the other, that fetishizes what Foucault calls reverse discourses,

oppositional politics in the U.S. have been swallowed up by the new orthodoxy of Nobrow culture: subversion.

Rather than end an essay on the ever-dazzling Wooster Group on such a sober note, I would like to conclude by noting that the apocalyptic, utopian promise – as attenuated as it may seem at the present moment – remains more powerfully present in their work than in that of almost any other theatre artist. After all, isn't that also one of the reasons why so many of us love them? This utopian promise is kept alive precisely by intense, unmitigated pleasure, by the unexpected, by moments of rupture when you never know what will happen next, by children running wild at a cocktail party or a game of badminton dropped into the middle of a Racine tragedy. One of the most explicit articulations of this promise in the Group's work – and one that continues to haunt me – is a passage from *L.S.D.*, the piece of theirs most explicitly about the utopianism of the 1960s (a kind of utopianism that has, especially since the triumph of Reagan-Bushism, been increasingly displaced by a neoliberal and right-wing anarchist brand; see Amin). In Part I, Norman Frisch reads a 1961 letter of Allen Ginsberg about the revolution of which he believed William Burroughs and Timothy Leary to be in the vanguard: "I think Bill & Leary at Harvard are going to start a beautiful consciousness alteration of the whole world – actually for real – Leary thinks it's the beginning of a new world." (Savran, 1988: 185). Some forty-odd years later, Ginsberg's words smack of madness. But the dream behind the words remains as powerful today as it was then. And who knows? He may yet be proved right.

L.S.D. (Let's Say Deconstruction!)

Narrating Emergence in American Alternative Avant-Garde Theatre History

Mike VANDEN HEUVEL

University of Wisconsin-Madison

Ask a reasonably well-informed theatre graduate student in the U.S. these days about the Wooster Group, and chances are you will hear one of two things (and sometimes both things). First and foremost, you will be told that "they're the ones who do deconstruction"; and second, that of late they're becoming more conventional in their approach to dramatic texts – that is, that "they're the ones who *used* to do deconstruction." Together, I think such observations indicate how the Group's work has been institutionalized, specifically in the American academy, and in particular how its long history has been narrated to present and future generations of American theatre scholars. This discursive process is an important one, given that the Group's rise to prominence has developed alongside an academic critical practice which, if it has not shaped the work itself, has certainly provided frameworks for responding to and appreciating the Group's performances.

The subtext of both these comments is complicated, and when taken together would seem largely to duplicate the mythology surrounding much of the historical avant-garde, in which an origin based in radical experimentation and a willful disregard of convention is eventually dispersed into moderation or lost altogether. Depending on one's perspective, this route is either valorized as a sign of growing artistic maturity and "getting more real" as time passes, or else is elegized as a waning of some tangible quality called "avant-garde-ness" into something less edgy and unpredictable, that is, a "style" that can be repeated and elaborated.

The Wooster Group has been somewhat unique, however, in rewriting this narrative (which should hardly surprise us) by essentially having it both ways: the work, particularly as regards the acting and the integration of video and sound design, seems to grow in assurance *even as* an emphatic deconstructive textuality has recently receded into more-or-less "straight" readings of Chekhov, O'Neill, and Racine. Despite the more conservative approach to texts, however, the Group's work is still universally acclaimed as the "most" avant-garde theatre produced in America today. Still, even as the evolution of a signature production style (minus the aggressive stance toward source-texts that characterizes especially the second trilogy) has allowed audiences to develop the means to appreciate with greater nuance the Group's artistry, the simultaneous waning of an overtly deconstructive agenda has nevertheless occasioned more than a a few elegies on the passing of the Group's radical edginess, or at least a suspicion that late capitalism has accommodated its brand of avant-garde theatre and left it without a center to contest.

Thus, whether one wants to praise the Group or bury it, the relative presence or absence of a deconstructive dramaturgy is important in assessing where the work stands today relative to its past. This follows, in part, from the Group's unique relationship with the academic arm of the culture industry. Arising at roughly the same moment that postmodern theory was making its mark on the academy, the Wooster Group has evolved alongside a critical discourse that, for better or worse (and somewhat belatedly), hitched its wagon to the star of avant-garde theatre and performance as a productive object for its modes of analysis, interpretation, and further theorizing. The results have been, on the whole, positive and sometimes admirable. But because the Group's avant-garde stature has been so successfully associated with particular kinds of aesthetic and cultural theory, in a sense it has become bound up with the fortunes and market histories of those theories.

The narratives that produce comments like the ones that began this essay are the result, I would suggest, of this shared history. Because the Group has outlasted the heyday of French theory in the academy, it now sometimes finds itself implicated in its decline: and while it is rare in academic theatre discourse to hear the Wooster Group explicitly censured in the same way one hears certain forms of high theory denounced, there's a sense that the Group's move away from the radical evisceration of canonical texts is positioned as a kind of empirical proof that postmodern theories have had their day in the sun. Perhaps the best evidence of this can be seen in general introductory texts of American theatre and on contemporary course syllabi which – in those I was able to survey sporadically on-line at department websites – regularly emplot the rise and further adventures of the Wooster Group along these trajectories.

An abstract of this typical overview might look like this: the Wooster Group develops out of the ritual-based, anthropological research into theatre that characterized the American avant-garde theatre of the 1960s and included in its vanguard the Living Theater, Joseph Chaikin's Open Theater, and Richard Schechner's Performance Group, from whence the Wooster Group issued. The reasons for the demise of the Performance Group, some of them articulated by Schechner himself in his 1981 book *The End of Humanism*, are related in some respects to the rise of post-humanist theories imported from France (in the work of Barthes, Lacan, Derrida, and somewhat later Foucault, Cixous, Irigaray, Baudrillard, and Deleuze). These theories, as they cluster together and begin to shape the larger category of "postmodernism," deflect some performance work (and just as importantly the critical discourse surrounding the work) from the earlier agenda of an avant-garde devoted to the older humanist pursuit of presence and authenticity. In its place comes the cooler, more detached and heavily mediated exploration of fragmentation, discontinuity and deconstructed textuality that the Wooster Group, among others, explores with such zest.

It is questionable whether or not this story fully incorporates the many other possible contexts in which the Wooster Group's work is shaped; more importantly for the moment, this narrative also drives one somewhat into a corner, and becomes another kind of "plot" when one has to incorporate into the tale the more recent decline of French theory in academic theatre discourse, as well as the oft-repeated argument that postmodernism is dead (usually accompanied by strong sentiment of "and good riddance to it"). In this context, one is asked to adopt one of the two positions I mentioned at the outset: that is, either to associate the Group's movement from radical deconstructive theatre to more conventional use of texts *positively* with the "Escape from Postmodernism" school of thought; or else to fashion a *negative* critical discourse based in a notion of a (yet another) "death of the avant-garde" narrative.

Neither of these options seems fully satisfying, but then I have little to offer in terms of an alternative narrative to project forward, so long as the narrative *donné* established thus far predetermines the outcome. Instead, I want to look retroactively at the establishment of the affiliation between French theory and the Group's work to see if by tinkering with that genealogy one might develop a different perspective on the Group's present status and future prospects as an object of critical discussion. I might add that what drives this project is an eminently practical desire: to provide myself with some traction in order to change the way I narrate the Wooster Group's history and heritage to my students.

Let me begin with an admittedly sketchy and selective history – JUST THE HIGH POINTS as it were – of the critical reception the Wooster Group's work received in the American academy, one which leads me to conclude that, indeed, deconstruction (of a kind) did become established as an important pivot point for responding to and contextualizing the Group's work during an important period of their evolution. From its beginnings in 1975 as a subset of the Performance Group and continuing for almost a decade, the Group's work was not at all well known in America outside New York. More specifically, the early work was almost utterly unknown to those in American universities most likely to have encountered early manifestations of poststructuralist thought: faculty and students in departments of philosophy, comparative literature, and English. The usual reasons for this mutual lack of awareness prevail. Such departments are heavily invested in the study of primary texts, and as an experimental group initially devising its own texts, the Wooster Group did not publish primary materials in typical formats and print venues. Arnold Aronson's descriptive review of *Sakonnet Point* was published in the December 1975 number of *The Drama Review*, but almost nothing in terms of national exposure followed until *The Rhode Island Trilogy* was completed by the end of 1978: at that time, *Performing Arts Journal* published a sketch of *Sakonnet Point* (with commentary by Spalding Gray) and a text of *Rumstick Road*. Almost a year later, in the March 1979 number, *TDR* published James Bierman's essay on the trilogy along with an interview with Gray.

To this point, then, little of the Group's work was in circulation, and, moreover, little had been done to develop an appropriate format to reveal what was actually being done with the texts in performance. In a sense, however, it hardly mattered, because given the unfortunate disciplinary purity of departments in American universities, along with a still healthy antitheatrical prejudice in the academy in general, it was usually the case that a journal devoted to Off-Broadway theatre reviews and criticism would not be widely read by literature or philosophy students and faculty. There are obvious exceptions to this generalization, but nevertheless, outside the confines of these journals specifically devoted to alternative theatre and performance, there was little awareness of the Group's groundbreaking work, and many people like myself – assiduously studying assigned readings in Barthes and Derrida in literary theory seminars taught in departments of English many, many miles away from the Performing Garage – had no contact with what was happening on Wooster Street and no means to link the theory we were learning with that exciting work.

Things began to turn, somewhat, in 1981-1982, when, first, documentation for *Point Judith* appeared in *Zone* and, soon after, *Route 1 & 9* appeared in its idiosyncratic entirety in a small (and soon-to-be defunct) arts magazine, *Benzene*. The latter was the first attempt to record a performance score using a non-traditional text layout, and although the success was limited, it nevertheless had the merit of boldly announcing that something different was being attempted by the Group that struck at the very nature of textuality.

(A short digression: As it happens, the *Benzene* text was also the "route" by which I (living and studying in the Midwest at the time) discovered the Group's existence, not to mention a future dissertation topic. Not surprisingly, however, the path thereto was crooked, and arrived at mainly through happenstance and coincidence. While conducting research on *Othello* in the University of Wisconsin's fine small magazine archive, I stumbled into conversation with a librarian who told me she had just catalogued "something about a contemporary play done in blackface that has everyone in New York pissed off." And so, while I found myself reading that work more or less hot off the press, I have since concluded that this was likely not a widespread coincidence likely to be repeated elsewhere, and certainly not to be counted upon to produce a large readership for the Group.)

Critical remarks on the performances as they progressed through staged readings and presentations-in-progress were also restricted early on almost entirely to local sources: reviews in *The Villager* and *SoHo Weekly News* and the like. In fact, what we might consider to be the Wooster Group's coming out party for a regional and finally national audience occurs only in the early 1980s when they were forced to publicly defend the use of blackface in *Route 1 & 9* before the New York State Council on the Arts. The event occasioned coverage in the *Village Voice*, most memorably when Don Shewey penned an article entitled "Elizabeth LeCompte's Last Stand?" (One wonders how Shewey feels about this rhetorical question twenty-two years later).

I have not yet exhaustively researched this early, local commentary on the Group's work between 1975-1981, but from the evidence at hand I can say with certainty that almost nobody was writing emphatically about the similarities between *The Rhode Island Trilogy* and deconstruction, although some may have been groping in those directions. The situation was not much different in academic writing. As Gerald Rabkin pointed out in a groundbreaking 1982 article in *Performing Arts Journal*, "The Play of Misreading," the response of academic theatre critics to the potentialities of poststructuralist theory had been to this point somewhat atrophied in comparison to other genres. But the lull was only temporary, and in the same year as Rabkin's article Herbert Blau's one-two punch – the publication of *Take Up the Bodies: Theatre at the Vanishing Point* and *Blooded Thought: Occasions of Theatre* – opened up the floodgates for a sustained and rigorous application of the new theory to seemingly all problems related to dramatic texts, experimental performance, and the epistemological grounds of criticism itself. Between 1982 and 1985, essays by Josette Féral ("Performance: The Subject Demystified"), Chantal Pontbriand ("The eye finds no fixed point on which to rest..."), and Bernard Dort ("The Liberated Performance") had appeared in *Modern Drama* (a periodical not given to theoretical work), and the two leading journals of theatre theory in America, *Theatre Journal* and *Performing Arts Journal*, had published important essays grounded in poststructuralist theory by Rabkin, Elinor Fuchs, Jonathan Kalb, and Philip Auslander, among others. Coinciding with the Wooster Group's rise to prominence and notoriety, this academic critical discourse soon both appropriated their performances as paradigmatic of one or another element of the new theory, while also lending the Group's work cultural capital and intellectual cachet.

And so it is that, around 1984 – perhaps in response to the debates surrounding issues of textual authority made public by Arthur Miller's intervention in the Group's adaptation of *The Crucible* into *L.S.D.* – reviews, journals, and books increasingly refer to deconstruction as the Group's primary *modus operandi*. Most hedge their remarks by repeating or paraphrasing Arnold Aronson's 1985 observation that, "although not overly influenced by the deconstructionist theories of Derrida and others (LeCompte says she is aware of this critical movement but has not read any of the sources), the Group's recent work provides virtually the only example of deconstructionist ideas put into practice in the American theatre." This loose, osmotic process of interaction between French theory and the Group's practices – for myself, this always meant imagining LeCompte having coffee with Richard Foreman and surreptitiously taking notes – becomes more or less the standard model for establishing connections between the two (although by the time of *Brace Up!* LeCompte is somewhat out of the closet and reading to the performers in rehearsal from Barthes's *Empire of Signs*).

However, even if the interactions between the Group and French theory might be casual, the critical discourse unflinchingly sought more rigorous connections, and in reviews and articles by Rabkin, Fuchs, Auslander, and others from the middle of the decade, the deconstructive intervention against the presence of the text and the actor became, in critical discourse at least, the signature practice of the Group's aesthetic. Importantly, however, by 1986 the connections between the Group's work and deconstruction were also being rigorously questioned and critiqued, as part of a larger shift in the academy that occurred when theorists in all disciplines began to interrogate the terms and assumptions both of French theory and of postmodernism itself. Focusing on what Auslander has aptly called "the uncomfortable line between deconstruction and reification," academic scholarship became more explicitly embroiled in the political issues and debates regarding cultural and ethnic representation, textuality and authority, and so on, that had long preoccupied the public response to the Group's work, especially after *Route 1 & 9* and *L.S.D.*

When David Savran's book appeared, which more than anything introduced the Group's work to a wide readership outside New York, the widespread acceptance of an alignment between French theory and the first two trilogies was cemented, in fact, more by omission than commission. *Breaking the Rules* (1986) makes only passing reference to the Group's deconstruction of texts, the authority of the lecture-demonstration, and traditional theatre practices, and in none of these passages did Savran feel it necessary to back up and explain these analogies to deconstruction in anything resembling poststructuralist terminology. The implicit assumption is that such terms and critical orientations could by this time be deployed casually, without weighty explanatory armature: indeed, I have always thought that the success of the book was surely in part owing to Savran's facility in showing how deconstructivist practices emerged from the work itself, in performative terms, rather than having to be applied externally from a theoretical perspective.

Thus, while not wishing to impose too strict a causal link, it still happens that, by 1988, even newspaper and mass-market magazine reviewers of Wooster Group performances regularly drop "deconstruction" into their headlines and commentary. Interestingly, many of the reviews that deploy the term in their headline do not explain, or even repeat, the term in the body of the article, and often when they do it is to dismiss it as cumbersome, yet somehow necessary, academic jargon or shorthand. (One example will have to stand for many: from a headline in the *Valley Advocate* at Smith College, reporting on a campus perform-ance of *Frank Dell's The Temptation of St. Anthony*: "Dazzling theatri-cality combines with 'deconstructed' texts on the cutting edge of the avant-garde." The term "deconstruction" never appears again after this sub-headline, and the scare quotes suffice to locate the term in its somewhat unsavory academic origin.)

This would seem to provide evidence that, as one might expect, the use of "deconstruction" or any of the catchphrases by which it is indi-cated, are anything but consistent during these latter years, especially as poststructuralist theory and its terminology leave scholarly discourse and become more common as catchphrases. In the specific case of its application to the Group's work, however, I see no reason to bemoan this process of mass-market popularization: in general the alignment of the Group's work with deconstruction and French theory in critical discourse has been illuminating and healthy, and even when it descends to what Patrice Pavis describes as "the banal sense of deconstruction" (316) it has always seemed to me a fine example of the potential reciprocity of academic and popular discourses which, every so often, come to inter-animate one another. While scholarly applications of deconstructionist thought have illuminated (for the most part) the aspects of linguistic and textual play in the Group's work, as well perhaps as the potential political and ethical positions it assumes, it was often the case that versions of deconstruction owing less to Derrida and more to one's knowledge or experience of Yiddish radio performance, "banal" community theatre, and low-budget television were equally instructive in their comments on the Group's multiple performance styles and its use of video and acoustic technology.

Nevertheless: by the mid-1990s, for good or ill, the Wooster Group had become, in popular and academic discourse, "that group that does deconstruction," and the groundwork was established for them to ride the theory bear market while it lasted, but also to come under different kinds of scrutiny when things became bullish. This essay hasn't the scope to explore the varied reasons for the eventual decline of French theory and the loss of faith in the explanatory power that seemed once to reside under the rubric of postmodernism. But if I have no space to speculate as to the reasons for this decline, there is ample – yet simple – evidence that the ebbing of postmodern theory has certainly affected critical discourse around the Wooster Group. That is, simply, that in America these days hardly anyone publishes on the Wooster Group's work in anything resembling theoretical terms. As early as *Brace Up!* in the early 1990s, there is a notable turn in commentary on the work, in the periodical literature anyway, away from theoretically-oriented criticism and toward more empirical forms of reviewing: descriptions of the work in progress, commentary from the artists and translator, and the like. As well, I noticed a good deal more attention being paid specifically to the main source text, Chekhov's *Three Sisters*, and to the particular changes being wrought upon it, rather than to the ideological work resulting from the adaptation. Jim Clayburgh, the Group's designer, said to one interviewer: "this is the most accurate rendition of a script we've ever done. The folks in Europe jokingly said that it was because *Three Sisters* was so much better than the other scripts we had done that we couldn't tear it apart as much." (Arratia: 125). This *reportage* mode of inquiry generally carries over to *The Emperor Jones* and *The Hairy Ape* as well, and to what I have seen thus far of commentary on *To You, The Birdie!*, and therefore would seem to indicate a sustained trend. When theoretically-informed work that still foregrounds poststructuralist ideas does emerge in the late 1980s and in the 1990s, it is usually in chapters of books devoted to the Group's earlier work, that is, prior to the "return to the text" phase after *Frank Dell's The Temptation of St. Antony* (for example, in Auslander's *Presence and Resistance*, my own writing, Nick Kaye's *Postmodern Performance*, John Rouse's essay in the anthology *Critical Theory and Performance*, and so on).

It is possible that this waning of theory simply parallels the decline in the very kind of avant-garde performance with which its vocabulary and thematics seemed so in tune; or perhaps, as Arnold Aronson suggests in his *American Avant-Garde Theatre: A History*, a "well-intentioned academia" may have done more damage than good in supporting experimental performance by bringing the latest theory to bear upon its reflections regarding the new forms of textuality, stage-craft, and acting. Even more problematic than the sometimes obfuscat-ing jargon of the theorists, says Aronson, was "the attempt to apply poststructuralist theory to theatrical production," where the rigidly formalist methods of deconstruction appropriate to studying static genres like the novel or lyric "began to encounter complications when applied to a [...] complex and modulating form such as theatre, with its multiple layers of 'text,' interwoven and sometimes conflicting sign systems, multiple 'authors' [...] multiple simultaneous 'readers' and the fluid and virtually ungraspable object known as performance." (201) Concluding with the interesting observation that "In a sense, reading theatre had always been a deconstructive exercise" (perhaps here echoing Pavis's similar claim that "there will necessarily be deconstruction of the text by the stage" [317]), Aronson neatly captures both the principal reason why poststructuralist ideas enjoyed a natural conjunction with avant-garde performance and, in particular, the work of the Wooster Group, while also suggesting how deconstruction, as it hardened into a method, could limit the fluidity and complexity of the very object it deconstructed .

This still leaves the issue unresolved about what might be done in the wake of deconstruction's ambivalent relationship to the Group's work, but I would like to end with, first, an invitation to discuss this brief genealogy to see where other plots and subplots likely have been left out; and second, to offer a speculative conclusion by suggesting how we might re-engage the narrative I have sketched here in ways that allow us as teachers both to pay homage to the theoretically-informed work already mentioned, as well as to locate *aporia*s out of which different pathways may retroactively emerge. While I do not think we can main-tain any useful narrative of the Wooster Group's evolution without reference to the impact of poststructuralist thought on the critical dis-course that shapes it, I do believe we can revise that narrative by causing the pivot point of deconstruction to wobble enough that it might be made to point in directions that deconstructive criticism never followed with sufficient rigor.

To my mind, somewhere along the way in the complicated reception of poststructuralism, in America and in performance discourse, decon-

struction became associated with a kind of anti-scientific mode of
thinking and writing that stressed, to the exclusion of everything else,
the shortcomings of logic, the failure of analytic approaches to meaning,
the breaking down of rules and rationality, and – perhaps most damag-
ing – the notion that if something is "fluid and ungraspable" it means it
cannot be interpreted and even modeled in useful ways. While this has
served to enliven the discourse of avant-garde performance, which often
shares a similar subversive agenda and a corresponding drive toward
sublimity, it has also helped to create just the sort of dead ends already
mentioned when this specific element of the avant-garde urge begins to
wane. Deconstruction has been very good at helping us to respond
imaginatively to the movement in theatre from the *lisible*, readerly
works of conventional drama to the more *scriptible*, or writerly texts of
avant-garde theatre and performance art – that is, the movement from
order to disorder, linearity to spatiality, text to performance. However, it
remains to be seen if it can be equally helpful in our understanding of
systems that swing back to new kinds of order, that is, those that evolve
through a complex interaction of stability and disorder into more complicated or complex structures.

Fortunately, from a variety of interdisciplinary perspectives, poststructuralism is currently undergoing reconfiguration: once deployed
merely as an anarchic form of discourse analysis, elements of deconstruction are instead being conceptualized as a style of thinking that
actually contributes to certain kinds of scientific progress and pragmatic
knowledge. The kinds of science it contributes to, not surprisingly, are a
far cry from classical physics or even the modernist, yet still linear and
analytical sciences of relativity and quantum mechanics. Instead, the
growing number of sciences dedicated to nonlinear systems and to the
understanding of self-organization, complexity, and emergence, have
recognized the need for philosophy and science to conjoin in order to
effectively model biological, social, and aesthetic systems that are too
complex and variable to represent via a single narrative or concept.
Complex systems, in which many variables interact in nonlinear and
asynchronous ways, cannot be understood analytically or represented by
a single path or outcome – that is, by a single narrative that connects all
the parts. Even when a narrative is twisted and tangled, if it can relate all
the parts to a single function, then the system it describes is not complex
but complicated (a Frenchman was once heard saying that jumbo jets are
complicated, while mayonnaise is complex).

Acknowledging that poststructuralism evinces a special inherent
sensitivity to complexity, Paul Cilliers, for example, has argued that
Derrida's rejection of traditional notions of representation and his insistence on the unstable and relational nature of language and discourse
might be linked to the kinds of so-called "distributed representation"

that characterize the intricately-connected neuronal networks of the brain. His argument is, essentially, that rule-bound and descriptive modes of representing complex systems necessarily leave out many of the contingent aspects of these systems, and also depend upon a system of centralized control to decide which rules become active at each stage of a given representation. Cilliers posits instead that the more distributed a complex system is, the more rich in information, memory, and what he calls "robustness" it is likely to be. Without a stable control center, and operating through a dynamic process of difference, distributed represen- tations share much with poststructuralist notions of the trace and of *difference*, and their claim that complex systems like language are inherently self-organizing and adaptive. And, like deconstruction (although not always in the popular understanding of it) these adaptative systems do not merely become increasingly disorderly, but instead allow new forms of structure to emerge even as former structures break down.

This emphasis on the emergence of new structures, and the possibil- ity of modeling a complex system's behavior as it self-organizes, distin- guishes this use of deconstruction from what we find familiar in literary and theatrical discourse. Cilliers points out that, at a stage he refers to as "self-organized criticality," a complex system will reach, after a series of adaptations and evolutions, an optimum state of distribution, around which it stabilizes and maintains itself. Although the system may appear to be at equilibrium, the smallest addition or subtraction may possibly create a huge structural change – or it may not. The point is that, when a truly complex system – and by now you have probably gathered that I consider the Wooster Group's work to comprise such a system – reaches self-organized criticality, it has a history that has driven it, by force of a simple need to survive, adapt, and evolve, to a point of very sensitive stability. At this stage, it may remain structurally stable for some time, and yet at the *same* time exist at the critical point where single events have the widest possible range of effects. In this state, says Cilliers, "the system tunes itself towards optimum sensitivity to external inputs," thereby preparing itself for large-scale changes that require the least amount of effort."

I end, then, with this speculation: what if a deconstructive drama- turgy were not understood as the endpoint of the Wooster Group's evolution, but rather simply as an important evolutionary mechanism that, working nonlinearly with other variables, has pushed the Group's work to a stage of "self-organized criticality"? In this scenario, the current treatment of texts as (relatively) stable entities need not indicate a more conservative agenda, but instead could signal that the work has reached a state of such advanced robustness that the complexity lies, not solely in the deconstruction of an existing text or pattern of meaning, but rather in the new structures of densely patterned order that emerge in the interactions between textual order and performative chaos. I will always admire and remain vastly entertained by the Group's deconstruction of canonical dramatic texts, but I also feel that the current work shows evidence of true complexity developing – complexity that, as the biologist Henri Atlan reminds us, requires both a global structure that can be interpreted and known with some stability as well as a superabundance of variety and indeterminate variables to interact with that structure to produce emergent and unpredictable results. This in turn might suggest that, far from a waning of avant-garde energy, the Wooster Group's more recent work presages a system optimally tuned toward new forms of robustness.

What Is This Dancing?

The Pleasures of Performance in the Wooster Group's Work

Greg GIESEKAM

University of Glasgow

The title of this essay is taken from the placard which appears on screen in the Wooster Group's *L.S.D. (...Just the High Points...)* while Kate Valk and others perform their Donna Sierra and the del Fuegos routine. The question was originally asked by Justice Danforth in Act 3 of *The Crucible*, when he heard of the girls dancing in the woods. I will contend that criticism often finds itself in the same situation as this puritan judge. Unable to cope with the dancing in Wooster Group productions (and similar performance-derived pleasures where the production begins to "dance" before our eyes as we attempt to retain some sort of monocular spectatorship), criticism resorts either to ignoring or marginalizing such pleasures and the disturbance they cause, or to instrumentalizing them.

From Where to Here?

It starts in 1986: I am concluding a year researching participatory community theatre projects in the housing schemes of West Scotland, areas amongst the most deprived in the European Community – some have 70% unemployment, infant mortality rates four times the average, life expectancies eight years lower than in adjoining middle-class suburbs. I write a 60,000 word report for the Arts Council, a few pieces for socialist journals, and do a week's workshop with Augusto Boal; I am active establishing a network of people involved in community arts activities in the region. I also attend the Wooster Group's *L.S.D. (...Just the High Points...)* at London's Riverside Studios.[1] I am bewildered by

---

[1]   In Britain the show was presented as *The Road to Immortality (Part Two)*, without reference in the programme to its previous *L.S.D.* title; in this essay I will refer to it by the more commonly used name, to which it reverted on its return in 1990.

it, puzzled, excited, agitated, enthralled – the usual responses of many encountering the Group for the first time.

1990: I am working on a reminiscence project with elderly people in Clydebank – a run-down former ship-building community on the banks of the River Clyde. The Woosters bring to Glasgow's Tramway the final performances of *L.S.D.*, an early version of *Brace-Up!*, and *Frank Dell's The Temptation of St. Antony*. I send 100 first year students to see them, arrange a session at Tramway where Liz LeCompte chats with them, and have Kate Valk and Peyton Smith up to talk. One student says to Kate, "It's all very surreal, but what does it mean?" Kate, with practised evasion replies, "You tell me." Half my students hate me for sending them, half think it is wonderful. I think *Brace Up!* is the most enjoyable Chekhov I have seen for a long time (and paradoxically, very Chekhovian). The audience collapses in laughter at the Cook Island dance sequence and bursts into applause – the sort of behaviour we might normally expect at a West End musical rather than an avant-garde performance. Nancy Reilly stays on for a few weeks to work with my students – they do a delightful short piece based on Madonna, mixing video, a Vogue dance routine, and personal material.

1992: The return of *Brace Up!* – all our students go and I lead a discussion between Liz LeCompte, the cast and 400 people in Tramway. I complain to LeCompte that she's cut much of the Act IV material, including Peyton Smith's wonderful, double-coded, ironic yet poignant, rendition of Olga's final words. She says it will probably re-appear in *Fish Story*.

2000: I am writing another 60,000 word report for funding agencies on community and amateur theatre – and I find myself writing an article on the Wooster Group for an anthology on postmodernism. *House/Lights* comes to Tramway, another generation of students join the former students who now flock to it *voluntarily*: most are thrilled, though few can really tell me "what it's about."

Why the selective autobiography? Partly, to illustrate my limited encounters with the Group's work: my view is conditioned by what I have seen situated on the edge of Europe rather than in downtown New York; partly to highlight what some colleagues have seen as the rather schizophrenic nature of my interest in them. How can I have been so involved in developing practices around cultural democracy in Glasgow's desolate schemes and yet be fascinated by a bunch of self-indulgent New York avant-gardists, as some would call them? It is also defensive. Roland Barthes has commented that,

> No sooner has a word been said, somewhere, about the pleasure of the text, than two policemen are ready to jump on you: the political policeman and

the psychoanalytical policeman: futility and/or guilt, pleasure is either idle or vain, a class notion or an illusion. (Barthes, 1987: 57)

Immediately, of course, the policemen jumped on him, notably Fredric Jameson, who condemned Barthes for his "complacent, stubborn commitment to the *instant*, [...] his blissful renunciation of the high seriousness of the Anglo-American critic's sense of the moral vocation of criticism itself." (1983: 5) Jameson laid down the proper course for good citizen-critics:

> A given piece of textual analysis must make a punctual or occasional statement about its object, but must also, at one and the same time, be graspable as a more general contribution to the Marxian problematic [...] The right to a specific pleasure, to a specific enjoyment of the potentialities of the material body, if it is to evade the complacencies of "hedonism" – must always in one way or another also be able to stand as a figure for the transformation of social relations as a whole. (1983: 14)

Jameson's shadow looms large over discussion of the Wooster Group and attempts either to dismiss or defend its place within a wider politics of performance – where it takes on an iconic role for postmodern performance generally. I am conscious, therefore, as I question the focus placed on the supposed politics of the Group's work at the expense of acknowledging and celebrating the vaudevillian and libidinal pleasures of their performances, that I am in danger of seeming a "complacent hedonist," despite my past involvement in various forms of political theatre practice and debate.

It would take a different essay to explore broader issues of political theatre in postmodernity and engage fully with the sort of arguments traversed, for example, in the Auslander (1987), Schechner (1987), and Birringer (1988) debate of the late 1980s. For the moment, a brief assertion of my own position would include recognizing some constraints which postmodernity has placed on the potential of earlier models of transgressive theatre, and acknowledging that some notions around resistant postmodernism have a certain persuasiveness. I do, however, find that some oppositions posited between different approaches fall into essentializing polarities, often based around *forms* or *subjects* of theatre, at the expense of arguments about *context* and *conditions* of performance. For me, politically challenging theatre embraces a wide range of forms and contexts: whether it is the politics involved in a group of elderly people doing a superficially non-political performance in a local community centre, the explicit politics of a professional production of a play by Edward Bond, or the resistance found in Brith Gof's postmodern spectacles, with their layerings of fiction, history, the local and the autobiographical. Different tactics are appropriate in different times, places and contexts.

From There to Where?

I want to start with two sets of parentheses in works by David Savran and Michael Vanden Heuvel, two writers to whom we owe much for their explorations of Wooster Group productions. The first set of parentheses is found in *Breaking the Rules*. Discussing the "First Examination" in *Rumstick Road*, Savran writes,

> In a way both frightening and sardonic (it is very funny in performance), it shows how an individual, prone to "bodily malfunctions," is objectified by those who attempt to help her. (1986: 87)

He goes on to describe the scene as "demonstrating" various ideas.

My next parentheses are found in "Waking the Text," Vanden Heuvel's elegant discussion of analogies between chaos theory and the way the Group challenge the orderly presence of texts "by infiltrating their field of signification with various disorderly performative insurgencies in the form of dance, vaudeville routines, live and recorded music, simultaneous live and video performance and so on." (1995: 63) Discussing *Route 1 & 9,* he suggests,

> The implication is that the process of constructing meaning in an unpredictable universe, like the blind building of the skeletal house in Part 2, is a haphazard but stimulating (and even funny) experience. (72-3)

One might also compare an equivalent (without actual parentheses) in Arnold Aronson's account of the splendid visual gag in *L.S.D.* in which Michael Kirby's arm on video shoots a revolver across stage at Nancy Reilly (recalling William Burroughs's shooting of his wife). He suggests that this "forces the audience to interpret the moment on many realistic, theatrical and social levels. It is *also* funny." (1985: 77, my emphasis)

The similarity of all these is striking – and perhaps puzzling from authors who are alert to the way Wooster Group productions embrace conflicting tones in their work and draw on popular entertainment traditions. What's wrong with funny? Why is it always an afterthought? I would argue that it is symptomatic of a tendency, even in the most sympathetic discussion, to bracket off the audience's experience of the comedy in Wooster Group performances. Equally, I would suggest the *felt* experience produced by the frequent dances found in the Woosters' work, the spectatorial pleasure and dislocation they bring about, is often bracketed off, while their local thematic productivity is what is sought or noted.

"Productivity" is in fact the central issue which arises in critical accounts of the Wooster Group (and not just of them). Despite references to the challenge the Group poses to traditions of interpretative criticism, despite discussion of the onus placed on spectators to attend to their own responses, despite disclaimers to the contrary, much writing on the Group eventually seeks to *render an account* of its performances. It "renders an account" in a double way: first, it constructs some sort of cohesive way of viewing/interpreting the potential confusions of the piece, a way which "makes sense" of the collisions of dissonant materials, which captures them discursively. But the phrase also suggests a financial transaction: the critic's rendering of an account is concerned with making the expenditure of time and effort – the company's, the spectator's, the critic's and the reader's – a worthwhile expenditure. (A cynic, or a reader of Bourdieu, might argue that such accountancy helps consolidate the cultural capital which we acquire in attending the performances or studying them.)

I am not disputing the possibility that Wooster Group performances might be productive in some of the ways suggested: accounts of different productions (in both senses) are more or less persuasive at times. What concerns me more is the drive to establish productivity *above all else*, the underlying assumption that non-productivity is to be disdained – with the consequence that those elements of performance which lie outside such "accountability" are relegated to the sidelines, to parentheses. In the very moment that the Group's challenge to hegemonized thinking is celebrated, it is arguable that a mode of thinking which derives from a capitalist hegemony re-inserts itself: only that which is "productive" is to be valued.

This, of course, is not peculiar to scholarship on the Wooster Group. It is a product of the whole *habitus* of academic commentators on theatre. We are expected to be productive, our productivity is measured by various assessment exercises, and we measure others' productivity similarly. Furthermore, Theatre Studies as a subject has often been beleaguered by external perceptions that we are a marginal "non-subject," dealing with a trivial, illusionistic form (the whole bag of post-Platonic prejudices come into play). In response, it is not surprising our productivity focuses on the realm of ideas, on what is discursively productive in performances – not bodily pleasures. Moreover, some of us may nurse subversive thoughts and imagine that our working through of such thoughts in our writing and talking may ultimately prove subversively productive. And so we attempt to produce subversive texts out of the work which we view – as in discussion of the Wooster Group.

The Jamesonian view of production versus pleasure clearly informs Vanden Heuvel's *Performing Drama /Dramatizing Performance*. As he criticizes performance of the 1960s and 1970s for reversing or bypassing history, he asserts, something akin to the reality principle is lost in the penitence of ritual and the pleasure of play, and with it goes theater's essential commitment to remembrance and history. (1992: 53)

(I pass over the notion of theatre having an "essential commitment.") For Vanden Heuvel, what "'matters' about play is how it is made to function within culture by a perceiving subject." Acknowledging its deconstructive potential, Vanden Heuvel says, "there simply isn't much to be accomplished by that function of play." Textual deconstructions only serve

> "to bounce the rubble." They perform no significant cultural work beyond their particular deconstructive exorcism. [...] Deconstruction's success or failure must be tied [...] to its productiveness. (1992: 53-54)

For Vanden Heuvel work of the 1970s "pursued desire rather than seeking to understand its power structures." While the best and most mature work, including the Wooster Group's, "achieved a particular order of complexity or genuine substance in which play was not simply gratuitous," even in such work "much was often lost." (1992: 55)

Behind Vanden Heuvel's dialectical narrative of the emergence of performance theatre from the confrontation of traditional theatre by performance lies his *own desire* for play always to be productive, to accomplish something. In this scenario, a return to meaning becomes the thing which validates the emergent form.

A similar outlook informs David Savran's accounts, from the continual search in *Breaking the Rules* to discover productive meaning in the Group's work, to establish it as "deeply political," as it "demonstrates," "stages" and "dramatizes" the various themes he discovers (1986: 219), through to his serving of the Group with divorce papers in a 1991 article, as his desire to see them as revolutionary is disappointed by *St. Antony's* "endlessly skeptical cultural critique." (1991: 55)

Without exploring the particularities of individual treatments of productions, I do find problematic the Jamesonian conviction that "the pleasure of play" is *only* acceptable if it is socially productive. Perhaps I am reminded too much of the contemporaneous injunctions by that arch workaholic Margaret Thatcher that all Britain needed was to "work harder" – poor old pleasure becomes like one of the shiftless, undeserving poor who should be booted out of society for being unproductive.

Behind the assumption that theatre only becomes worth discussing if it is usable lies a binary opposition between the generative and the sterile. Here I call to mind Lyotard's discussion, in his 1973 essay "Acinema" of Freud's account of pleasure, where he notes,

But the motion of pleasure as such, split from the motion of the propagation of the species, would be that motion which in going beyond the point of no return spills the libidinal forces outside the whole, at the expense of the whole. (1989: 171)[2]

In contrast, Lyotard introduces Adorno's endorsement of pyrotechnics. He differentiates a child who lights a match for the pleasure of it from someone who lights it to boil water for a cup of coffee. The child's diversion, his mis-spending of energy is seen as producing "a simulacrum of pleasure in its *so-called* 'death-instinct' component." Such an action is portrayed as artistic because,

> this simulacrum is not an object of worth valued for another object. It is not composed with these other objects, compensated for by them, enclosed in a whole ordered by constitutive laws. On the contrary, it is essential that the entire erotic force invested in the simulacrum be promoted, raised, displayed and burned in vain. It is thus that Adorno said that the only truly great art is the making of fireworks: pyrotechnics would simulate perfectly the sterile consumption of energies in *jouissance*. (1989: 171)

In passing, we might note the child's play of Adorno contrasted with Vanden Heuvel's idea of "mature" work eschewing non-productive play. While I am reluctant to endorse a wholesale swing towards embracing only a politics of *jouissance*, I confess to delighting occasionally in a good display of pyrotechnics – even if when watching them I sometimes have a melancholic sense of waste: thus setting in train a, usually unresolved, conflict between my ethical and aesthetic habits of mind and body. (This perhaps underlies the, again unresolved, ambiguity or discomfort one may feel, along with the excitement and pleasure, when watching the Group.)

It is, of course, often choreographic and musical sequences, usually comic or grotesque, which provide such pyrotechnic moments in Wooster Group performances: Jump the Line, Mashed Potato and other wild gyrations in *Route 1 & 9*, along with the various silent comedy routines – yes, for all the offensiveness of the use of blackface, I will admit to laughing at these, being energized by the music and dance; the Donna Sierra and the del Fuegos routines in *L.S.D.*; in *St. Antony* the comedy routines with the bed, the various nude dances on the videos, and the door-swinging routines with Michael Stumm and Anna Kohler playing out the melodrama of Pierre's death under Peyton Smith's direction; the stick dances and Cook Island routines in *Brace-Up!*, and of course, the superbly timed cartoon-chase sequences in *House/Lights*,

---

2   Speaking of spilling libidinal forces, we might note that Framji Minwalla's 1992 attack on the Wooster Group and other postmodern work was subtitled "the revenge of the onanists."

along with its wonderfully apposite, but hilariously incongruous rendition of "Burning Ring of Fire."

While Michael Stumm might be reported as saying the dance sequence from the end of *L.S.D.* could be shown on the Ed Sullivan show, or while the effects on an audience of the dance in *Brace Up!* might be similar, say, to the big dance number "Heat" which opens the second half of *Kiss Me Kate* – i.e. it is a "show-stopper" (even a "clap-trap") which has no diegetic import – the tendency of critical discussion is either to ignore such moments or only to comment on what they bring to the table of meaning, or to feel confused by their absence of meaning, as in a review of *The Emperor Jones*:

> The best moment of the production comes in the very first scene in which Smithers stands alongside Jones and they perform a rhythmic, synchronized dance together. The precision of the movement and the grace of the moment is a joy to watch. Meaning remains unclear and this interlude does not advance any narrative. (Brietzke, 1998: 385)

It is interesting to note here the mention of "the precision of the movement": a notable thing about most dance sequences in Wooster shows is the combination of a high degree of precision with an air of casualness which distances the dances from seeming to attempt the virtuosity associated with dance companies; as Susan Letzler Cole reveals in her account of *St. Antony* rehearsals, there is a deliberate attempt to break the dances down a bit once the routines become familiar.

Vanden Heuvel might well protest that in his articles in *New Theatre Quarterly* and *Journal for Dramatic Theory and Criticism* he does give credit to the way in which the dances operate as part of the "disorderly intrusion" visited by performance upon the texts used in *Nayatt School* and *Route 1 & 9*. Drawing on chaos theory, he views the relation between disorder and order in the work as a dialogic one of complementarity, which leads beyond the limitations of textual order and the potential anarchy of disorderly performance, towards "a more complex orderly structure." For him, the dances and other moments where anarchy threatens are tools in the Group's project not just to expose existing texts as inadequate, but to "recuperate them as elements within evolving (and more complex) representations for knowing the world." (1993: 265)

Note here, however, that the focus of his argument is what the dances and other aspects of performance do *to the texts* – not what affective impact they may have on us, the spectators. Their impact, then, is returned to the world of ideas and notions of representation, and in turn such a reading demands an idealized spectator who reads the performances in this rather disembodied way. While Vanden Heuvel explicitly rejects the idea that such an approach sees disorder as merely order's negative other, I am not sure that the use of order and disorder as complementarities avoids a binary way of viewing them, and a reinstatement of a dialectical reading, as opposed to the dialogic one which Vanden Heuvel suggests he is doing. For me, there is an implicit hierarchy not just in the words themselves, but also in the move to transcend them in a "more complex order." Disorder – which is identified with the performances, the dancing, the music – has to function critically and ultimately contribute to a new world order. Performance once again is instrumentalized, rather than being allowed to produce pleasure in its own right.

While there is much that is tempting in such attempts to "make sense" of the sort of associative rather than causative or logical, linkages which occur between elements in Wooster productions, what if we were to reverse the way of looking at it and focus more on what Barthes might see as the "obtuse" elements of the productions? In doing so, we might take more note of how certain moments of performance impact on us as spectators, rather than see them primarily in the light of how they contribute dramaturgically to some larger over-arching structure.

In his essay on the Third Meaning (meaning other than informational or symbolic) Barthes speaks of it as:

the "one too many," the supplement that my intellection cannot succeed in absorbing [...] the *obtuse meaning*: [...] analytically, it has something derisory about it; [...] it belongs to the family of pun, of buffoonery, useless expenditure. Indifferent to moral or aesthetic categories (the trivial, the false, the pastiche), it is on the side of carnival. (1977: 54-5)

For Barthes, "obtuse meaning disturbs, sterilizes criticism," because it is:

Discontinuous, indifferent to the story and to the obvious meaning (as signification of the story). [...] It maintains a perpetual erethism, desire not finding issue in the spasm of the signified which normally brings the subject voluptuously back into the peace of nominations [...] it does not theatricalize meaning; [...] obtuse meaning appears necessarily as a luxury, an expenditure with no exchange. (1977: 61-2)

For me, Barthes's ideas reflect more my experience in seeing Wooster Group productions and the experience I observe in others with whom I discuss them afterwards. What I encounter is a tendency to comment first on the "pyrotechnic" or "obtuse" elements – which are mostly to do with performance – whether gags, dances, the incongruous use of particular styles of movement, voice or costume, the virtuosity of performers' mode-switching, or certain uses of videos and other technologies. Only afterwards, gradually, do we start to attempt to "read" things which may somehow hang together discursively; but frequently such attempts are met by various gaps, contradictions and incommensurabilities, along with a recognition that, in fact, it is these very areas which have been the ones which have most *bound us* into the production. I think, for example, of how we experience the acid-scene in *L.S.D.*, not as a demonstration or a "theatricalizing" of something, but as an immersive experience, in which we join the performers on the roller-coaster experience of a trip (while at the same time fearing for Kate Valk as she hyperventilates and marvelling at the performers' stamina, skill and seeming Artaudian self-sacrifice). Our resulting exhaustion leaves us all the more ready to experience the contradictory emotions of the final juxtaposition of the Earl Sandle story with the fierce hilarity of the del Fuegos' dance and the melancholic dousing of the lights over the farewell dance – an ending that has us leaving the theatre both vitalized and experiencing a sense of loss. (While we can, of course, recuperate some of these sequences discursively, I would suggest that the perfor-mances themselves exceed whatever meanings we might take from such post-event meaning-production.) Obtuse buffoonery might be seen in the childish thrill of the cartoon-like sequences in *House/Lights*, the constant punctuation of the language with the computer-generated quacks, the fascination induced by the precision reconstructions of the Olga film or some of the hallucinatory play between Kate Valk live and her video image, all complementing the sense of bathing in the waterfall of Stein's language. Or perhaps the excessive is found in the contradic-tory emotions we may feel when confronted with the pornographic video in *Route 1 & 9* and the Channel J dance routines in *St. Antony* – where we may be caught between the temptation to indulge in voyeur-istic thrills and a sense of panic at finding ourselves in a public place watching such material. Again, these moments work in ways which operate beyond their potential diegetic role within an overall structure.

Furthermore, there is the sheer virtuosity of the performers: surely one of the principal pleasures we take in watching a Wooster Group production is our fascination (I use this word advisedly) with what we might see as the performers' "shape-changing." They may not seek a text or character-based presence, nor the sort of "authentic" presence sought by some strands of performance, but they all exhibit a sort of showmanship, a sort of charismatic vaudevillian presence which derives from their very ability to "switch on" different modes of performance, from indifferent reading or "bad acting" to the carefully naturalistic, from the casually comic or parodic to precisely pointed Meyerholdian grotesques. There is always a playing with the boundaries, the edges between the "masks" they adopt (Valk qtd. in Rosten) and their presen-tation of themselves, or at least their Wooster Group personae: it is not that we actually get them there in front of us as themselves, even though this is the conceit at times. But it is this very playing between these staged selves and the figures and styles they adopt which is so pleasurable, charismatic, seductive. It is hard not to project ourselves into such combinations of wit, skill, humour, "sexiness."

In an interview with Lin Hixson LeCompte herself sees such playing as similar to the sort of performing found in the *Jack Benny Show* or *I Love Lucy* – where the lead performers continually shifted personae and audience address. And indeed, many of the sources of pleasure in the Wooster Group are derived from popular traditions of vaudeville, television, cartoons, film and so on. But it becomes clear when watching the group devise, that this is not out of some popularizing desire, where the avant-garde artist "from above" decides to reach out or to adopt "popular" techniques of immediacy, comedy, sentiment etc. as part of a political project, à la John McGrath, for example. It seems to arise from a genuine delight in such traditions – and it is this which, at base, criticism has trouble with. Criticism is happy enough to recognize popular pleasures when used strategically, or to examine them for their potentially retrogressive politics when examined in popular forms such as the Broadway musical or popular film, but it has problems when they seem to be used "for their own sake," for their pleasure.

Here I would return briefly to Barthes for a last time, to his notion that for the "reader who appreciates controlled discontinuities, faked conformities, and indirect destructions," the pleasure of the text emerges from a cut or gap between two edges: "Neither culture nor its destruction is erotic; it is the seam between them, the fault, the flaw, which becomes so." (1976: 9-10) It is the intermittence of skin flashing between two articles of clothing – not the skin itself but *the flash* of skin, which seduces; or rather, the staging of appearance-as-disappearance. With the Wooster Group also, I would suggest it is just such "flashes" which contribute to the "thrill" of the performance: here we might see Kate Valk's continuing with a half-wiped blackface in *L.S.D.* or a similar technique in the final dance of *Route 1 & 9* as emblematic of the way in which productions show the flashes between deconstructed performance, dance, faked errors, as well as faked conformities and the perfectly "good" representational acting which occasionally appears. Such flashing also applies to the way they stage themselves just as they disappear themselves – we think we are getting a real glimpse of them but realize we are not. And, above all, it applies to the way which we glimpse the appearance and disappearance of texts, meaning, and culture in amongst the performances.

It may be complacently hedonistic of me, but long after some of the more localized thematic productions of the dramaturgy have become assimilated into my ideas about *Our Town*, *The Crucible*, or the politics of representation and presence, or the collapse of the Enlightenment project, it is these haptic pleasures (and the discomfitures which come in their wake) which still live on, which will bring me back to see the Wooster Group.

I am not arguing that there are no discursive meanings to be generated from the productions; and these may at times be political, whether in their topical matter or in their overall challenge to conventional representational practices. Such meanings are there to be made or sometimes found – even if sometimes they emerge almost by accident, as in some of the political debates generated by their use of blackface and pornographic imagery or their handling of Arthur Miller's text. But I would argue that a mode of criticism which primarily focuses on these and brackets off the obtuse elements, the pyrotechnics, does a disservice to the role of the performers in the nightly creation of Wooster Group productions (as opposed to just the usual recognition of their dramaturgical input and acknowledgement of their skills); it also re-installs a fairly traditional mode of hermeneutic criticism in which the critic is our hermeneut guiding idealized spectators to the governing Ideas of the production, and serves, despite disclaimers, to re-enforce a legitimating regime which is based on various hierarchical binaries around the rational/irrational, mind/body, high/low, political/non-political and so on.

I would suggest the Group's work demands a criticism that at least makes room for our bodied emotions, contradictory and politically incorrect though they may be at times, that acknowledges that we exist in bodies that fear and desire, that catch our minds off guard, that perhaps shape our thoughts as much as concepts do, that have consumed acid or engaged in pornographic sex, that have danced and taken pratfalls: a criticism that likes to dance like the Wooster Group.

Task and Vision Revisited

Two Conversations
with Willem Dafoe (1984/2002)

Philip AUSLANDER

Georgia Institute of Technology, Atlanta

In the latter part of 1984, the late Michael Kirby, then the editor of *The Drama Review*, commissioned me to write an essay based on an interview with the actor Willem Dafoe for a special issue devoted to the concept of the performance persona. I no longer recall why Kirby called on me, if I ever knew. I was at a very early stage of my career – a newly minted PhD in Theatre with two articles in academic journals and two years of full-time teaching experience under my belt. Certainly, I was (and remain) very interested in actors and performers, what they do and how they think about what they do. And I had done an article on the Living Theater, based on an interview with Judith Malina, during their not-so-triumphant return to New York City, published in *American Theatre* earlier in 1984. Whatever motivated Kirby, I owe both him and Willem Dafoe a debt of thanks. The impetus Kirby gave me to think about the concept of persona and the conversation I had with Dafoe both provided important fodder for my subsequent thinking. In much of the work I have done since – whether focused on performance art, stand-up comedy, or rock music – the idea of persona has served me well as a way of conceptualizing a performed presence that is not a character (in the usual sense) but that also is not quite equivalent to the performer's "real" identity.

I was a young and unknown academic at the time I first interviewed Dafoe, and he was a young (we are around the same age) and not generally well-known actor who had gained some repute around the downtown New York performance scene and was just embarking on what would prove to be a highly successful parallel career as a film actor.[1]

---

[1]   At the time I first spoke with Dafoe, he had acted in several independent films and one fairly high profile feature, Walter Hill's *Streets of Fire* (1983). He was about to go to work on *To Live and Die in LA* (dir. William Friedkin, 1985) and would

We met in his drafty, underheated lot in New York's SoHo at the time the Wooster Group was performing in *L.S.D (...Just the High Points...)* and had a vigorous, caffeine-fueled conversation that lasted several hours. From this discussion I distilled the article entitled "Task and Vision: Willem Dafoe in *L.S.D.*" Although the special issue on persona for which I wrote it never came to fruition, an edited version of the article did appear in *TDR* in the summer of 1985, in an issue that featured a special section of essays on the Wooster Group, including pieces by Arnold Aronson and David Savran.

My 1984 conversation with Dafoe revolved around several themes. One was the particular role he played in Wooster Group performances and the way that role evolved from aspects of his own personality and his relationship to other members of the group. Although Dafoe talked about his own experience, his conception of the process by which performance personae evolved in the group's work can be gleaned from his comment on Ron Vawter:

> When we make a theatre piece, we kind of accommodate what [the per-formers] are good at or how they read. They have functions, so it's not like we treat each other as actors and there has to be this transformation. We just put what Ron brings to a text and formalize it: it definitely comes from Ron as we know him, as he presents himself to the world and then, of course, when you formalize it and it becomes public in a performance, that ups the stakes a little bit. That's not to say Ron is just being himself, but you're tak-ing those qualities that he has and you're kind of pumping them up and put-ting them in this structure. (1997: 41)

This quotation points to another issue we discussed extensively: dif-ferent modes and registers of acting and performing characterized by different degrees of illusionism or anti-illusionism. Acting, Pretending, Transformation, Enacting, Presenting, and Sketching were all among the key words Dafoe used to define a range of different possibilities for describing what performers do. Placing his own performances with the Wooster Group on the anti-illusionistic end of the performance spec-trum, he suggested that his satisfaction in performance, his version of catharsis, comes from the execution of a role conceived as a series of tasks. "It's just about being it and doing it," he said; my own gloss was:

> This leaves the mind free – instead of trying to fill the moment with emo-tions analogous to the character's (Stanislavsky), the performer is left to ex-plore his own relationship to the task he is carrying out [...] The possibility of meditativeness leads to a kind of catharsis, defined entirely in terms of

---

achieve stardom with *Platoon* (dir. Oliver Stone, 1986). According to the filmogra-phy, at <www.rottentomatoes.com>, Dafoe has been featured in 40 films, including two documentaries about cinema and one about yoga, from 1983 through the middle of 2002.

the performance structure: "The way I get off in the performances is when I hit those moments of real pleasure and real clarity and an understanding about myself in relationship to the structure; it is work, it is an exercise of me for two hours, behaving a certain way, and it can become meditative." The creation of persona from self results in a measure of self-understanding. (1997: 43-44)

In the article, I went on to note that "Film acting is the unavoidable point of reference for a definition of performance as the development of a persona" (1997: 44); Dafoe's ideas concerning the relationship between live performance and film acting became another major theme of our conversation. Dafoe draws parallels between the process of making a film and that of making a theatre piece. Typecasting, "the fact that they've cast me in this role, is not unlike a certain kind of tailoring that we do at the [Performing] Garage" (1997: 44).[2] The technical requirements of film acting correspond to the score of a Wooster Group performance and provide Dafoe a similar opportunity for reflection on his relationship as a performer to an inclusive process. "When you're doing a scene, you've gotta hit that little mark and if you don't hit the mark it spoils the shot. And, somewhere, I respond to that. Most people find that distracting, but that allows the frame for something to happen; it cuts down on my options and I'm a little more sure about what I want to do at any given point" (1997: 44-45). As in Wooster Group pieces, the imposition of a specific task creates a degree of freedom within the structure. "You get no sense of having to produce anything. What you're thinking about in a funny way is your relationship, almost literally, to this whole big thing, the 20 guys around, the black box, you're dressed up in a suit or you're dressed up in leather. You get some taste of what they want you to come across with, but what energizes you is the whole situation" (1997: 45).

Dafoe's saying that there was no significant difference for him in terms of process and affect between performing in a Wooster Group piece and acting in a film was surprising and provocative to me. I was much more used to the stage actor's ideology, according to which film acting is a different and somewhat debased form of acting, and the activist ideology of the experimental theatre of the Vietnam era, according to which participation in mainstream media was tantamount to selling out. Dafoe's attitude seemed to me to represent a new way of thinking about the artist's relationship to cultural politics, an idea that proved pivotal to the central argument of my essay "Toward a Concept of the Political in Postmodern Theatre," first published in *Theatre Journal* in 1987.

---

[2] During our second conversation, Dafoe told me that he no longer feels typecast in films now that he has had the opportunity to perform a wide variety of screen roles.

The seeming ease with which the post-1960s generation of American theatre experimentalists has adapted itself to the demands of commercial film and television may seem disturbing; certainly, the ability to move back and forth fluidly between commercial and political/aesthetic performance was not considered a worthy objective by the sixties generation. This is not to suggest that theatrical experimentalists of that decade did not participate in commercial projects, but only that the current generation clearly no longer feels the need to justify such work on the grounds that it makes other, politically subversive, work possible. [...] From a postmodernist point of view, this adaptability is arguably symptomatic of a healthy lack of distinction between high and popular art in postmodern culture; from the perspective of a more traditional analysis of political art, it could be seen as implying an alarming lack of integrity on the part of young experimental artists. Certainly, the phenomenon raises the question of whether or not the avant-garde or political artist need claim to take up a position outside of the dominant discourse; my argument here suggests that such a claim has no clear utility under postmodernism. In order to address a conception of culture as a conjuncture of adversarial cultural practices, the artist must position herself among those practices. (1997: 68)

I elaborated this argument further in my book *Presence and Resistance: Postmodernism and Cultural Politics in Contemporary American Performance* and returned once again to Dafoe's comment in my later book *Liveness: Performance in a Mediatized Culture*. This time, I argued that Dafoe's lack of interest in making distinctions between performing with the Wooster Group and acting in films is symptomatic of the closing gap between the cultural contexts of avant-gardism and mass culture – as well as the cultural categories of live and mediatized – in a media-saturated society (1999: 29). Dafoe's remarks on his relationship to live performance and film acting have been important touchstones for me in my own thinking about the relationship between live and mediatized modes of performance.

Since that first conversation with Willem Dafoe had fed my thinking about performance and its contexts in so many important ways, I seized the occasion of the Brussels Wooster Group conference (16-18 May 2002) as an opportunity to meet with him again, which we did in February 2002, once again at his loft in SoHo, now a more elegant place than the one I remember from our earlier encounter. The circumstances of this conversation were considerably more formal than the first one – the interview had to fit into Dafoe's complex schedule and time for it was limited. As I had chosen to videotape the conversation, we were surrounded by equipment and camera people (a situation in which Dafoe was perfectly comfortable, of course, but I was not) and so on. We revisited many of the questions we had discussed in 1984 and talked about Dafoe's current perception of the Wooster Group, his sense of what kind of performing he does with the group, the Wooster Group's use of technology, and his current impressions of the relationship between his work as a Wooster Group performer and a well-known movie actor.

Many of Dafoe's comments were very consistent with his earlier ones. He still describes performing, whether in theatre or film, in terms of the pleasure of carrying out tasks that gain meaning from the discursive structure that contains them; as a performer, Dafoe remains concerned primarily with the integrity of individual moments rather than their thematic relationship to a whole. He does not see performing as a form of interpretation or intentional communication; his job, rather, is to make specific images available to the audience, which is left free to interpret them. Some of his remarks clearly reflected the years of experience he has accumulated with the Wooster Group and as a film actor since we first talked, particularly when we discussed the Wooster Group's status as an institution and the importance of the opportunities and inspiration it has provided to younger performers. I thoroughly enjoyed resuming the conversation we had begun almost two decades earlier and found Dafoe to be as thoughtful and eloquent as ever.[3]

*

A: I was thinking back on the last time we talked which, indeed, was some time in the mid-1980s and at that point the Wooster Group was hardly a fledgling operation. It had quite a few significant productions under its collective belt and was getting a fair amount of notice and respect within the experimental theatre audience and community. Here we are, almost twenty years later, and the Wooster Group is still going strong. I guess I'd like to start by getting some of your thoughts on the Wooster Group as an institution all these years later. Correct me if I'm wrong in anything that I say, but I have the sense that the Wooster Group is now very highly regarded within the world of people interested in experimental theatre, as almost a matriarch of experimental theatres. Certainly, it's been mentioned to me in the last couple of years how influential the Wooster Group has been on other younger companies in other parts of the world and locally. So I thought we might begin with some reflections on that.

D: Sure, depends who you talk to. But I'm conscious that we've been around, some of us have been working together for over twenty-five

---

[3] The text was transcribed from the edited videotape by Dawn Pendergast (who also edited the video) and edited by Philip Auslander. Material removed from the text to maintain flow and avoid redundancy is not indicated. Ellipses indicate pauses in speech, not absent words. All text that has been added to the transcribed text appears between brackets. The titles applied to sections of the interview also appear in the video.

years. Still, as I experience it personally, only up until recently, Liz [LeCompte] always approached every show like it was our last and it's sort of been a case of boy-crying-wolf or the woman-crying-wolf. We see that she does continue to work. But for many years it really felt like [the piece] we were working on was the last. This wasn't some coy way to make us concentrate. It was really very hard to make pieces. We don't work from a particular philosophy or methodology. It's a fluid thing. It evolves. It was very hard for her to project into the future. And I speak of her – I could as well speak of Kate [Valk], who figures very largely in the decisions of the group. There has been a change in that recently; I don't feel that so much. I feel like I can anticipate being very old and still making theatre pieces with Kate and Liz. You're just aware of the longevity and you're also aware that some people that are making work started out as interns for us or worked with us for a while. There's quite a few groups in New York City that actually do quite good work that came through our *system*, our interning system. I'm aware of that, but beyond that, I get a little self-conscious because you know you're half blowing your horn. The word institution makes me nervous because I don't think of us as an institution.

A: Okay. Why don't we talk about your personal involvement in terms of your having done this for twenty-five years. What is it that keeps you doing it?

D: I think I still love to perform. And I love to perform in these pieces. Certainly my ideas about what I do and how I approach what I do have changed through the years but the thing that remains is that I like the sensation that I have when I'm performing. I like the sort of single purpose feeling that you have, the kind of concentration, the kind of grace that can be possible that you can accomplish through gesture. You feel useful. You feel unified. It's a state of being that I like a lot. It's a very selfish thing. It's a way to get away from myself to get to myself. It's a state that I like. It's a physical state. It's a mental state. And I can only find that... only certain situations present those opportunities. And the Wooster Group's work is one where I continually find it. I've always maintained that I'm more interested in dance than acting. That still holds true.

A: In other words, in the physical.

D: In the physical. The sensation. I think I'm interested in sensation.

On Acting

D: I find when you talk about approaching performing through task or you talk about action and you kind of get away from personality and psychology and interpretation, people get very cold and say "oh I get it, you're like a technician or a craftsman." It's not true; I think it's true in task that emotion comes, just like a character's revealed through the story. Sometimes I feel like an athlete. The task is very simple. Do you want to tell me that watching a guy or a woman run a 100-meter race isn't emotional? What are they doing? They don't want you to think in a particular way. What are they concentrating on? They're concentrating on getting from here to there. But to watch them in the task can be a very emotional thing.

A: There are certain things that interested me a lot [in the earlier interview]. One of them was your saying on that occasion that in the live performances you felt that your relationship to the audience was a very abstract relationship, that you didn't have the same need for audience or connection to audience as some performers do. I was wondering if you continue to feel that way.

D: I think that's sort of true because I'm not charming and I don't want to learn how to be charming. And I think that if you think about the audience too much you get into this personality game of charming them. Also, there's this feeling that with a certain kind of contact with the audience, it's an unfair social relationship. Because they're sitting there and you're presenting something to them and it's as if you know something and you're going to impart this experience or this idea to them. I don't think in terms of that, particularly; the Wooster Group work doesn't work that way either. These are constructs that I can't quite account for. They interest me and they may have a point of view, but as an actor I don't have to know what that is necessarily. So I'm not an interpreter, I'm more like someone who is performing these tasks in front of these people in these different frames. And the audience will watch it. So that's a lot different than, I think, a lot of traditional theatre. Sometimes when you do interviews, people ask you, what do you want the audience to feel? What do you want the audience to get from this? I never think in those terms.

A: They get what they get.

D: Yeah. Which sounds kind of glib or snotty, but I wouldn't presume to know what they need. I just assume that I'm a human being and they're human beings and we're coming together which has the great dynamic which I do love. It's not like I'm cold to people watching. It gives you great energy. But specifically, do they feed me? It's still an abstraction. Because if I start to get in their heads then I start to be too concerned with the *value* of things and the *meaning* of things.

On Technology

D: People will tell you different things but, for example in this piece
[*To You, The Birdie! (Phèdre)*], our video stuff is home video stuff. Our
sound stuff is home sound stuff. We started out quite humbly. Our
computer stuff is home computer stuff. It was stuff that we had around.
And when we get in a room and we make a piece, we bring our stuff
with us. And it really doesn't involve ideas as much as these are wonderful tools to use to help us problem solve. The impulse is basically to
get something on the stage. In some cases, to tell a story or work out
something that we're playing around with to find our relationship to the
text. But, as a performer, they're just tools, and sometimes we use them
to actually take us away from ourselves, to take the control away from
us. We have to cooperate with them. In this piece in particular, there are
video screens that the audience does not see and there's a video that we
use as subtext basically, physical subtext. They aren't things that we
necessarily copy but they inform how we're doing something. It's like if
I'm talking to you, I'm talking to you but I may be looking at a Bugs
Bunny cartoon. That's going to affect how I'm talking to you and
particularly if we play around with some imitations, some dialogue, with
that unseen technology. If I'm watching, you know, a porno film, it's
going to change how I talk to you. So we play around with that. We do a
lot of mix of live and prerecorded stuff and that really is interesting
because you have to figure in the mix all the time. You're a little off-
balance. You're always a little fluid. You can't hunker down and abso-
lutely control the performance because you've always got to reconsider
the mix. Because even though you're working maybe with the same
tracks, how it gets mixed each night by the technicians, who are basically performers – unseen performers – and how you feel that according
to your feelings and how it comes to you. That's the tension and that's
the play of performing in one of the theatre pieces. So technology is just
a... it's a wonderful go-between that helps us bounce stuff off of each
other.

A: Just to go back a few minutes to what you just said with respect to
the sort of dynamic of the actor behaving as if they had something to
impart to the audience. I'm not sure if this is really connected, but I was
thinking as I was going over things in my mind, of the frontal presentation of the Wooster Group.

D: Well, one thing [that] is very specific about the Wooster Group is
[that] we work with a lot of technology and it's never hidden, which is
an enormous difference than most theatre. Particularly now that the
commercial theatre uses more technology, they make great efforts to
hide it more and more.

On Theatre and Film

A: Another thing you said the last time we met which really interested me and which I got, truthfully, a lot of mileage out of in terms of
my own thinking about things was when we were talking about how you
feel about theatre performance versus film performance. Now that
you've made a *lot* more movies than you had when we first met, I'd like
to talk some more about that... how you see the process of acting in
films. At the time you basically said to me that you saw no difference, in
terms of process, between what you do in the Wooster Group and what
you do in films.

D: I'm a little bit still there.

A: It's okay. It's not a problem. I'm just curious.

D: I'm a little bit there and all the films have such different...
they've got their own rules. Each film kind of makes its own rules and
makes its own process. You know the huge difference that I feel, the
useful way to think about it, the simple way, is film is like a musician in
a recording studio. Stage: you're performing in a bar. You know, that's
what it comes down to. Film, of course, is totally fragmented and you're
basically making these things and then someone else orders them. But
the biggest difference lately that I keep on thinking about is in film
you're often addressing, basically, your first impulses, you're hitting a
scene. Okay, you rehearse and all that stuff, *maybe*. But basically, on
most films you walk in the room, you check it out, you block the scene,
you maybe talk about it, you do some things, and then you shoot it. And
that's it. And you never visit it again. Of course, the editor visits the
material but you as an actor never visit it again. Where, in theatre, no
matter how loosely structured the performance you're doing is, you keep
on visiting the same things over and over and over and over again. And
you have to develop a way to receive and to reinvest and not only is that
a helpful talent to learn in life, but that's the magic of the theatre. That
never gets tested in film because basically you're dealing with everything for the first time. So sometimes we joke that what we do is the
New Naturalism in the Wooster Group. Because basically we're traditional in that even though the scenic elements and a lot of things [are]
anti-illusionistic, let's say, we still have that thing that everything is
created for the first time. There is that illusion and it's not really an
illusion because usually the mix, no matter how tight, how meticulous
the score, the mix always shifts around. Your investment in it always
shifts around and that's the pleasure of performing for me.

D: What's interesting about film is that constantly, you're always
anticipating what it's going to be *later* when you first start out and try to
craft the performance with those things considered. And after a while

you realize you can never anticipate so you might as well deal with what's in front of you. It's like if I decide that... I'm trying to think of a clever little example... Let's say if we know that I'm going to kill you at the end of the movie, I may say "well it'd really be cool to do some kind of gesture or something" so when you see me kill him you can say "Oh yes! I saw that in that scene because there was that moment where he grabbed his hand a little too hard or something." It gets into kind of schticky bullshit stuff because then you're anticipating the effect of things. I mean it's like when I go back to that thing about identifying with being an athlete. I trust sort of biological truth. When the guy runs from here to here, you know, he runs and stuff happens to him and that's what you see.

A: I think you've been clear on what the pleasure [is] for you in performing in the Wooster Group, but what is the pleasure for you in acting in film?

D: Similar. It's also the life adventure stuff. I've really always been attracted to location movies. I've attended to my *career*, let's say, less than I have to working with interesting people. I like the adventure of it. And there's something beautiful about a bunch of people getting together with this equipment, with this General. You know, I always think of it like an invading army, it's so single purpose. Even on a low budget movie with very few resources, it has a schedule. It has deadlines. These people have to come together [in] different roles... It's a real collaboration. Each person comes, bringing their expertise to this event that's happening right before your eyes. You figure into that event. It's romantic. It's more like how we make our theatre pieces. A bunch of people come into a room and make this thing. And I like that kind of community that comes together to make a thing. And I think that's true in a more personal way in the Wooster Group because we own the place. We tell our stories. Our impulses are ours. And although we have economic concerns, [we] don't have the same kinds of business concerns that film does because it's such a popular medium and it's such an expensive medium. I think the pleasure has to do with the adventure and in the crudest way, once again, the pleasure of being an actor is to experience these different things. It's a great exercise in empathy. It's a great exercise in the possibility of transformation. I mean, I argue with people that know me whether I'm a narcissist or not. But you know, I'm always fascinated by this – you got to get away from yourself in order to find the commonality, to find yourself. It all sounds like so much New Age stuff, but I am interested in this stuff because it keeps on occurring to me. I just finished a movie in December. They said "Where are you going? What are you doing next?" And I said "Well, I'm going to work with this company that I've worked with for quite a while." And the guy said [condescendingly] "That's *great*. You're doin' some theatre. That's *great.*" You know, that's the attitude. If they don't know, they don't know, that's all I can say.

A: Well, there are a lot of different dimensions to this, but there is this weird way of thinking in this country, particularly from the film industry point of view, about going *back* into the theatre.

D: Well, yeah. I mean, nobody does it. I mean I'm lucky because I had this company before and it functions and it's functioned all the way through. People have been dedicated to keeping it together. We're still functioning. Most people will only go to theatre when there's nothing interesting going on in film where that's not the case with me. The only thing that I'm conscious of is, once again: I've been doing this for long enough that I always felt like I was the young kid passing through and now, all of a sudden, overnight, I've become the old man. I'm only forty-six years old, but this kind of theatre is a young person's game. Because there's no money in it. It's a very poor theatre. It's very uncertain. There's not a lot of social cachet so people that are ambitious, they have to really do it for the work. So if there's a persona, I'm conscious of the life persona of a guy that's chosen to stay in this young man's game.

A: I was also thinking, in terms of the idea of community, [of] the films as being sort of temporary communities and the Wooster Group as an ongoing…

D: Yes, that's very true.

A: Can I say permanent community? I don't know.

D: It's true. Film is a series of one-night stands and the Wooster Group is my wife. With all that's great and horrible about the difference between those two things.

PART II

THE WORK

The Wooster Group
A Dictionary of Ideas

Bonnie MARRANCA

PAJ

Anthology

The Wooster Group brings together the intertextual, the intercultural, and intermedia in a new definition of the *liber mundi*. This theatre chooses all species of texts from the cultural heritage, then stages their dissemination in new spaces and environments, generating a multitude of narratives and images.

This is the legacy of John Cage's "library of sounds" and of Rauschenberg's mixed-media works. Early on these artists understood that in using the archives of art and culture as a database the issue is not one of ownership, but of distribution. Viewed in another light, the deterritorialization process of this kind of theatre, if extended into the world of cyberspace, changes the very nature of the way we think of art and authorship, composition and interpretation, and the notion of boundaries between art forms, art and everyday life, one culture and another, the created and the ready-made. This approach highlights process – the artwork and the *work* of art.

It is more and more apparent that the post-war American avant-garde model, based on the cutting up, quoting, redistribution, and recontextualization of the world archive of accumulated texts, images, and sounds prefigured the digital mode of perceiving space and time and meaning. This is the new design of information.

Books

Inside *House/Lights* is Gertrude Stein's *Dr. Faustus Lights the Lights*, inside *Nayatt School* is T. S. Eliot's *The Cocktail Party*, inside *Point Judith* is Eugene O'Neill's *Long Day's Journey into Night* and Jim Strahs's *The Rig*; Thornton Wilder's *Our Town* is the center of *Route 1 & 9 (The Last Act)*; *The Crucible* shapes *L.S.D. Brace Up!* stages Chekhov's *Three Sisters* and fragments of *Brace Up!* itself appear in *Fish Story*. Then there are the films, the paintings, the songs, the dances, the television shows. All of them fragments – replacing, restructuring, recreating, pushing the frame. The text of *Frank Dell's The Temptation of St. Antony* includes a long compilation of writings and other media: the Flaubert classic, Lafcadio Hearn's "Argument" which prefaced his early translation of the French text, material by Lenny Bruce who was sometimes known as Frank Dell, books on magic and spiritualism, original writing by Jim Strahs (the Group's in-house playwright), and scenes based on Ingmar Bergman's film *The Magician*. The frantic voice of Dell at the end of the text explodes, "the the books in the library the the they run they play they see radical things."

Foucault characterized Flaubert's work as "the book of books" (1977: 87-109), a fanciful library of books that can be "taken up, fragmented, displaced, combined, distanced by dreamy thought... " It is this French tradition, and the later English-language examples of Joyce and Pound and Burroughs, that are the antecedents for the Wooster Group's textual and rhetorical styles. Even as it breaks open and reconstitutes literary material, the Wooster Group staging still exudes a modernist belief in the significance of art as a "language" within a work.

Books read, books open, books turned inside out, texts cut apart, turned upside down; books on the floor, words spilling underfoot. The trilogy, the epilogue, parts one and two, parentheses, exclamation point, a work-in-progress. Pull a quote from here, take that paragraph, take out the whole section, cut the play apart, redo it, retranslate, show it on video, record it, perform it live, do it all at once. Collage is the aesthetic strategy at play.

This is *texture* rather than text; theatre "pieces," precisely. The Wooster Group are not beloved readers. They are browsers who skim the pages of books, randomly collected. They like the sound of words rather than their meaning. They are more interested in *passages* than in writing. This is the contemporary style of reading – scattered, naive, non-linear. Texts that can be interrupted. A book that can be opened to any page.

As group autobiographies ("lives of the performers"), the productions reflect a collective intelligence, duplicated on the literary level by the anthology-like scripts that are staged. The most Pirandellian of performers, the Wooster Group is always in search of an author.

Conversation between Elizabeth LeCompte and Richard Foreman

RF: I want to use language to escape language.

EL: Yeah, but I've already escaped language.

RF: Well, I feel trapped.

EL: It's not that I feel trapped. I find it *is* a trap, that I have to constantly move around. But language to me is like what for a child the color red is. I don't have any association of its power... I don't look to it for anything but entertainment.

RF: I feel ruled by it. I look at language as if it were a kind of Ping-Pong game in which there are a lot of little balls hitting things and going off in strange trajectories and you're dominated, your life is ruled by the fact that these things are accidentally hitting this way, that way, that way. And I want to figure out the scheme of that so I can be clear of it.

EL: And that's what you write about.

RF: You could make the case that this perverse historical period we're in produces serious art only if it's perverse. And I'd like to think that I am forced into what I know is a perverse strategy by the times. I'd like to think that in happier, healthier times maybe I wouldn't even be an artist.

EL: You've said that a lot to me, but I haven't really understood it till recently. I've had this feeling of not being an artist. I don't know what it means to me... Maybe it's age. I've had a vision of just doing landscape architecture. It has to do with figuring out how to replant the earth the way it was. Returning it. You know, some obsessive thing like that. Returning it to the way it might have been naturally.

RF: Practically every moment I'm conscious, I have the urge to say, "Wait a minute – This life that is passing through me, I want to be more jewel-like." What I mean is that I don't want things coming in and passing through my head the way they are doing now. I want there to be other surfaces inside me that they bounce off of – like light bounces around inside a jewel. So a new structure is made by that bouncing around. And that's why I have to write, to evoke that, to turn myself over to that imagined "thing."

EL: The closest I come to that is landscape architecture. I want to organize space. I can't think unless I'm organizing space. Now obviously I've thought, "Oh, I'll go outside." I realize now, that's a big change. I'd no longer be an artist. I'd be somebody organizing landscape... But it's the same, yours with words, mine with space.

RF: I don't see the difference between doing that and what I think other contemporary artists do. Just messing around with materials until you find what turns you on, what gives you a thrill.

EL: Yes, but I always have in the back of my mind these people who will be sitting and watching. And I know when I'm messing around and I don't care that they're there – and I know when I'm messing around and I do care.

RF: I've always thought, perversely again, that my moral task in life was to dare to show more and more of the messing around that just turned me on. Without caring what the response is.

EL: Oh, yes. Me, too.

RF: I do care. But that's a failure on my part.

EL: That's right, yes. And I've always felt that way, too. (140-142)

Dramaturgy

The Wooster Group incorporates different technologies – writing, drawing, audiotape, video, film, telephone, record player, computer – into theatrical form. Built on the transformation of the fragment into an anthology, this is a new conception of *dramaturgy*, not merely a play or text, and more than drama. If the Wooster Group is a theatre that looks like it only cares about its image, it is just as interested in rhetoric.

The differentiation and inner dialogue of speech styles and perform-ance languages (live and mediatized) is at the heart of its dramaturgical process. Dialogue is shifted from the relationships of the performers to the relations between theatrical elements. Often, a play-within-a play or a game structure acts as interlocutor. In *House/Lights*, on-stage "charac-ters" from Stein's play have their speeches punctuated by a computer-generated sound score of "quacks" and "bings" and "blips." The Mac-inTalk voice demonstrates its potential as yet another audio track to add to the many forms of production constituting the narrative tracks of a Wooster Group work. (The script as powerbook.) At the same time it situates within the new media the tradition of sound poetry that includes Stein.

Ecologies of Place

Wooster Group pieces are rooted in the articulation of different kinds of performance space. In their evolving ecology of theatre, the kinds of spaces most used are:

Indoors:
House
Tent
Hotel room (usually Miami)

Outdoors:
Sea
Backyard
Highway (the Wooster Group has developed its own version of the "road play")

Media spaces:
Film
Video
Phonograph
Tape player
Photograph
Computer

Lecompte, a visual artist, starts with the construction of space as a way of conceiving design as structure. Her project is aligned with the American avant-garde tendency to regard space as a field of revelation (social, political, or spiritual). *Three Places in Rhode Island*, and those locations which refer to Maine, outline emotional geographies that are played out in theatre works elaborating abstract versions of the performers' actions.

The tension between nature and culture in the works is paralleled in the relationship between inside and outside (or between three-dimensional design and video) . Sometimes, the performers need to get outside the live event and find freedom in filmic space. The contrast between different spaces offers a key to the individual works. Another space of freedom is the hotel room to which a theatre troupe is escaping, at times functioning as a place of sexual license or fantasy. Increasingly, the touring company in the hotel room performs the general condition of Wooster Group life on the road. The frequent shifting of locations mirrors their working process, which pulls texts and images from here and there, traveling through but never inhabiting them. The incessant production of imagery and text is a variation on the idea of construction in their built environments.

A single text or site is too confining and claustrophobic for the Wooster Group. Putting more and more complication into it, by way of other texts and other media, points to a way out of it. They don't want their pieces to end and so they rehearse and rehearse and divide them into parts, then make them into trilogies, and carry along objects and costumes, music and leftover texts, putting them into the same house, turned this way and that. They build and rebuild the house that is not a home in a struggle with the elusive sense of place. And when moving becomes unbearable, they create an afterimage of the landscape they left behind or the echo of voices in it.

Figures of Speech

The Wooster Group actors are "figures of speech" more than "characters." Their plenitude of discourses is manifested in modes of direct address, dialogue, monologue, sermon; the interview, the letter, the lecture-demo and talk show; drama, non-fiction and novelistic writing, computer-generated sound and digitally-altered voices. They are *lazzi* for the contemporary theatre. (The performer's mask/face duplicates the techniques of layering and texturing that characterize other aspects of the staging.) Dramatic classics, religious, scientific, literary, and instructional texts are referred to indiscriminately, even interrogated. The production of affects is more important than representation.

The forms of speech employed by the performers are drawn from many sources: conceptual performance, vaudeville, soap opera, film acting, cabaret, musical comedy, melodrama, television, rehearsal as performance. Varieties of speech style and performance style overwhelm narrative in productions whose tension grows out of the juxtaposition of acting and reading, live performance and mediated presence, and competing forms of media. The Wooster Group takes to heart the idea of theatrical production and reproduction, offering both the performance and its documentation within the same event. A live performer may interact with others in real time, on film or on pre-recorded video, or the voice may be separated from the body. At times the same scene is enacted in two different media, film and live performance or live performance and a radio play of the same text. Some speeches are heard on tape or telephone or records or computer. A live actor and an actor on video converse in real time. In one sense, this is a post-actors' theatre in which the live performance situation forces performers to confront images and recordings of themselves in an ongoing analysis of the nature of "presence."

In *Route 1 & 9* a romantic scene between the young couple in Wilder's *Our Town*, which serves as a point of departure for the piece, is performed on video by the actors. What is notable about the scene, acted in an intense, soap opera style, is its inherent commentary on performance languages. Namely, the distinctions between stage speech and video speech and between acting and performing. The highly-charged expressive language of Wilder challenges the medium of video. It is simply too intimate and full of emotion for the flatness of the video screen. If *Route 1 & 9* recreates and mocks the educational approach of Clifton Fadiman's fifties' lecture on *Our Town* – indeed, the clichés of arts education itself – nevertheless, the Wooster Group, here and elsewhere, substitutes its own kind of "lesson" in the production.

Ground

LeCompte uses the floor as an active element of performance space, treating surface like a canvas. The stage picture is always framed and the borders of the space defined, but the desire to extend the event outside the frame reveals itself in the shifting ground of the set design. The performer's body is the figure in the ground, moving between portrait and landscape, private and public self.

In *Sakonnet Point, Nayatt School,* and *Route 1 & 9,* reality is diagrammatic – marked out on the floor. Electrical chords trailing the TV monitors in *Brace Up!* form tracks along the floor. In *The Hairy Ape* sound travels upwards from the lower depths, the floor tilts, the performers disperse in rows, only their upper bodies visible. In *North Atlantic* the ship heaves.

The ground is always shifting beneath the feet of the performers which is why dance defines their movement, not walking. Dance is often used to animate the sense of place, or simply to kill time or speed up a scene, whether in the house music of *Route 1 & 9* or the eccentric dance of *Brace Up!* or the mock ballet of *House/Lights.* And, not surprisingly, since reading texts or watching fellow performers from the edge of the stage has so prominent a role in the productions, the typical Wooster Group performer is seated, automatically creating a special relationship with performance space.

House

In the house there is a table: A sculptural element. A site for reading, playing records, sitting, chatting, examining the body, writing, telling stories, drinking. From this place setting all narratives begin. But, the Wooster Group will have none of the domestic realism of American drama. Their beloved house remodels the old box set and the ordered cosmos visible through the open houses of Renaissance painting.

The house splits apart and fractures, like the texts performed inside it, spatially duplicating the literary structure through the use of multiple platform levels, corridors, steps, scale, depth. With each new work the design of raw space moves toward architecture. From production to production, there is the tripling of perspective: textual material presented in several media, the same set/house turned to different angles, intermixing of live and mediated performance. Wooster Group staging practices, from their grounding in the environmental theatre of the Performance Group, extended the "rough cuts" concept of Gordon Matta-Clark's deconstructed houses into performance space, bringing theatre design closer to installation art and away from Schechnerian ritual.

Jim Clayburgh: "The ground plan for *Rumstick Road* became the ground plan for *Nayatt School,* only reversed in the space and lowered. Then the house finally fell apart to a skeletal structure on legs at the end of *Point Judith* and moved from wood to tin. The *Route 1 & 9* house – built of tin studs and tin 2x4s – was the same one built at the end of

Point Judith. It's a constant evolution of the same ground plan, with just a transfer to another space or the change of an angle. Even when I designed *L.S.D.*, the ground plans of all the other shows were on the stage as my reference for working it out." (1984: 6)

The house no longer appears in *House/Lights* and *To You, The Birdie! (Phèdre).* Ron Vawter and Paul Schmidt have died, Spalding Gray left home and then died, too. Third generation performers from different countries and continents now make up the theatrical family, open to "adoption," as it were.

Image

1. Body, text, image, sound, environment are denied the feeling of wholeness – it's the fragment, the angle of perception, that matters. The tension in a performance is manifested in the anxiety of the audience searching for an image of the whole (text; house).

2. The image of the stigmata in *Flaubert Dreams of Travel But His Mother's Illness Prevents It* (the film in *Frank Dell's The Temptation of St. Antony*), refers to a wound (martrydom), aestheticizing the inner life of the Wooster Group.

3. Re: *Brace Up!* "In Chekhov's time a samovar was as ordinary an item of domestic life as a television is today." (Schmidt, 1992: x)

Just the High Points: Willem Dafoe Says a Few Words about *L.S.D.*

"The more I perform, the more my relationship to the audience becomes totally abstract. Different performers, actors, need different things. For example, Spalding [Gray] loves an audience. He really feels them out there. I don't. It's a totally internal thing. Even when I have a character, I'm always curious to see how I *read*, what people think I am, who I am, and then you lay the action on top of that so you're confronting yourself in these circumstances. It's open-ended. I'm not presenting anything: I'm feeling my way through. If you were acting something, if you were very conscious of acting a character, somewhere you would close it down, you'd present it. You'd finish it. In this stuff, you never know."

"The way I get off in the performances is when I hit those moments of real pleasure and real clarity and an understanding about myself in relationship to the structure. It is work, it is an exercise of me behaving a certain way for two hours, and it can become meditative." (Qtd. in Auslander, 1985: 96-97)

Kate (Valk) on the Found Object

"First Liz asked me to make a copy of a satin dress that had been worn in *Three Places in Rhode Island*. When it was finished, she tried the dress on Willem but liked it better on Matthew, who wore it as 'the family dog' in *Long Day's Journey into Night*. A lot of the costumes worn in *Long Day's Journey* were taken from earlier parts of the trilogy and used in a different way. Willem wore a purple dress around his neck that Libby had worn in *Nayatt School*. Ron wears the same striped shirt as Jamie did in *The Cocktail Party* section of *Nayatt*. Liz had me sew gold furniture trim on a lot of the costumes. She had me make a black silk lampshade for the standing lamp in the *Long Day's Journey* house. It had the same shape and was constructed like the Red Tent from the Trilogy." (Published text of *Point Judith*)

LeCompte and Video/Performance

The visual artist Joan Jonas appears as a performer in the role of Celia Coplestone in *The Cocktail Party* scenes of *Nayatt School* and as Masha in *Brace Up!*. More significantly, she has another performance history underlining her presence with the Wooster Group: Jonas's early performances featured many of the techniques that would become media strategies of this theatre. In her video performance, entitled *Organic Honey's Visual Telepathy/Organic Honey's Vertical Role* (1972), audience members could watch various versions of it on tape on multiple monitors. The process of image-making was a part of the performance, duplicating and altering the information of the performance as it was being performed.

Another contemporary antecedent to this way of working is Carolee Schneemann's performance/installation *Upto and Including Her Limits* (1973). During the performance one of her own films was shown on a double screen projection; audiotapes documenting real life situations were played; 3-6 monitors showed moments of the performance in a replay or as they occurred. There was a continuous projection of slides relating to the work and to Schneemann's early paintings and collages. A reading area in another space away from the performance included Schneemann's notes, posters from past works, business and artistic correspondence. She was seen live, on tape, on film, and heard on audiotape.

The so-called "deconstruction" mode of LeCompte's style derives from film and video editing and collage which is a spatial rather than a literary impulse. It is not so easily domesticated in poststructuralist theory, where some theatre critics have tried to contain it. In the genealogies of performance, the existence of two different and often exclusive histories of performance – one in the theatre and the other in the visual arts – shortchanges the influence and achievement of cross-media artists. What is needed is a view of American performance that brings together the two traditions for a more comprehensive history of performance ideas.

Medicine/Mania

Doctor, priest, teacher, author – they are variations on the dreaded authority figure at the center of the productions. The fear of death and of loss of control is played out in the refusal of closure, of meaning, and, ultimately, of accountability for the work.

The characters in the productions exhibit a fear of succumbing to irrational forces that masquerades as chaos. Extremities of their behavior show up in an hysterical, manic speed of delivery weirdly at odds with the "cool" surface look of the world they inhabit. The works are full of paranoia, anxiety, rage, and a notable absence of decorum that co-exists with the acknowledgment of sin and a functioning moral order. Pleasure is not so much an expression of joy as as act of transgression, bordering on the pornographic.

Dance is an essential activity for the company, not only to relieve the dramatic tension but also to cover over the lack of resolution of cultural problems. The "social dances" performed create a sphere of freedom, bracketed off from the world, carnivalesque in spirit.

Non-Acting and Acting: Gray Analyzes Himself as a Performer

"Could I stop acting, and what was it I actually did when I acted?" Spalding Gray asks. "Was I, in fact, acting all the time, and was my acting in the theatre the surface showing of that? Was my theatre acting a confession of the constant state of feeling my life as an act? What was the reality of myself on the other side of that 'act'? [...] I began to use all these questions as a sort of creative energy source from which to work. These identity questions became a foundation for more personal work.

"The perception of acting as being a 'lie' became, in itself, a kind of dramatic conflict, a tension, the old protagonist-antagonist theatre construct. The conflict between acting (active interpretation) and non-acting (just doing the actions) created a new thesis, a new 'act.' The separation I had experienced in theatre previous to this was transformed into a kind of Gestalt. It was closer to the bone. It was a dialectic between my life and theatre rather than between role and text. The 'figure' became myself in the theatre and the 'ground' was the contingency of everyday time out of which this timeless, and therefore 'saved,' figure grew.

"This is not to say a new 'gap' was not emerging. Now there was the new space between the timeless, poetic me (the me in quotes, the self as poem) and the real-time self in the world (the time-bound, mortal self; the self as prose). The ongoing 'play' became a play about theatrical transcendence.

"It was, for me, a grand play between love and death. Love became the act of giving myself away to the work and to our audience. This act was always played off the great wall of prosaic time, the massive flatness of it all, the indistinguishable 'thing-in-itself.' This was the not-self or the place of death in life. The figure became the individual creation and the ground was the allness-of-it-all from which this figure grew. The play was the movement in and out of those two realities.

"This was the new 'play' which I found more interesting, and certainly more immediate, because it was going on all the time. I only had to stop it, and look at it, and any number of theatre situations would present themselves. It was learning how to make frames, to frame the mass of reality. I saw this act as composition. I thought of myself as performer/composer because this interplay from which this set of actions grew did not necessarily take the form of text but more often took the form of a conglomerate of images, sounds, colors, and movement. I did not choose to work this way. I found it to be the only way I could work." (1979: 33-34)

Lee Breuer of Mabou Mines once said that Spalding Gray had the third great acting idea of the century. He went beyond Stanislavskian psychology that joined the actor and character, and Brechtian technique that separated the actor from the role, to use his own life as material for conceptual performance.

On Working as a Dramaturg

Norman Frisch: Although one may pretend that one is attempting to stage some fragment of a text – or even an entire play by O'Neill or Chekhov – what is actually being staged in a Wooster production is the life of the rehearsal room. So the material – that life – that one is staging is being manifested in the very moment one is staging it. It is never static. It is never really knowable. The nature of it is rarely, if ever, agreed upon by the players involved. So the dramaturg, in projecting some order or pattern onto all these fluid, disparate, multidimensional elements, takes on a difficult role in interpreting the very private impulses and gestures of one's colleagues. You may think your're making an observation about Masha, or Jones, or Tituba, but if the lines between performer and performance have been intentionally blurred, your observations may be taken quite personally.

Marianne Weems: I think, too, that as a dramaturg with the Wooster Group, you quickly discover that there's no "outside" vantage point from which to view the piece. It's like a physics experiment where your mere presence affects the atoms as they interact – you're part of the process, and so you're implicated in a way that doesn't allow for a kind of clinical dramaturgy. There's no point in stolidly maintaining a scholarly approach. (Jonas, Proehl, Lupu, 1996: 499)

Pedagogy (Subversive)

The Wooster Group reveals a gnostic project: to foment doubt and confusion through the performance, quotation, and collision of images, texts, and styles, thwarting habitual responses to complex ideas. The goal is not the acquisition of knowledge as a civilizing activity or foundation of cultural and social values, but exactly its opposite: the decentering of the human being and the destabilizing of knowledge and beliefs. In its own way, *Route 1 & 9*, through the lessons of *Our Town* recreated from an *Encyclopedia Britannica* educational film analyzing Wilder's play, undermines the conventional notion of the "humanities."

The teaching play – or anti-teaching play – has a long history in modern theatre, especially in the varied pedagogical scenes of eighteenth-century and nineteenth-century drama by the likes of Lenz and Büchner. Closer to our own time, Peter Handke reinvented this form in his "speak-in" plays and Heiner Müller mocked the pedagogical authority of German drama by reconceiving Brecht's *Lehrstücke* in his own re-education plays which articulate post-Stalinist views of Marxism.

In contemporary American drama, Richard Foreman has most directly taken up traditions of the teaching play as a formal device. Besides the Brechtian model, one of his influences was the artist Jack Smith, who pioneered a mode of performance in the sixties – and prevalent in the performance art of the next decade – in which he used autobiographical fragments, slides, and collections of texts, in a lecture-demonstration format. But, a fascinating aspect of Smith's work was the way he incorporated an aesthetics of "failure" as part of the performance. His equipment was constantly breaking down; he would stop and reset or redo a part of his performance (albeit in unrehearsed asides), or give technical instructions. His bizarre staging of *Ghosts* in the late seventies is one of the earliest examples of "deconstruction" in the American avant-garde theatre.

The Wooster Group retains this way of working that confounds real time and theatrical time, stylizing it in the frequent onstage interplay between technicians and performers that highlights changes, glitches, revisions, and restagings of the kind that occur in *Frank Dell's The Temptation of St. Antony*. LeCompte, in fact, likes to make aspects of a performance seem unvirtuosic and beset by mistakes. This is a visual arts attitude toward performance, anathema to most theatre. Paul Schmidt, who translated *Three Sisters*, which forms the basis of *Brace Up!*, and acted the part of Dr. Chebutykin – another Wooster Group medical man dispensing advice – made several interventions in that production. He would correct a line reading or pronunciation of a word, summarize a scene that is unstaged, describe the mental state of characters, or discuss the meaning of a speech. The translator then became a "character" in the production, offering an ongoing critical perspective.

LeCompte descends from a tradition of subversive or anti-pedagogy that began with a critique of the Enlightenment. In her theatre, she undermines the role of art as the articulation of moral values or as a statement of "truths" about the human condition. Refusing the role of director as critic because she is more interested in amplifying modes of perception than in any singular meaning, she plays with the very notion of "interpretation." In their own way, however, in the pedagogical forms of the "lesson," "examination of text," and "rules" that wind their way through the productions, the Wooster Group has been educating audiences in a new understanding of theatrical experience joined to mediated experience that is closer to reality than the realistic theatrical style inherently criticized. Exposing multiple forms of cultural production to embrace the canons of high art and the sentimental kitsch of popular culture, the works extend the legacy of the dark side of the Theatre of the Ridiculous by pointing to the impact of imagery on the American psyche.

What energizes this pedagogical mode is not the wisdom of books. Rather, it is the manner in which texts and tropes are catalogued in the Wooster Group's own library and treated in its satirical dictionary of received ideas. Their works are satyr plays to be set alongside the classics of the dramatic repertoire. This ethos is well-suited to the classics because of their sense of order and control: the productions are, in effect, the bringing to order of disruptive realities – a profoundly classicist project. (LeCompte's formalism is a variety of classicism.)

Questions I've Asked Myself over the Years

• How much of the work is sheer problem-solving and willful complication of the narrative and how much a serious deliberation on the material?

• Why does this theatre company still need to rebel against authority, whether in the form of the text, or through the themes of education, medicine, and religion, at this stage of life?

• What is the sincere nature of spiritual inquiry in the works?

• Is the incorporation of an afterimage an aesthetic strategy or a form of narcissism?

• Is the work of the theatre overpoliticized by critics in order to legitimize it as theoretical subject matter?

• Do I want to do the detective work it takes to figure out their references? Can they be known?

• Where does the difference between critique and reference situate itself in the productions?

Religion

One of the great themes of the Wooster Group is spiritual crisis. *Rumstick Road,* the first major company production, explored the agon of matter and spirit that was dramatized in the Christian Science beliefs of Spalding Gray's mother, whose suicide was the work's emotional heart. In *Nayatt School,* the use of *The Cocktail Party* as intertext highlighted the anguished Protestantism of Celia Coplestone. And *Point Judith,* the epilogue to *Three Places in Rhode Island,* revisited the Catholicism of *Long Day's Journey,* featuring Ken Kobland's film with nuns. *To You, The Birdie! (Phèdre)* ends with a search for redemption. As a matter of course, the complex maneuvers of the Wooster Group raise religious and moral issues, just as they challenge legal, scientific, intellectual, and medical authority and values.

When Frank Dell asks, "Can matter be part of God?" one has to wonder if this is Ron Vawter's own voice crying out in the wilderness. If the Wooster Group pieces can be understood at the level of autobiography, this work is a particularly soulful commentary by Vawter, who, having once studied for the priesthood, acted the role of Frank Dell until he died of AIDS, in 1994. In one sense, *Frank Dell's The Temptation of St. Antony* stages spiritual crisis at the hour of his impending death. The character Sue reads to him: "There are also certain others who linger in Hades, but not unhappily as a rule. I refer to certain young men of a careless, animal, and occasionally, vicious life who die violent deaths [...] These poor fellows are suddenly wrenched from their bodies while still they are in the prime of manhood. They are not, in any sense, capable of grasping, for a while, the difference between earth life and the Afterlife."

Subsequently, in *Brace Up!,* as the character Vershinin, Vawter gives one of Chekhov's bittersweet speeches about the "future" in the style of a sermon, directly addressing the audience. "In two or three hundred years, well in a thousand, maybe... a new and happier life will begin. Of course, we'll never see it, but we are working towards it right now. We work for it, we suffer for it, we create it, in fact. And that's the whole point of our existence. That's what happiness is, I think." The translator/doctor, Paul Schmidt, who was also dying of AIDS, discusses its meaning in what can only be described as a scene of tragic irony.

The waywardness of appearance and reality that energizes the work of the Wooster Group is not merely a theatrical conceit but a staging ground for the genuine interest in the performance of the self. It was elaborated initially by Spalding Gray and Ron Vawter, both traditionally-trained theatre actors with a propensity for self-reflection. The nature of acting on the stage would evolve as fundamental questions about human actions – the crisis of identity and belief – in the world. They brought a quality of emotion to the productions that is no longer there. Both actors, from the alternating prism of Christian Science's refusal of materiality and Catholicism's word made flesh, inserted the issues of moral struggle and shattered belief systems into the collective Wooster Group mind. Dance, then, could be understood as a form of ecstatic performance.

Speaking Voices

Speech acts, though not in the dialogues of conventional drama, have a substantial impact on the Wooster Group conception of theatre: speech and gesture brought together, but as autonomous acts, often separating gesture and meaning, and parts of the body. In *To You, The Birdie! (Phèdre)*, one actor speaks in an electronically-modified voice on behalf of another actor, the director communicates from her seat in the audience to the actors through their wireless microphones, the actor's body interacts with a video camera to create an image on stage that is part digital, part live. The strictures of neoclassical drama are parodied by the reading of badminton rules during the production, exactly the sort of in-your-face rebellion this theatre is drawn to. As if to further confound performance styles, videos of Merce Cunningham and Martha Graham dances are being played for the performers while the stage events transpire.

The Wooster Group revels in the rhetorical play of text and image and hearing and sight, as they demonstrate the very process of "articulation." Meaning is less important than the contrapuntal and polyphonic "voices" each aspect of the staging expresses. What matters is the intensity of presence.

On one level, the theatre experience plays out the competition between the spoken and the visible, the aural and pictorial, the live and digital. The issue of perception was addressed by Gertrude Stein in her 1934 essay, "Plays," as an aspect of emotion. In other words, how do we receive information in the theatre: through seeing or hearing? How do these senses work together? In a Wooster Group production, how does one experience the various performance styles and modes of production, live and mediated?

In *House/Lights*, which brings together Stein's own *Dr. Faustus Lights the Lights* and the grade-B porno film *Olga's House of Shame*, performers wear earpieces in which they hear a recording of the text from the play and the soundtrack from the film that cues their speech. Several video monitors are placed above the audience, in and around the space, and off-stage, guiding the performers who are watching them and synchronizing their actions with film or video.

"Your sensation as one in the audience in relation to the play played before you your sensation I say your emotion concerning that play is always either behind or ahead of the play at which you are looking and to which you are listening. So your emotion as a member of the audience is never going on at the same time as the action of the play." (xxix) Stein's words read like a Wooster Group manifesto.

Temptation of St. Antony, Frank Dell's

The ecology of place is relocated from Flaubert's desert to a hotel room, and the illuminated manuscript is no longer a text but a chrestomathy. Its mystical structure of seven scenes erupts in simultaneous discourses: literary, filmic, video, and audio vocabularies that employ the media technology rhythms of rewind, fast-forward, cut, and freeze frame. The actors in this narrative within narratives, which never comes to an end, are making a film, replaying audio tapes, reading and being read to, performing, and rehearsing a text which is divided into sections, parts, and episodes. It is alternately narrated and dramatized in monologic and dialogic form. The activity is one of cutting and pasting, rewriting, and recontextualizing.

From the start the Wooster Group developed its experimental attitude through the manipulation of textual materials, autobiography/fiction, mediated experience, and the contraventions of writing and speech. What propels the works are competing forms of narrative, allegory and the critical impulse. In the world of Frank Dell "appearance is the only reality." The intention is not to make anything meaningful, but to empty everything – the body, the word, the object – of meaning. It is not unseemly that its members should take as a point of departure the writing of Flaubert, who had searched for the text that would exalt form over matter, a text emptied of meaning: subjectless.

Fundamentally, the theatre's own aesthetic strategy is constituted by the struggle between form and subject matter, presence and absence, and, on the visual level between light and darkness, black and white. For sure, subject *matter* is always problematic in the Wooster Group whose theatrical style moves toward dematerialization, aligning itself with the aims of conceptual art. What Baudelaire said of the Flaubert text – that it represented "his spirit's secret chamber" – might equally describe their relation to the work and to their own interiority. In its extreme aestheticism the Wooster Group enters the realm of the spiritual.

Remarkably, the Wooster Group has improvised around and retained many of Flaubert's essential themes, which, as it happens, have been central to their own work over the years. Not the least of them is the obsession with style. A brief account of such concerns includes the ambiguities of appearance, magical reality, multiple identities, the conflict of science and faith, sexual frenzy, and the interplay of religious crisis, hallucination, and ecstatic experience. There are also the scenes bearing on temptation and depravity, the use of language as obscenity, and the symbology of monsters and witches. Flaubert's great classic, a compendium of different kinds of texts and voices, literary canon and church canon, the profane, sacred, and the heretical, is the ideal work for the Wooster Group's own glossolalia.

Urban: New York School, Seventies and After

Color: downtown black
Temperament: ironic, self-involved
Mood: subjunctive
Style: conceptual
Legacy: post-Cagean
Mode: documentary, interrogatory
Performer: authenticity (expressive) vs. artificial (impersonal)
Politics: high/low
Ideal: Nietzschean redemption through art

Vawter's Spirit

"I'm not a practitioner of any organized religion but I have a great many spiritual ambitions although they remain mysterious and invisible to me. I'm searching for the invisible [...] I feel that yearning in the audience. That's where I get my fuel. It's unfashionable to speak of these things and also very difficult. And it's taken a few thousand years to pull religion and theatre apart anyway. So now they're separate let's not confuse it with people going to church, because we're not going to church [...] I've always felt that the great influences of my life have reinvented, or created, their own sense of spiritualism [...] I think audiences have great desires towards the spiritual and all they need is the slightest excuse from the stage to open them up. So, I try to find a place between character and in front of the audience which would trigger spiritual or meditative experiences." (Etchells: 90, 87)

Wilson and LeCompte

Both visual artists, they create two different approaches to a theatre based on the idea of the archive. Robert Wilson is a symbolist, a seeker of truth and archetypes. His dramaturgy of the dispersed texts of different cultures and continents dwells in the realm of allegory. LeCompte is a materialist, an iconoclast, spreading confusion and skepticism. Her theatre elaborates the critique of the text. His subject is civilization, hers is society.

If Wilson studies the cosmos, LeCompte is interested in hell. Wilson's theatre is one of decorum, the Wooster Group lacks social grace. He loves the dream world, she can't get enough of real time. Myth, his guide; hers, popular culture. Minimalism is their sculptural inheritance, bands of black and white light.

How they regard media is the dividing line between these two kinds of theatre-making. Its usage creates the distance between the attainment of knowledge and enlightenment (the aim of Wilson) and the multiplication of information and doubt (the desire of LeCompte).

X

The Wooster Group works in a form – theatre – that is rooted in the process of discovery. There, everything is supposed to move in the direction of becoming visible. But, this theatre refuses the option of revelation and instead performs the tension between being known and not being known. The Wooster Group invites you into their house but you are always a stranger, a witness to the inbred eccentricity and suspicion. There is no sense of intimacy, no comfort, no hint of what may occur from one moment to the next. Something reclusive and self-contained, something very private, even secretive about this theatre/family encourages a theatricality of narcissism, reflected, curiously, in recurring images of water and the echo.

"You Must Have a Shoe Fetish..."

I said to Elizabeth LeCompte one evening. She readily owned up to it. I had just seen Phèdre try on several pairs of shoes. "So do I – that's why I recognize it," I said to her. We didn't speak of it anymore. Sometimes girls just want to have fun.

Zero Degree of Performance

The Wooster Group began its life with the blank sheets of *Sakonnet Point* that flutter all the way through *Point Judith*, like book covers enfolding *Three Places in Rhode Island*. On these bedsheets Spalding Gray writes the narrative of his life; LeCompte stages it. This is the story of a family. The Wooster Group starts on the road to immortality.

Now the blank pages have been refunctioned as the virtual web/badminton net of *To You, The Birdie!* (*Phèdre*). Play-within-a play.

Is *Phèdre*'s web a new formal device masquerading as sport or does it signal a coming transparency in the life of the players and in the rules of their game?

Theatre
as an Allegory of Unreadability

The Wooster Group's
The Road to Immortality Part Three,
Frank Dell's The Temptation of St. Antony

Markus WESSENDORF

University of Hawai'i at Manoa

The relationship between text and performance has been problematic at least since the early 20th century, when Vsevolod Meyerhold's theatre experiments established the director as the actual *auteur* of the performance text. The director's rise to main creative and aesthetically unifying force in modern theatre not only ended the *mise en scène*'s traditional subservience to drama by shifting the focus towards the particular artistic vision expressed on stage, it also led to a heightened awareness of the performativity of the theatrical event itself. The radical anti-textual gesture flaunted by so many theatre artists in the wake of Meyerhold, and later Antonin Artaud, furthermore implied that the dominance of the dramatic text had to give way to the creation of original and non-representational theatre pieces. A survey of avant-garde and experimental theatre productions in the 20th century, however, would show that most of these works – from Artaud to Jerzy Grotowski to Robert Wilson – were still based on textuality, i.e., self-scripted performance "scores" or, even, conventional drama. As Michael Vanden Heuvel has argued in this context, the ideological divide between "conventional textuality" and "transgressive performativity" does not appear as clear-cut in theatrical practice. Few directors "with even the strongest investment in performance theory are likely [...] to insist on the absolute freedom of performance to transgress authors and texts in the project of releasing an unlimited play of significations" (2000: 132). Even if we consider, with Erika Fischer-Lichte, the performance text of avant-garde theatre "a quasi-autonomous 'fabric of floating signifiers'" (90) that "lack an independent semantic dimension" and "bring no previously established meaning into the production" (93), the specific quality of the

relationship between the self-generated intrinsic textuality of that production and its external textual referents would still have to be determined.

This essay will examine the relationship between text and performance in one production by the Wooster Group that can be considered
their most radical theatre experiment with the "unlimited play of significations" so far: *Frank Dell's The Temptation of St. Antony*, a production
that Elizabeth LeCompte developed with the group between 1985 and
1987 and that became the concluding part of a trilogy titled *The Road to
Immortality*. *St. Antony* can be regarded as the culmination and endpoint of a series of Wooster Group-projects that pushed the boundaries
of stage "translation," representation, and interpretation of dramatic
texts to the limit, just stopping short of losing any referential link to
those texts that they were dealing with. The series included *Nayatt
School* (1978), *Point Judith* (1980), *Route 1 & 9* (1981), and *L.S.D.
(...Just the Highpoints...)* (1984), productions that, respectively, deconstructed dramatic texts by T.S. Eliot (*The Cocktail Party*), Eugene
O'Neill (*Long Day's Journey into Night*), Thornton Wilder (*Our Town*),
and Arthur Miller (*The Crucible*). *St. Antony* itself started out as an
adaptation of Gustave Flaubert's early modernist drama, *La tentation de
saint Antoine*. This play had been suggested to the group by director
Peter Sellars, who also initially collaborated on the project. By comparison to *St. Antony*, most later Wooster Group productions were more
linear, coherent, and straightforward in character (this certainly applies
to *Brace Up!* [1991], based on Anton Chekhov's *Three Sisters*, the two
productions based on and named after O'Neill's *The Emperor Jones*
[1993] and *The Hairy Ape* [1995], as well as to *To You, The Birdie!*, the
group's interpretation of Jean Racine's *Phèdre*). Three different aspects
of the performance-textuality binarism as they appear in *St. Antony* will
be examined in the following pages: the correlation between Flaubert's
text and the Wooster Group performance; the interrelationship between
textuality and theatricality in both works; and, finally, the allegorical
character of *St. Antony* as an overall performance text. The discussion of
allegory will mainly draw upon Craig Owens's influential essay from
1980, "The Allegorical Impulse: Toward a Theory of Postmodernism,"
which itself drew upon Walter Benjamin and Paul de Man's theories of
allegory to produce a critical reading of contemporary art and performance.

The specific relationship between performance and text in *St. Antony*
is already spelled out in the program notes to this production. Since play
synopses in most programs seem to "match" the performance that we
are witnessing on stage, we tend to overlook the fact that program notes
shape, inform, and guide our reading of performance, that they always
already contribute to what Brecht has called "the literarization of the

theatre" by "punctuating 'representation' with 'formulation'" (43), adding a dimension of writing even to those performances that supposedly celebrate presence and an anti-textual stance. The program notes to *St. Antony* included a glossary of the texts, authors, historical figures and dramatic characters that the production alluded to, providing information, for example, about St. Antony, Gustave Flaubert, the Irish author Geraldine Cummins, Lenny Bruce, and Ingmar Bergman.[1] The visual design of the program notes, however, directly addressed and rendered problematic the notion of performance as the representation of a text by juxtaposing two very dissimilar plot summaries that visually, through their episode-by-episode alignment on the page, suggested that they were analogous.[2] The plot outline on the left dealt with a theatre troupe rehearsing and finally performing a "magic show" in a hotel room in Washington D.C. The summary on the right, by contrast, referred to Flaubert's *La tentation* and indicated some of the visions and hallucinations that the protagonist of this epic drama experiences in the desert. The assertive quality of the juxtaposition of these synopses in the program did not only suggest to the spectator that each summary had to be read through the other one, but also that both synopses referred to and described the same performance. As it later turned out, the synopsis on the left related identifiably some of the incidents that actually occurred on stage, while the outline of Flaubert's narrative was far from being recognizable in *St. Antony*. To determine the specific relationship between both plot summaries – and, by extension, Flaubert's text and the Wooster Group production – I will examine the narratives of *La tentation* and *St. Antony* more closely.

Flaubert wrote three versions of *La tentation de saint Antoine*. He conceived the first version in 1849 and published the last one in 1874. The protagonist of all three is the historical figure St. Antony who, in the second half of the third century, retreated to the Egyptian desert to lead a hermit life. In Flaubert's epic drama, the sins, temptations, deities and monsters of various mythical ages and religious traditions parade before the passive, almost mute anchorite; labyrinthine palaces, vast crowds of people, the shadows of former disciples and the devil himself appear in his hallucinations. Divided into seven "acts" or "chapters," the narrative of *La tentation* unfolds as a continual stream of phantasmagorias that is triggered by St. Antony's reading of the Bible at the beginning of the drama and only comes to an end with the final epiphany of Christ.

---

[1] Since I attended several performances of *St. Antony* in 1988-89, I am referring here to the program notes of that version.

[2] For an extended version of the 1988-89 program notes, see the Wooster Group, *Frank Dell*: 262-268.

St. Antony, by contrast, is structured around an extended rehearsal that the members of a small theatre company, headed by a character called Frank, conduct in their hotel room. The performance is episodic and loosely structured: Frank (played by Ron Vawter) works on some of his monologues by dubbing video segments that show himself and other members of his troupe imitating a show on a sex channel; Frank intermittently chats with his assistant Sue (M.A. Hestand) and later rehearses a dance with the "girls" of the troupe, Onna (Kate Valk) and Phyllis (Peyton Smith); towards the end of *St. Antony* the whole company performs a pantomimic and highly melodramatic dance sequence, the already mentioned "magic show." These rehearsal and dance scenes frame other incidents: Onna and Phyllis invite the hotel maid Eva (Anna Kohler) and her boyfriend Jacques (Michael Stumm) to participate in one of their routines which involves the loud banging of doors to which Eva and Jacques are strapped; Onna and the sound technician Dieter (Jeff Webster) reminisce about past experiences with the troupe; Frank repeatedly takes calls from Cubby (Willem Dafoe), another member of his troupe who only appears on video and who is supposedly calling from the set of a film in which he plays Christ (a direct reference to Martin Scorsese's *The Last Temptation of Christ* from 1988 in which Dafoe indeed played the title role). The performance concludes with a *deus-ex-machina* ending: The troupe receives a job offer from Europe and starts packing.

There are, obviously, not many surface similarities between Flaubert's narrative and the Wooster Group's performance. The only recognizable elements that both text and performance share are those passages from *La tentation* that have been directly incorporated into *St. Antony*. Sue, for example, reads several passages from Flaubert's text to Frank;[3] other, smaller quotations from Flaubert have been integrated into Frank's ruminations on metaphysical and spiritual questions;[4] some of the characters that appear in the video segments of the production bear the names of *dramatis personae* in *La tentation* (St. Antony's sister Ammonaria, the Queen of Sheba, the Chimera, the Sphinx, the Unicorn). There are some lines of dialogue in *St. Antony*, however, that are not direct but highly modified borrowings from Flaubert's text. At the

---

[3]   The page number announced by Sue ("Page 226") before she goes on reading a lengthy passage from Flaubert's *Temptation* to Frank (*Frank Dell*: 280) refers indeed to the correct page in Kitty Mrosovsky's translation.

[4]   Frank's meditations on the Milky Way, attraction and repulsion, the infinite and the absolute, the indivisibility of God, the relationship between appearance and reality etc. (*Frank Dell*: 270-272) parody the metaphysical dispute between St. Antony and the Devil in Flaubert's text (*Temptation*: 205-212). Frank's statement, "Form is perhaps an error of your senses, and Substance an image in your mind" (272), is a direct quotation from Flaubert (212).

beginning of *La tentation*, for example, Flaubert's saintly protagonist says the following lines, "and as I prayed with outstretched arms I felt as if a fountain of mercy were pouring into my heart from the height of heaven. It has now dried up. Why?" This is followed by the stage direction, "*He slowly walks about within the rocky enclosure*" (Flaubert, 1981: 62). In the Wooster Group production this passage has been transformed into Frank's more casual statement, "Y'know, I find prayer intolerable, I find it hard as a rock. My heart is as hard as a rock. I used to be so overflowing with love and now I don't feel anything" (Wooster Group, 1996: 272). The rocky enclosure of Flaubert's stage direction referring to the setting of the scene has been turned into a figure of speech in Frank's monologue – the rock as a metaphor for spiritual barrenness. As these examples demonstrate, the adaptation and incorporation of textual fragments from *La tentation* into the surface structure of *St. Antony* not necessarily establishes resemblance between both works. The question, however, remains whether *La tentation* and *St. Antony* may not be linked on a deeper level of organization.

By choosing to work on *La tentation*, the Wooster Group picked a text that was not only not dramatic in a conventional sense but had been considered impossible to stage when it was first published (the fantastic imagery of the play required stage technology that has only become available in the late 20th century.) Michel Foucault has pointed out, in his essay "Fantasia of the Library," that *La tentation* contains "the indications marking a possible performance: division into dialogues and scenes, descriptions of the place of action, [...] blocking directions for the 'actors' on stage" (93) etc. These markers of a dramatic text, however, are misleading since *La tentation* was not intended for theatrical presentation. The staging of the text was supposed to take place *within* the text itself, in the act of reading the text: "an insidious spectator takes the reader's place and the act of reading is dissolved in the triumph of another form of sight. The book disappears in the theatricality it creates" (93). The question arises, of course, how a text that supposedly has nothing to gain from a future performance but enacts – and exhausts – its own performativity in the very act of reading, can be profitably transferred onto the stage. It appears that Flaubert, in writing *La tentation*, approached the relationship between theatricality and textuality from a writer's point of view, while the Wooster Group in their response to Flaubert's text seem to have inverted the perspective. If the book in *La tentation* "disappears in the theatricality it creates," the performance of *St. Antony* in return continuously teeters on the brink of vanishing into the multi-layered textual references that it has set up. These references, however, are not exclusively of literary character, they also include audiovisual systems of writing such as film, video, and sound recording. If, according to Foucault, Flaubert's *La tentation* "was responding to an experience of the fantastic that was singularly modern and relatively unknown before his time" (90) – the discovery of the imaginary as a "phenomenon of the library" (91) – then *St. Antony* can perhaps be considered an up-to-date interpretation of Flaubert's text that not only translates a 19th-century literary text into a 20th-century language of the stage but also, simultaneously, converts the paradigm of texuality in Flaubert's time into a contemporary textuality that encompasses non-literary media. Both works reflect self-referentially upon their own media conditions. While Flaubert refers to the book that triggers most of St. Antony's hallucinations right at the beginning of his epic drama (1981: 61), the Wooster Group production opens with Frank checking his microphone: "Testing for sound. Testing the Sony dynamic microphone at one foot, testing the Sony dynamic microphone at two inches... testing, testing, testing..." (1996: 269). Frank's seemingly random decisions to play, fast-forward, repeat or skip certain video passages in *St. Antony* are similarly prefigured in the random reading technique with which Flaubert's saint leafs through the pages of the Holy Scriptures: "Shall I take... the Acts of the Apostles?... yes!... starting anywhere" (1981: 66). While Flaubert's St. Antony is driven by a quest for eternal theological truths, Frank's assistant Sue mocks his desire to find the "tape with the answer to everything on it" (1996: 275).

The distinction between the literary paradigm of textuality of the "Gutenberg Galaxy" (McLuhan) and post-literary textuality based on audiovisual media is of major concern to the German media theorist Friedrich Kittler who has analyzed extensively the effects of different "discourse networks" on subject formation and the human imagination.

> As long as the book was responsible for all serial data flows, words quivered with sensuality and memory. It was the passion of all reading to hallucinate the meaning between lines and letters: the visible and audible world of Romantic poets. [...] Electricity [...] put an end to this. Once memories and dreams, the dead and ghosts, became technically reproducible, readers and writers no longer needed the powers of hallucination. (10)

Kittler suggests here that modern media technologies have rendered the culture of literacy obsolete since they allow for a full visualization of phenomena that were merely fantasized by the reader before, as supplements to the book provided by the imagination. Kittler, however, seems not to consider the possibility that different technical reproductions of "memories and dreams, the dead and ghosts" may themselves be arranged or integrated into an incomplete configuration with the characteristics of a hieroglyphic text, with the reader trying to establish the meaning of the overall text by filling in the gaps between each fragmentary component. *St. Antony* uses audiovisual media, but not to technically reproduce as spectacle those imaginary worlds that Flaubert could only indicate in writing 150 years ago. On the contrary, video images and sound-scapes in *St. Antony* never form a whole – neither by themselves nor in combination with other semiotic levels of the production – that would allow for a coherent and unified reading of the performance text. The Wooster Group rather treats the *mise en scène* as another, extended form of writing, a post-literary performance text the meaning of which could only be hallucinated, arising from the gaps between divergent signifiers on stage. (These include, for example, the segments from Ken Kobland's video *Flaubert Dreams of Travel but the Illness of His Mother Prevents It*, the lounge music that plays in the background of Frank's monologues, the piercing shrieks of Onna, and the hydraulic wall that is raised repeatedly with a loud drone, etc.)

The part-by-part arrangement of images, sounds, bodies and objects in *St. Antony* and its preclusion of any totalizing reading of the overall performance text point to the conceptual link between the Wooster Group aesthetic and the notion of allegory. In the modern era, allegory has often been considered inferior to its opposite mode of representation, the symbol. While the symbol "represents the supposedly indissoluble unity of form and substance which characterizes the work of art as pure presence" (Owens: 62), allegory negates such notions as indissolubility, unity and presence. Any kind of theatre in which a part (be it a dramatic text, the characters' inner life, or the body of the performer) comes to stand in for the whole event could be considered "symbolic" in this context, and it could be argued that many types of modern theatre (from naturalism to symbolism to "poor theatre") have aspired to an experience of presence as "the mystical instant in which the symbol assumes the meaning into its hidden [...] interior" (Benjamin, 1998: 165). Nevertheless, there has also been an "allegorical" tradition in modern theatre that would range from the Dadaists to Bertolt Brecht to Richard Foreman and that could be characterized by "compartmentalized" (Michael Kirby) performance texts, an emphasis on writing/ reading, and the absence of a stable meaning. As the description of the disjointed and centrifugal structure of *St. Antony* may have indicated, it is the allegorical mode that best describes the Wooster Group's performance aesthetics.

Craig Owens has claimed that "allegory occurs whenever one text is doubled by another" (53), whenever "one text is *read through* another, however fragmentary, intermittent, or chaotic their relationship may be; the paradigm for the allegorical work is thus the palimpsest" (54). Apart from the conflicting plot summaries in the program to *St. Antony* that I have already mentioned, it is the double-title of the production that indicates its palimpsest-structure from the outset: *The Road to Immortality Part Three: Frank Dell's The Temptation of St. Antony*. The references in the title to "The Road to Immortality" and "Frank Dell" both relate to the American stand-up comedian Lenny Bruce, who was a figurehead of the emerging American counterculture in the late 1950s and early 1960s. Albert Goldman's biography of Bruce is one of the two major sources in *St. Antony* by which Flaubert's *La tentation* is doubled. Goldman writes that during the time before his death, Bruce's secretary Sue read passages to him from Geraldine Cummins's 1932-book, *The Road to Immortality: Being a Description of the Life Hereafter, with Evidence of the Survival of Human Personality.* (In *St. Antony* the character named Sue reads passages from the same book to Frank.) The name "Frank Dell" refers to one of Bruce's many stage personae, a character in one of his early monologues. The second part of the double-title of the Wooster Group production implies a reading of Flaubert's text through Lenny Bruce – as if Bruce himself had turned the story of St. Antony into one of his routines: "Frank Dell's The Temptation of St. Antony." The persona Frank Dell, by the way, had already appeared twice before in Wooster Group productions, namely in *Route 1 & 9* and *L.S.D. (...Just the Highpoints....).*

The other major source that doubles *La tentation* in *St. Antony* is not indicated in the production's title: Ingmar Bergman's film *The Magician* (orig. title: *Ansiktet* – "The Face") from 1958. In this film a troupe of magic performers arrive in Stockholm only to be subjected to severe questioning by local authorities in an attempt to expose them as frauds. The "Invisible Chain Routine" that is part of the "Magic Show" in Episode VI of *St. Antony* parallels the inspection performance that the troupe in *The Magician* has to give to the authorities, whereas the job offer from Europe in Episode VII of the Wooster Group production recalls the *deus-ex-machina* ending of the film when the troupe suddenly receives an invitation to perform at court. (Other characters, scene elements, and dialogues from Bergman's film have also been incorporated into *St. Antony*.) The palimpsest character of the Wooster Group production becomes particularly evident in those lines of dialogue that seem to refer to Flaubert's text but are actually taken from Goldman's biography of Bruce. Sue's already mentioned remark to Frank regarding "the tape with the answer to everything on it" (1996: 275) comes across as a modern translation of some of St. Antony's lines in *La tentation* but is in fact a direct reference to a recurrent tongue-in-cheek joke between Bruce and his secretary.

The notion of palimpsest also applies to the character dramaturgy in *St. Antony*. Ron Vawter in this production, for example, not only played "Frank Dell" but also, and without any discernible distinction between the various characters, St. Antony, Pierre (from Jim Strahs's *Have Seen the Tree*), and Dr. Vogler (from *The Magician*), etc. Even the manner in which the Wooster Group used and assembled Flaubert's texts recalls a palimpsest: the passages read by Sue are taken from Kitty Mrosovsky's

1980 translation of the third version of the text; the synopsis of the play appearing in the program notes, again, is an edited version of Lafcadio Hearn's summary of his own translation of the play from 1882; whereas the hotel maid's appearance in a pig mask refers to the first, unpublished version of Flaubert's drama – the only version that featured a pig.

The palimpsest character is also reflected in the production process that led to the performance text. *St. Antony* was developed over a 2-3 year period during which time it took on the character of a permanently over-written text. Various people were involved in creating the different segments of the production. The dance sequence (i.e., the "magic show") at the end, for example, was choreographed by Peter Sellars during the company's residencies at M.I.T. (Boston) and the Kennedy Center in Washington, D.C. Davrid Savran, in his excellent documentation of the group's early work on *St. Antony* (1986-87), describes an early version of the production that is much more linear, narrative and comprehensible in character than the final version. Some components of the at first intelligible fable of *St. Antony* were later omitted or substituted by elements that did not fully replace the missing parts but were only linked to them on a metonymic or associative plane. The dying actor, for example, who joined the troupe in the earlier version, no longer appears as a full character in the completed production of *St. Antony* but has been incorporated as another character fragment into Ron Vawter's multi-faceted performance, a change that may be partly explained as a result of Vawter's discovery in the fall of 1986 that he had AIDS, thereby literally becoming the "dying actor" himself. Another change is the later omission of the skeptic doctor who originally interrogated the troupe. Michael Stumm, who played this role, only appears as the hotel maid's boyfriend Jacques in the final version.

Another allegorical element of *St. Antony* is the concern with death and the "transience of things" (Benjamin, 1998: 223) that runs through the entire production. Even though *St. Antony* was originally dedicated to Ursula Easton (one of the former child performers in *Nayatt School* who had recently died), it was Vawter's sickness that would finally become the undeclared epicenter not only of the completed performance text but also of each performance of *St. Antony*. Not that the theme of mortality, though, would ever be confronted or represented directly in any particular scene or tableau, but references to death occur frequently throughout *St. Antony*. Vawter as Frank ruminates about death repeatedly, but in a laid-back if not slightly ironical manner that plays down the seriousness of the topic. The video segments contain morbid scenes in which people probe a corpse with poles. Onna and Phyllis in a later scene based on Jim Strahs's *Have Seen the Tree* repeatedly refer to a deceased person named Pierre, but their descriptions of his passing are highly inconclusive: Pierre may have fallen in battle, but he may also have overdosed in a bathroom. Not only the obscure circumstances of Pierre's death but also the melodramatic *tremolo* with which the performers converse about it, help to underplay the gravity of the topic.

> ONNA: I think again of – PHYLLIS: Pierre.
> ONNA: Dead.
> PHYLLIS: – dead Pierre. Dead in a trench – (The Wooster Group, 1996: 282)

Some of the allegorical characteristics of *St. Antony* are already apparent in Flaubert's text: the foregrounding of reading; the over-writing of one text by other texts; the counter-narrative; a concern with the transience of matter, etc. But *La tentation* and *St. Antony* are also linked on another level, since both can be interpreted as failed attempts to achieve the artistic ideal of an autonomous, self-contained and self-explanatory work. Both endeavors, contrary to the stated intentions of their creators, finally crystallized into allegorical configurations. When Liz LeCompte set out working on *St. Antony*, her driving idea was that in "this piece the story had to rise to the surface. Or as in an etching: the story had to be hard black lines that impress out of the confusion, so strongly that you would go away with the impression of not a world created, but of a story told" (qtd. in Savran, 1986-87: 38). Flaubert, on the other hand, dreamed of writing a book that would fully suspend its textual limitations: "What strikes me as beautiful, what I would like to do, is a book about nothing, a book with no external tie, which would support itself by its internal force of style, a book which would have hardly any subject or at least where the subject would be almost invisible, if that can be so." (1997: 170). This passage from a letter by Flaubert to Louise Colet from January 16, 1852 is quoted in the pub-lished version of *St. Antony* (265). It not only describes Flaubert's own intention in writing *La tentation*, it also suggests a possible key for understanding how the Wooster Group approached Flaubert's text. The stage adaptation of Flaubert's "book about nothing" "where the subject would be almost invisible" has led to a performance text in which not only the adapted source material but any narrative structure has become almost imperceptible. Two other passages from the same letter by Flaubert that are not included in the published version of *St. Antony*, however, reveal the writer's frustration with not having achieved his goal. Discussing his recently completed first draft of the novel *L'édu-cation sentimentale*, Flaubert complains to Louise Colet that "there are too many things missing and it is always an *absence* that weakens a book" (1997: 170). Flaubert then continues, extending this criticism to *La tentation*: "How lovingly I chiseled the beads of my necklace! I left out only one thing, and that's the string" (170). Flaubert's comparison of his epic drama to a necklace without a string is only another metaphor for the allegorical character of *La tentation*. This metaphor – evocative of Benjamin's characterization of baroque literature as the ceaseless piling up of fragments "without any strict idea of a goal" (1998: 178) – also seems to describe the organizing principle of *St. Antony*, since the episodes of the final version of the production were clearly not linked by any hard "black story line" supposedly aimed for by LeCompte.

As regards the relationship between performance and text in *St. Antony*, the Wooster Group did not imitate Flaubert's text on stage but rather applied a recursive strategy of adaptation that re-induced the allegorical structure of *La tentation* into the composition of the perform- ance itself. As an obtuse, deferred and metonymic representation of Flaubert's text, *St. Antony* cannot be clearly identified as a mimetic staging of that text, since the similarities are not detectable on a surface level. The many evident connections and intersections between both works, however, make it equally impossible to prove that the Wooster Group performance does not somehow "paraphrase" Flaubert's text in theatrical terms. The representational status of the performance with regard to the text cannot, in the final analysis, be decided with certainty. Liz LeCompte, in her staging of *St. Antony*, seems to have approached *La tentation* like an allegorist who, in Owens's definition, "does not restore an original meaning" but rather "adds another meaning to the image. If [s]he adds, however, [s]he does so only to replace: the alle- gorical meaning supplants an antecedent one; it is a supplement" (54).

Yet, if we come to understand *St. Antony* as a supplement of Flau- bert's text, this is only possible because the program notes – to return to the beginning of the essay – have made us aware of such a possible link in the first place. The specific interdependence of program notes and performance in *St. Antony* recalls, in this context, the allegorical emblem. Paul de Man, in *Allegories of Reading*, analyzes a particular episode in Marcel Proust's *À la recherche du temps perdu* that refers to a fresco by Giotto supposedly representing Charity. This representation, though, is highly ambiguous since the "facial expression of the 'heavy and mannish' matron painted by Giotto connotes nothing charitable" (1979: 74). De Man concludes that we "know the meaning of the allegory only because Giotto, substituting writing for representation, spelled it out on the upper frame of his painting: *KARITAS*" (77). The plot summary of Flaubert's *La tentation* in the program notes to *St. Antony* functions similarly to the emblematic INSCRIPTIO, or motto, in Giotto's fresco. Without the synopsis, the audience's reading of the production would be radically different since no indicator in the performance (or better: PICTURA – "picture," to stay within emblem- atic terminology) itself would suggest any specific direction for its interpretation. According to de Man,

In a metaphor, the substitution of a figural for a literal designation engenders, by synthesis, a proper meaning that can remain implicit since it is constituted by the figure itself. But in allegory [...] it seems that the author has lost the effectiveness of the substitutive power generated by the resemblances: he states a proper meaning, directly or by way of an intra-textual code or tradition, by using a literal sign [...] which conveys, in its turn, a meaning that is proper to it but does not coincide with the proper meaning of the allegory" (1979: 74).

Allegory, in de Man's understanding, results from the possibility to establish two mutually exclusive proper meanings for the same text, a literal and a figural (or rhetorical) one. The plot summaries in the program to *St. Antony*, in a comparable manner, assert the simultaneous validity of two conflicting readings of the actual performance: a close, "literal" reading of the performance (provided by the synopsis about the theatre troupe in a hotel room) and a figural one (represented by the summary of Flaubert's text). Since these two suggested "proper meanings" of the performance cannot be closed off by one final, definite reading, they render the overall production of *St. Antony* an allegory of the impossibility of reading or, in de Man's words, an "allegory of unreadability."

Fugacity

Some Thoughts towards a New Naturalism
in Recent Performance

Simon JONES

University of Bristol

Ever since Copernicus man has been rolling down an incline,
faster and faster, away from the center – whither? Into the void?
[...] All science, natural as well as *unnatural* (by which I mean
the self-scrutiny of the "knower") is now determined to talk man
out of his former respect for himself, as though that respect had
been nothing but a bizarre presumption. (Nietzsche, 1956: 291-2)

This article uses the Wooster Group's *Brace Up!* as the event
through which to explore analogies between recent performance and the
sciences of complexity. In 1984, Ilya Prigogine and Isabelle Stengers
described these sciences as "a new naturalism" (22). This article takes
the deconstructive practice of the Wooster Group upon a classical-
canonical Naturalist text, *Three Sisters*, as a radical continuation of the
pseudo-scientific Naturalist project of the last century, rather than as an
aesthetically oppositional undertaking. It analyzes the performance
Brace Up! in terms of (speeded-up) time and (the edges of) space,
describing the show's dynamic as centrifugal, its nature as fugacious.
By using the setting, both literally and metaphorically, it elaborates an
idea of "center," both as space-perception and Text-conception, viscer-
ally and ideologically, in the constant state of *being-fled*. Using ideas of
time, it figures this aptness to flee as *the character* of the New Naturalism in performance; and the performance of *Brace Up!* itself as the
expression of a "third person" beyond the subject-object dilemma of the
old Naturalism, away from the centripetal pull of the Chekhovian stage,
its spatial-temporal organization, with Irena at the close of Act Two, at
the dead center of the play, *alone, with intense longing,* "Moscow!
Moscow! Moscow!"

fugacious, *adj.* apt to flee away: fleeting: readily shed. *ns.* fuga-
ciousness, fugacity. (L. *fugax, -acis*, from, *fugere*, to flee.)
fugitive, *adj.* (*Chambers Twentieth Century Dictionary*)

The Naturalist(ic) Stage

Look at the stage. Or rather, look at Jim Clayburgh's design for the
set. Since none of the performances I experienced allowed this relation
to the stage, you have to imagine yourself turned some forty-five
degrees clockwise. And lowered some thirty to forty-five degrees, so
that one is at a shallower angle to the plane of the platform, to use
common sense orientations. Indeed, the platform, inspired by Noh
theatre, folds back onto Brecht and his presentational rostra, that in their
"turn" had deferred to Noh. The leading line of the raised level runs
parallel with the seating configuration. The lines of the reading table
upstage and the flown bars above the platform add to the dominant
perspective insisted on by this relation.

This is a version of Zola's experimental cage in which Chekhov's
animals can be put and observed from the scientific safety of the auditorium. A perspectival genealogy traceable back to those theatres built in
Italy, France and England in the sixteenth and seventeenth centuries
which placed their monarchs and rulers at *the* point of optical convergence, which mirrored the vanishing point on stage where all the lines of
perspective illusion met. An orientation of sight and a deployment of
things and persons in the space, as a whole, that could only be sustained
by its exercise of authority, over the whole: the right of its ruler to *the*
best view in the house, all others placed further away, literally by degrees, from the plane and the attitude of the perfect vision, as they were
placed further away politically and socially. As long as theatre concerned itself with seeing the monarch, being seen by the monarch and
being seen being seen by the monarch, this reflexive relation of stage-
space/audience-space, the classical horseshoe mould of so many European theatres, was the complete *mirror up to Nature*. Its isomorphic
closure embodied the stabilization of political authority apparently
effortlessly and mathematically, thereby naturally, *folded back* onto
itself, the illusion of the stage *repeating* the fiction of power, the pro-
tagonist-actor player-king standing center stage with his "court" of
players so carefully arrayed out from him, *facing* the performer-king
with his competing aristocratic factions likewise deployed. Of course,
this was a fantasy, and everybody knew it.

But when the bourgeois classes claimed the playhouses for themselves, they set up king Nature as the earthly Representative of their god
Capital *in the place of*, or rather *in the seat of* the ousted authority, like

the early churches upon their pagan sites. The legitimatizing metaphor and the novel social procedures it accounted for changed; but the seat in the auditorium and its view of the stage did not. Under the influence of the so-called empirical sciences, the *mirror* became the *frame*, in Zola's terms from his 1880 *Naturalism in the Theatre* the transparent screen, through which the Subject viewed the Object. Under these rules, Nature no longer reflected back a stable vision of its unchanging disposition; it was forever severed from the experiencing *Cogito* of Man and subject to his examination by method of trial and error and the establishment of Laws, which were themselves only verifiable *within* the terms of this relation of severance subject-object: Man-Nature. That seat in the theatre was democratized: anybody could sit in it ... for a price the most expensive, because the best, in the house. What had registered, or maybe simply *marked*, the theatre event, the *whim* of the monarch in all its canny political complexity, the *pleasure* he derived from the show, was re-placed by *method*. This was social, or rather class-grounded, in its formulation, anonymous and relatively mobile in its use and application, given that the "parts" of the event fitted, or rather submitted to, the terms of the procedure. However, the relative idiosyncrasy of the whim of the one and the relative anonymity of the method of the other should not mask their shared *character* as agents *of* the event: that of *taste*. To democratize taste, to detach it from the "body" of the monarch, as was, in deed as well as in metaphor, his authoritative head from his subjugated body, to spread it out from the center, was not the radical dispersal it appeared, as long as the idealized spectator, soon to become *a critic*, remained in his seat. The reproduction of the feudal state of Mankind became the representation of the bourgeois states of Man. The former paying little heed to the *tain* of the silvered "surface" in the pleasure of the act of admiring its perfect reflection in the mirror; and the latter obsessed by the *crease* of the fold which imperfectly folded back or re-presented the experimental objects of its still-formulating laws of Nature. The transparency of Zola's screen thickened: it became a medium. The claims he made for its "transparency" and the evidential neutrality of the artist-experimenter's judicial "temperament" became the ultimate expressions of Newtonianism in the arts. And these acts of inevitable, necessary mediation *centered* themselves on the fort-da game of what was in and out (of) this frame. From Nora slamming the door in Ibsen's *A Doll's House* to the inspection of Annie Sprinkle's cervix in her post-porn performances, what came to concern the spectator was what could be seen on stage and what could not, what happened *off* scene: in short, a crisis of *proof*.

To this extent, the exterior possible worlds opening out to Nora and the interiority of Sprinkle's flesh speculating upon her essence come to *mean* the same thing: that the fold of the frame is turned ninety degrees

about the center point of the line of the proscenium arch, to make a
center-line that bisects the stage and the spectatorium. Upon this new
axis the scene is played; and the points are plotted along this center-line
in terms of *before* and *behind* the gaze, what is on and what is off scene,
interior and exterior. So the more one speculates the scene, literally goes
into it, the more one "discovers" that nothing is "really" there; and the
more one speculates upon the outside, the more one "realizes" the
actions that can only happen on stage before one's very eyes. The
center-line insists on this fold of two kinds of un-seen/scene: that of the
consciousnesses of the spectator and of the actor, at opposite ends of this
line, polarized; and that of the *behind* and *beyond* this face-to-face
encounter, the (possible) world(s). It insists on this, to the extent, that
every gaze is met with its equal, a like mind traceable back to that
Cogito, analogous to Newton's third law of motion; and that every
extension of thought can only be *realized* in its folding back onto this
(interior) stage. Of course, it is precisely within this equalized relation,
upon the surface of this plane, the geometry of which is bisected twice
by two lines, cutting at the dead center, the proscenium arch and the
center-line, the face-to-face, that re-presentation takes center stage. In
this position, more accurately a *point*, since it cannot actually be occupied, nor measured for anymore than one of its properties at any one
time, the terms of the equation are traded, and what was opposite
becomes the same, folded along the crease of the arch, facing me facing
myself: and reader becomes writer, and time can be stilled and then
reversed, in the accounting for of the terms, in the presentation of the
proof of the equation.

The *character* of the Naturalist stage is not to be found in its attention to surface detail, its fetishization of the *mise en scène*, its adherence
to various formulations of biological and economic determinisms. It is
to be found in its *cleaving* of the spectator and the actor, staged in both
senses of the term *to cleave*: a sundering along the fold of the proscenium, and a joining of the line between subject and object. Without this
double operation, with its demarcation, its axial-rotation, and its folding
back into, there could be no Naturalist theatre. The event is grounded
where these two lines cross; and the lines of force are centripetal, setting
the frame and dividing the participants, in order that they can bring the
outside in and be brought to join hands across the *dead center*.[1] What is
more, in the infinitive *mood*, in its supreme potentiality, *to cleave* is both
unto and *asunder*, a compossible tension, like the alive and dead cat in
Schrödinger's thought experiment, the Naturalistic stage's organizing

---

[1]   As Gilles Deleuze put it in *Bergsonism*: "The real is not only that which is cut out
according to natural articulations or differences in kind; it is also that which inter-
sects again along paths converging toward the same ideal or virtual point." (29)

geometry of cut-becoming-join, join-becoming-cut. However, in the past tense, the simple participles bifurcate into *clove unto* and *clave asunder* respectively, and what was once *in-the-future* potential becomes now the actually-having-happened past, the implicate becoming explicate, both-and becoming either-or, the join-cut the cut or the join. So, the Naturalistic stage, in its unfolding morphology, expresses both-and compossible subject-objects in-outs, along its two dynamic folds, complex potentials, that inevitably become simple pasts once we observe them with the benefit of critical hindsight.

In trying to avoid a *theme*, but seeking to roll with an *inflection*, I now trace the Wooster Group's relation to the Naturalist stage. They have sought to avoid the aestheticization of their work, despite occasionally slipping into oppositional stances when cornered by interviewers. Their refusal to submit to method has led to its being schematized variously as *bricolage* or multiple frame-breaking. These readings fail to recognize the place of *the center as staged* in their work.

Note on Texts/Side Order Politics

For many critics of the Wooster Group (Vanden Heuvel, 1991; Savran, 1988), there seems to be an anxiety about politics, a need to prove a political bent, as if there were a kind of "apoliticalness" in experimentation in theatre, disreputable in its naiveté and self-indulgence, improper for such a communal art of the *polis*. We find the work drawn repeatedly onto the stage of the political project, so central to Naturalism since its early days associated with radical nationalisms worldwide. Critics re-fill the decentered stage by claiming on behalf of the artists a teleology to these acts of gay abandon: namely, undermining the Text of cultural and thence political hegemony in the name of the Really Radical. But again, I do not see the oppositional in the way the Wooster Group handle these canonical texts, although micro-political effects probably do emerge from these events. There is a kind of going with the flow, that is both intensely intimate and intimately intense.

Take the Wooster Group's use of Thornton Wilder's *Our Town* in *Route 1 & 9*. By playing dialogues as soap opera in close-ups on monitors, suspended above eye level, the emotional suturing, insisted on by the text in its desire to naturalize its fictional community as the model America, is *extended* with a certain, clear technological logic, not denied, nor opposed, out of its conventional, hegemonic, centripetal theatricalization, into television, whither long ago the forces of Naturalism and the Method had fled. Whereas one can construct a regime of dialectical readings, engendered by the experience of the performance *as a whole*, one cannot deny the effect of the text *at work*, even in this

alien(ated) medium, even as the ideological and cultural limits of those
operations are made explicit *elsewhere* in the event. The techniques
Wilder used, or rather the way he inflected the Naturalist play-machine
is made all the more strange as it makes itself the more natural to the
audience, its intimacy amplified by their familiarity with the rhetoric of
the soap opera. To have parodied would have been to have parried or
blocked the force of *Our Town*, avoided, not harnessed, its attractive-
ness, as a satellite harnesses the gravity of a planet to fling itself far out
into the void.

Also, consider the use of time in Eugene O'Neill's *Long Day's Journey into Night* in *Point Judith*. The autobiographical and thematic
resonances between the play and the Wooster Group's concerns, about
the violence and love in families, gender and class roles, mental health,
drug addiction, memory, storytelling, have been noted. In speeding up
the text in Stew's Party Piece into a frenetic thirteen minute version, in
apparently reversing the play's ever lengthening languor, the Wooster
Group again extended, rather than undermined, the play's self-reflexive
decaying orbit, passing knowingly through the literally long night in the
theatre, ever closer to the dead center of its own hallucinatory performativity, the repeated re-telling of the past, lost forever outside off-stage in
the fog, by performers who have lost faith in their stories, lost the ability
to sever fantasy from actuality, and very nearly almost lost the power to
charm, to an ever less credulous, though more seduced audience of
actors, competing for one another's attention, in turns crazed, then
stupefied by drugs. In O'Neill's machine, the geometry of the event, its
dispositional logic is *fractal*,[2] with the triads actor-audience-character,
teller-listener-tale, consciousness-perception-exteriority, memory(time)-
(event)time-life(cycle), folding back onto themselves, not as reflections,
but refractions, whole versions, versions of the whole, turning in on and
out of themselves, rotating in ever more complex detail, at scales getting
bigger and smaller, depending on which way you are looking, around
the axis of the proscenium arch and the two-way gaze.

In a musical sense, this is *fugal*, expressing complexity out of the
simple line, which opens the event, and thence continues opening it out,
moving further away in time from its simplest expression, but always
expressing the essential relation of its *cleaving*. In speeding up the
duration of the play, the Wooster Group was inflecting, but not reversing, O'Neill's temporal aphasia, which itself broke the conventions of
"natural" stage-time, by etiolating the evening *of* theatre, turning its

---

2   See Vanden Heuvel's comment: "In LeCompte's fractal theatre, systems of order or
     'solidity' often conceived as well-shaped, Euclidean texts transform suddenly into
     strange fractal shapes that indicate that within such a seemingly orderly system exists
     an inherent turbulence or nonperiodicity." (1991: 100)

narrative progression into a cycle of dream-memory events, and revealing all its secrets by the end of the first act, all the characters turning
upon themselves in a collective *fugue*, that is, a form of amnesia which
is in flight from reality. By different means, the fast version enacted the
same *dislocation* of time from its center of relative and temporary
stability: the point is, the *essence* of the play could be experienced *only*
in fast-forward, since its essence is that distortion of orthodox time, its
extension from natural time to *super-natural* (uncomfortable, because
inhuman) time. This is not "real" time, but the time *of possibilities*; and
the possible events that emerge do so precisely because of those relations unfolding. In a narrative sense, the Tyrone-performers do and say
everything that it is possible to do and say around and about their
cleaving from and unto the Naturalistic stage. Only in escaping the
attraction of naturalized time can any performance of *Long Day's
Journey into Night* fully express the Naturalism of this play-machine
and its fractal disorganizing and re-organizing of the space-time fold at
ever emergent levels.

 Willem Dafoe's portrayal of "Yank" in *The Hairy Ape* extended to
the physical limits, or thereabouts, this acceleration of time. Technique
acts as a kind of reservoir-center for the performer, from which he draws
sustenance, and from which he ventures in occasional *dis-plays* of
histrionics, recognizable to his audience by their differential intensity,
activity and brevity, their *distance from* the center as constant *point of
reference*. He puts himself deliberately out on a limb, at the periphery of
what he knows, what he feels comfortable with, he risks embarrassment
in going over the top, in breaking the ever more tenuous and fragile
relation of what is proper (central) to his act and how excessive (peripheral) his performance is becoming, in order to *show* his skill, his depth,
his differential, and in order to revitalize these functions upon his *return* to the center. Dafoe, a microphone in each hand, in blackface,
white-eyed, clad in many layers, rarely left his downstage center position, cutting instantly from one extended pose to another, rarely slowing
the speeded, tripping, amplified articulation of the text: and yet, at the
same time, he never occupied this center libidinally, his flesh being but
a reminder, a ghost of what a center could once have been. He was
scattered at the edges of what it was possible for him to do *with-in* that
performance. His perceptual locus, which normalizes and naturalizes the
body at the center of agency and events, must have been likewise dispersed *fugaciously*, being in many places away from the center. The
intensity of this delirium disorganized the space-time fold of the (w)hole
event, placing all participants at these limits, with-out any re-turn to the
center, without ever giving time and space to such a place.

Bruce Wilshire writes about Heidegger's notion of *mood*:

The categorical condition which Heidegger locates in all attunements and moods is *Befindlichkeit*. Difficult to translate, it can perhaps be said to mean that one always finds oneself, one is always present to oneself, however obscurely or inarticulately. This manifests itself as mood. What we ordinarily think to be our "center" is really a hum of mood in which we are lost in a mimetic periphery which we cannot acknowledge. (124)

And it is *in* something like this *mood*, that Dafoe placed his spectator-audience. Here, where the mood of no-where was, rather than as *place*, better thought of as a *vibration with* or a *relation of* many possible-potential selves, an *out-of-body* experience. Centrifugal and fugacious, this mood re-placed the conditions and facts of the (any)body, who participated in the event, with the potentiality of a de-centered, super-natural self, without losing the specificities and personalities in-volved. We became *implicit* (not *implicated*, because that term suggests a time *before*, which *during* the event, in experiencing it we cannot actually feel because of our displacement from the center which organizes times into successions) in what the text had to say, about the sexualities of "Yank" and Mildred, their involvement with class and industrial politics and in the performances, and in our own histories, the "strong" and "simple" relation of ourselves to "ourselves" being disorganized into a weak and complex potentiality: a new triad of actual-possible-fictional selves, alongside those excited by (in part) Dafoe's performance.

A History of the Wooster Staging

The characteristic curvature of the space-time fold in the Wooster Group's setting emerged out of the spatial destabilizations and irruptions enacted by the Performance Group under Richard Schechner's direction. In a series of well-documented works, such as *Dionysus in 69* and *Mother Courage*, the geometry of the Naturalist stage was disintegrated in order to "environmentalize" the participatory relationship of the performers to the spectators (Schechner, 1973: 1-39, 87-124; Aronson, 1981: 195-199). By dismantling the proscenium arch, ironing out the *crease* which demarcated performer from spectator, by insisting on their physical inter-activity, Schechner intensified the idealization of that very *mise en scène* he was seeking to side-step or supersede, obliging participants, in their dislocation, to draw closer to the proper-center of the event, that is, the *interiority* of the consciousness of the performer-character (itself made more proper by daily exercises of "psychotherapy"), or else to leave the scene (either libidinally or literally). Out of the unpredictable intensities of such strategies of disorientation, the Wooster Group's inclination towards deconstruction and extension, rather than destruction and opposition, emerged, inflecting the curvature of the space-time fold once again, rather than attempting the impossible, unfolding it, to re-turn to a "purer," less "acculturated" participatory relation, an original scene.

> The same set as before (only dropped down and turned around). (Director's note, *Brace Up!* programme, 1991)

Indeed, *Sakonnet Point* (1975), as documented by James Bierman (14), began with the "environment" remaining from the Performance Group's *Mother Courage*. Jim Clayburgh commented in an interview with Euridice Arratia that "Liz [LeCompte] likes to start thinking about something with a set in mind [...] The easiest way to get that is to sort of look what you have in the closet and pull it out, and maybe turn it inside out, which is in fact what we did." (124) Bierman writes of the structures of *Rumstick Road* (1977) and *Nayatt School* (1978) being "architectural rather than linear" (17); of the repertoire of actions returning "like familiar landmarks in an unknown landscape" (30). He describes the "unity and integrity of the trilogy com[ing] largely as a result of a staging idiom [... being] the proliferation of spatial options and perspectives" (28). In a comparison with painting, he describes the development of this idiom from the three areas of *Rumstick Road*, with their "heightened sense of depth familiar in early Renaissance art" (17), to *Nayatt School*'s room on stage disorientating this naturalized view, as "some of the most perplexing Cézanne paintings, in which there are several perspectives in one picture" (22). LeCompte commented on Cézanne, in remarks made to Arnold Aronson, "He doesn't finish a line [...] It gives a space and an air; it doesn't solidify into a form that's not breakable. I can't stand it when something becomes perfect, enclosed. I like to leave the system open." (1985: 72) Michael Vanden Heuvel has noted the raised seating for *Nayatt School*, which obliged the audience to peer down at the performance "from above rather than receiving the illusion of being eye-level, as from a conventional auditorium." He likened this to "being positioned within a reference frame of scale and perspective that insists that the spectator be fully conscious of irregularities and disequilibrium." (1993: 262) So, from its emergence in the *Three Places in Rhode Island* trilogy, the Wooster Group inflection profoundly concerned itself with the *problem* of framing, rushing alongside painterly techniques in perspective from Giotto to Cézanne in just four works. Its trajectory came out of Naturalism and its attempts to idealize the perfect point of spectatorship, to ground its knowledge upon what could be learnt by observation of its objects and their relations to the *mise en scène* and each other; and not the environmentalism of counter theories of participation.

Hence *The Road to Immortality* trilogy progressively did away with frames within frames, rooms within rooms, perspectives within perspectives, which were turned off the center-line to acknowledge their "perspectiveness"; and came more clearly to formulate the problem of the *cleaving lines*, which cut as they joined and joined as they cut. The platform replaced the room: firstly, in *Route 1 & 9* (1981), a flat floor, marked out with perspective lines, the solid walls of the room stripped down to a frame, the remains of before; then, in *L.S.D. (...Just the High Points...)* (1984), a raised platform (Savran, 1988: 169-220); and finally, in *Frank Dell's the Temptation of St. Antony* (1987), a high wall which turned out, in the finale, to be the raised platform from before, this time folded up on an axis parallel with the proscenium arch, and then lowered horizontally to form a magician's stage, for a trick that was played away from the audience upstage, wires and all showing, an epiphany that revealed its magic in turning the wall into a platform on the vertical plane and the audience through a 180 degrees on the horizontal, suddenly to face the event the "wrong" way. The *cleft* itself underwent considerable transformations, as the intensified event-site of the cutting-join, the problem, the line replacing the frame: in *Route 1 & 9*, a fragile rail that demarcated floor from audience, performer from spectator, object from subject; becoming in *L.S.D. (...Just the High Points...)* the reading table with its lower ramp-fore-stage, events congregating at the table, before and behind it; becoming in *Frank Dell's The Temptation of St. Antony* a lower fore-stage, a narrow raised platform (in front of the high wall), between which the under-stage, an uncomfortable space which supported literally and technically the platform above, upturning the relation before-at-behind ninety degrees, making a below-inbetween-above, a precipitous and precarious plane, with performers swinging through doors, slipping through traps, doors becoming traps, walls becoming floors, and front becoming back. So, now the stage was set for *Brace Up!*, expressed in its essential relation, *the fugacious cleft*: whereas before all the activity was attracted to the literal proscenium line, before the audience, between us and them, folded this way and that; now this line was actively disorganized and became a series of points along a set of trajectories, rendering the platform as a place of performance only useful in reminding us of its vanquished power, and the edges of the space the dynamic attractors, turning not just stage back to front, but the whole space-event inside out, turning itself out along the double axis, proscenium arch/center-line, like the petals of a flower expressing their deeply informed morphology.

Fugacity

New Naturalism adds time to Naturalism, that is *irreversible* time, that cannot fold back on itself in reflection, that does not permit an uninvolved observer to stand outside the flow of events. For Merleau-Ponty, "the word perception indicates a *direction* rather than a primitive function" (12), a movement out towards encounter and implication. The empirical model of scientific objectivity, which silently inferred the character of its implied and hence invisible Subject *in* the grounding of its discrete and thence explicit Object, is re-placed by a *supernatural* objectivity, in which Subject-Object are *implicate*, not determined by mutual exclusion and its inevitable re-turn in eventual inclusion, but compossible in their potentiality at the ever-expanding periphery of the event. Whilst the center can be held to re-present the absent past, the absent self with its absent thought, in its re-writing of the absence of presence, the supernatural event supersedes this deconstructive practice in its *fugacious presencing* of the potential futures of potential bodies.

In *Brace Up!*, the Wooster Group performer becomes such a "body," which *inflects as it projects*. The presentational mode of the setting, the platform, the downstage center step, at which Vawter-Vershinin posed with poise and self-centeredness to declare his beautiful futures, this dead center, which seemed to be the most simple arrangement of performance possible, performer directly addressing audience, amplified the so-called transparency of the Naturalistic stage; so that in projecting intensely along the line Subject-Object, the Wooster Group body suddenly inflects, turning away outwards. Vawter's intensification of the line excited this presentational mode until it jumped its own reflective logic and emerged as a fan of trajectories radiating out from the center, his too subjectively embodied Object surpassing our objectifying gaze and objectifying it in its turn(ing): a super-naturalizing, that excited the Natural cleft and fold until they could no longer organize the energy therein, disorganizing themselves in the flight of the dislocated, scattered Subject-Object relation, the out-of-body of the superhuman.

This body is also *eccentric*, out of the center. A tension was formed between, at the one end, the performers who *exceeded* the center stage, those who occupied the platform too perfectly, too intensely, excessively, such as Vawter-Vershinin with his direct address; and Dafoe-Prozorov with his melodrama mediated on monitors with widescreen framing, emotions and sentiments both too big and too little for the small screen inadequately aping the big screen; and Valk-Narrator with her stage-management, organizing the narrative, the performers, the props, as if they were all equal objects of her gaze, through which everything appeared to us, with the oh-so-friendly maximized efficiency of a fast-food operative delivering the appearance of customization to her umpteenth hungry-to-be-different consumer. And, at the other end, those performers who moved about the periphery, off the platform, sitting on its edges or at the reading table upstage, turned away, facing away from the center and us, tentative and irruptive, bursting into the "action proper," as a comet, in its eccentric, wayward orbit, cuts across the path of our inward-looking planet and lights up the sky in a mesmerizing, but disturbing, "unnatural" burst of light, such as the overlapping dialogue from the reading table, with its alien rhythm and dislocation of amplified voices from distant, semi-obscured mouths, a fleeting *feeling* of personalities come and gone before they could be clearly discerned the one from the other, supra-individuals; and Schmidt-Chebutykin-translator, facing off, his face mediated on video, his commentary on his own translation yet another turn on his own inflection of the *Three Sisters* text-machine, as it flees the stabilization of its meanings into ever more complexity and complication; and the Smith-Olga-Jonas-Lashinsky-Masha-Roth-Irina-sisters, with their screens and their hospital chairs, marginalized and hidden by Valk-Narrator as she centers and reveals "their" story. This on-off center-eccentric tension was further excited by the interruption of Shelley-Fedotik-Renderer-Rohde, a "mistake" (perhaps from one that had happened in a rehearsal) stopping the flow of the text, a cue jumped, then integrated into the "body" of the event, the peripheral, "minor characters" bursting onto the platform, taking center stage through a "mis-timed" cue, the eccentric turning unexpectedly back on the center and challenging its stability, disrupting the triad that occupies the center of the (naturalistic) Method, that of Author's script-Character-Actor's improvisation, asking how much emergent activity can the Naturalistic text hold, and yet dependent on that indeterminacy to give it "life."

This body is thence, not a surface of inscribed events,[3] but *a periphery of becoming events*; not at the center of what is staged, but outside the performable, the characterizable; outside what can be timed and what can be spaced. It is not an op-position, but an evasion, an avoiding; not a meta-body, nor an out-of-body in the sense that one feels separated from one's body and is able to recognize it as Other. It is an *outside-of* body, projected, then turned, so that what was inside, inward facing, has been folded to face *outwards*, towards the void, vast, scattered, and full of times. It becomes a *differentiator*. It is *the monstrous* within Nature, that expresses Nature's endless creativity. It *feels* alien to us because we recognize its arrival from our very unspeakable interior, because it is *of* ourselves: the monster we are always about to become.

---

[3]   See "Nietzsche, Genealogy, History" in Foucault, 1977: 148; and Birringer's use of this disintegrating body in "The Postmodern Body in Performance" (1991: 205-231).

STAGE DIRECTION. *The alarm is heard again. The stage is empty.*
IRENA. (*speaking from behind the screen*) (*Three Sisters, Plays*: 310)

Disorientated Time-Space

New Naturalism adds time to the Newtonian machine, so that it can only be put into reverse in very special circumstances, such as in theatre practice, when the critical time of reflection is made after the event in a vain attempt to distil innocence from the ravishment. This new time function is forever *fractal*, being formed of manifold times, turning in on and out of themselves. Simple objective time is replaced by thermo-dynamic time, time relative to the curvature of space, and by quantum time. This is both instantaneous events, co-determined over distances without any means of communication, faster than the speed of light; and no time at all, where the experience of time passing cannot be accounted for at the quantum level, literally disappears from the equations, does not happen, events without time. These times happen (or do not) at different levels (scales) within the event, depending upon how one chooses to observe, that is, implicate oneself into, the event. As such, the Wooster event can be imagined as these many times manifolded. For instance, the many incidents of co-incidence, when two or more events are simultaneous, though not at the same time, happening at positions peripheral which one cannot view with a single glance, that I cannot remember, since memory, as Frances Yates has observed, requires *a fiction of a place*, in order to organize its sensations; and this is exactly what the Wooster Group sought actively to disorganize in their fugacity. What I do remember is this sensation of flight, of places only recalled as *having been fled*, and not the content of events, the topics of what happened, but their form, or rather, their re-in-forming, as my memory was *re-natured* by the theatre event, away from fixing place and conse-quence. In Barthes's sense (1976: 16, 23), this was blissful, because my textualizing of the event was both *atopic*, without place, and *asocial*, since this *being-fled* was riven through with the loss of community, the anxiety over the ongoing fragmentation of the consensus, upon which Naturalism, and beyond that the Real, ground their effect. This flight was thermodynamic, deconstructive in a molecular sense, since "we" were not allowed to reconfigure ourselves as a new community of individual readers, a readership of difference, opposed *as one* to the dominant and hence pleasurable reading of the Chekhovian text; but were required to encounter a series of bifurcating points, which took us progressively along our very own, idiosyncratic paths, hurrying away from being of one view, away from each other, each point of perceptual decision driven by the gravitational vector away from the center, and yet, by virtue of that vector, always in some sort of relation to that center, a kind of memory, carried along from point to point, accumulating like a kind of history, a genealogy.

So, in reversing this centripetal pull, our identification of naturalized time, with its causal succession of past, through present, into future, was displaced. The energy to effect this escape, like all good parasitic operations, was stolen from the center-host, as a satellite uses the gravity of a planet to fling itself out of orbit into the void, appearing to cleave unto its home, solely in order to be cleft from it; so, the Wooster event went right alongside the very heart of Naturalism, its generative principle, gathering speed in the *curve of its inflection in* the Chekhovian text, to use that energy stored there potentially in its relations, to deflect off into the more complex organization of New Naturalism.

The Wooster Group's theatre machine recognizes both this extension of the Natural, not into the technological, but *by way of* it, into the Superhuman; and its essential character, that of *speed*. So, the use of video in *Brace Up!* did not draw us into the delirium of ever more accelerated interpretation of signs, circulating ever more furiously the virtual center of all displaced cultures, the attractions of which cannot be resisted by many a postmodern critic. The Wooster Group took the modernist thrill of speed, inherent in the Naturalist's hopeless desire for transparency, that is, to collapse the distance between subject and object, to arrive at the ideal of events experienced without the twinned distortions of the medium and of the personality, the noises of language and humanity. They swung close by this delirium of picnolepsy, with their monitors mediating events off-stage, mediating Japanese movies, and with their auditorium of disembodied voices and isolated sound effects, only to steal energy from this sensorium, in order to scatter those very images and effects, which appeared to be orbiting that virtual center, into a fugacious constellation, that, in carrying us away from the center, placed us, by not placing us anywhere in particular, in those very inbetweens, which the current state of picnolepsy seeks to smooth over, to naturalize. In this way, by way of speed, the Wooster Group achieved *the third person* of New Naturalism, rather than a polyvalence which draws all meanings to the dead center of affective equivalence, a delirium sustained by drugs or by theory, where the one must equal the other, and the different is more of the same, your choice. This new person is not a synthesis of the old Subject with his/her Object, since it occupies no position, no seat in the theatre, let alone a gender, is not speaking, nor spoken to; but it *remembers, in the trajectory of its flight*, whence it came, from what places-topics it emerged, what stabilized centers, cultural, socio-political, sexual, it fled, and *about* whom and what it speaks. This third person looks to the future, in fleeing the past; but it does not rush towards this potentiality indiscriminately, since what informs, but does not determine its flight, is its nature.

> When I contemplate an object [...] I become aware that each perception [...]
> re-enacts on its own account the birth of intelligence and has some element
> of creative genius about it: in order that I may recognize the tree as a tree, it
> is necessary that, beneath this familiar meaning, the momentary arrange-
> ment of the visible scene should begin all over again, as on the very first day
> of the vegetable kingdom, to outline the individual idea of this tree.
> (Merleau-Ponty: 43-44)

The flight *towards the implicate* is always *from the implicated*: there can
be no innocent escape. The essence of this nature is precisely this relation. And even though the peripheral objects upon which the eye of the
participant comes to rest, are still, that is, placed in relation to the dead-
center-stage, the very movement of the eye, from that center to the
periphery, against the naturalized focusing-homing, is re-natured, creating a new vector in the eye's attempt *to position* these eccentric objects.
The character of this is fugacious, since in mov*ing*, *during* the event of
position*ing*, the potential is always *towards off*: the new nature of the
eye is to be in flight from its natural home.[4]

At every point one chooses and do not forget, the choice is always
ours to measure, that is, to make *of* the unoccupiable a place, to take
from becoming and bring *into* being, the inflection of Chekhov's play –
that old style again – *Three Sisters* remains intact. Nothing was denied
in opposition; but excited, intensified, sent fleeing, to constellate at the
ever expanding periphery of this New Objectivity. The stage emptying
upstage to the ballroom, only partly seen, for Irena's Saint's Day party,
becoming the Wooster Group's *fled* space. The ballroom table becoming
reading table. The careful orchestration of sounds off, the displaced
"working" world which the characters keep at bay, becoming effects
without causes, a still incomprehensible void. The marginalized and
thence dehumanized servant Anfisa becoming the mediatized (appearing
only on pre-recorded video) and hence sampled Buscemi-Anfisa; her
physical frailty becoming verbal fragility. The "strange character" of
Soliony, hanging around the edges of the action, causing trouble, disturbing and disorganizing, becoming the peripheral functionality of the
performers, getting into position, drawing attention from the proper
center. The screens that separate the sisters from one another and from
the center of the stage, becoming screens that separate them from us.
Irena forgetting her Italian becoming the forgetfulness of the fugacious
event. The repeated melodramas of Vershinin's wife's suicide attempts
and the Natasha-Protopopov extra-marital affair, happening off, becoming the melodrama-action of the samurai and godzilla movies on moni-

---

[4] "Off-center objects are characterized [...] by the forces of approach and withdrawal,
surrender and escape, and they establish fields of strong visual instability." (Garner:
77)

tors. Toozenbach's fear of his own German otherness in relation to his Russianness, marked in his triple-barrelled name, becoming:

> A Gaia-nin troupe (the house entertainment) in a hotel (Japanese-owned) in New York (sometime in the near future). They are putting on a Western classic (*Three Sisters?*) for an audience of out-of-town tourists. (Director's Note, *Brace Up!* programme, 1991)

Russia's uneasy relation westwards becoming America's westwards towards Japan, that is, eastwards, depending on whether you use an Atlantic or a Pacific centered map. Chekhov's mythical Moscow, viewed from the marginal provinces, becoming the Wooster Group's take on American culture, viewed from various displacements, not least, the trajectory American culture took from European, *via* Chekhov and Ibsen, through O'Neill and Wilder, and "back" to them; and thence their trajectory on their European tours, folding back one marginalized European into the center of a European culture, itself looking westwards, inflected by way of Americans looking both ways and suddenly outwards into the void. Since the future is out there, which is nowhere, if it is anywhere.

> ANDREY. I hate the life I live at present, but oh! the sense of elation when I think of the future.

> MASHA. We're left alone... to start our lives all over again. We must go on living... we must go on living. (*Three Sisters, Plays*: 323, 329)

Brutus Jones 'n The Hood

The Wooster Group, the Provincetown Players, and *The Emperor Jones*

Roger BECHTEL

Illinois Wesleyan University

Introduction

When the Wooster Group opened its production of Eugene O'Neill's expressionist classic *The Emperor Jones* in 1998, its notoriously "deconstructionist" style was still in evidence: the world of O'Neill's West Indies island was transformed into a white linoleum rectangle on which the Group's Kabuki costumes, minstrel show mimicry, and video mediations coexisted in provocative tension. *The Emperor Jones*, however, did mark at least two substantial departures from the Group's previous work. Most immediately, it was the first time they had presented a play under its original title, largely uncut and unaltered textually, and without the interpolation of any other scripted text. More subtly, the Group also deviated from its norm in the program for the production, which went to great lengths to historicize the play and O'Neill. It noted that *The Emperor Jones* was originally produced by the Provincetown Players in 1920, and, strikingly, used a whole page to reproduce the entire text of a W.E.B. DuBois essay entitled "The Negro and Our Stage," reprinted from the program of the 1923 Provincetown revival of *The Emperor Jones*.

Drawing our attention to these historical markers, the Group invites us to contemplate the genealogy of these two companies. Both of these companies were/are "downtown." Geographically speaking, this means below 14th Street; but more importantly, their ethos was/is "downtown," a term that has become synonymous with being nonconformist and noncommercial. The Provincetown, like the Wooster Group, was committed to experimentation, and was a, if not *the*, leading member of the American theatrical vanguard of its day. Similarities also exist in their performance spaces: the Provincetown occupied a converted stable, the Group a converted garage.

Once these surface similarities are exhausted, however, a comparison between the two reveals profound ironies, nowhere more prominent than in their treatments of race and the corresponding cultural receptions. Issues of race have become defining moments for both companies, but in antithetical ways. Blatantly transgressing the cultural norms of its time, the Provincetown's *Emperor Jones* became the first production by a white American theatre company in which a black character was portrayed not by a white actor in blackface, but by a black actor, Charles Gilpin. Later, in the face of public outrage and governmental opposition, the Provincetown presented an interracial couple in O'Neill's *All God's Chillun Got Wings*, in which the white wife kissed the hand of her black husband. If we consider the legitimate theatre's use of blackface in the 1920s as racist, then the prevailing social code demanded that representations of African Americans must, in essence, adopt a racist posture. Breaking this code resulted in an attempt at indirect governmental censorship of the Provincetown when the Mayor's office refused to grant a performing license for the child actors in *All God's Chillun*.

The Wooster Group's history with regard to racial issues is, on the other hand, like a negative image of the troubles that beset the Provincetown. In one of the Group's earlier pieces, the 1981 *Route 1 & 9*, white actors appeared in blackface, told dirty jokes, got drunk, and farted boisterously (Savran, 1988: 9-45). While *Route 1 & 9* has retrospectively come to be regarded as a challenge to racist attitudes, at the time it was blasted by the press for its racial irresponsibility. Juxtaposing the two theatres in this respect evokes a palpable irony: unlike the Provincetown, the Group depicted a black character using a white actor in blackface – the very thing the Mayor's office in 1923 demanded – and violated the social code by doing what the Provincetown refused to do. And, like the Provincetown, the Group fell victim to indirect governmental censorship when the New York State Council on the Arts decided to revoke its funding.

The irony created through the historical positioning of these two companies forces this history to leap out from the flat discourse of textual historiography and to imbue us with a sense of its non-discursive temporal dimension. In a sense, the Wooster Group is not only performing *The Emperor Jones*, but also performing the Provincetown Players, albeit in a historically refracted and reversed modality. The irony, however, is not simply that of the inverted double. What I want to examine here is how the Group's production goes on to create a dialectical constellation of historical positions between itself, the Provincetown, and Eugene O'Neill, in which the ironic doubleness is multiplied and activated in a complex circulation, piquing our historical awareness and invigorating our historical sensibility.

Representing Race

If the Group's use of blackface in *Route1& 9* provoked wildly antithetical readings in New York's intellectual and artistic communities in 1981, how are we to read their use of blackface today? To answer that question, perhaps it is useful to begin by asking another: how is O'Neill's representation of race in *The Emperor Jones* received today? There is a substantial critical movement that regards *Jones* as an exploitation and extension of the stereotype of blacks as primitive and atavistic. John R. Cooley argues that O'Neill "approached his black portraits with insensitivity and maladroitness, consequently perpetuating pejorative images of black life"(63). For Darwin T. Turner, O'Neill "seems to stress a fixed opinion that blacks will fail if they attempt to live according to white men's standards" (6). Other similar criticisms have been leveled by a number of writers (e.g., Bogard and Poole).

In many ways, the Wooster Group's production could be read as a deconstruction of the play which supports these contentions. The use of blackface and the minstrel-show attitude of Valk's performance immediately signify that this Brutus Jones is a stereotype of a particular American kind, one perpetuated by vaudeville and theatre in the first half of this century, and certainly part of the cultural milieu in which *The Emperor Jones* originated. The production also turns the balance of power between Jones and Smithers on its head, which has the effect of exposing Jones as a kind of dupe or braggart buffoon. In the long first scene between Jones and Smithers, Dafoe is only vaguely recognizable in the ambient light at the back of the stage, while his electronically enhanced voice, along with the variety of burbling and hissing noises he makes while Valk is speaking, give him a kind of ubiquitous, disembodied quality. The impression is that Jones is already being controlled by the spirits of the forest, and the forest is the world of the white man. When Smithers does step into the light, we see that he is sporting, *a la* Eugene O'Neill, a penciled-in pencil mustache. Moreover, in a manner that might allude to Eugene O'Neill as the "voice" of this script, Dafoe will also become the disembodied voice of every other character in the play except Lem, the native chief. Finally, in an interpretive gesture contrary to O'Neill's text, rather than having Jones in possession of the revolver with the silver bullet throughout, Smithers gives Jones the gun at the end of the scene, and utters the line that he will repeat after each successive scene: "'E's got 'is bloomin' nerve with 'im, s'elp me! Ho – the bleedin' nigger – puttin' on 'is bloody airs! I 'opes they nabs 'im and gives 'im what's what" (23-24).

The Wooster Group *Jones*, so far as this reading goes, does seem to expose the latent and not-so-latent racism inherent in the play. But to end the reading here would be to miss the much more complex and provocative intersection of race and representation in this production. From the outset of the performance, virtually every representation is in some way destabilized. Valk may be in blackface, but her neck is shaded red, her hands remain white, and she is wearing pre-modern Japanese robes. Similarly, Dafoe's eyes are made-up to appear Asian, but his feet are red. Most stunningly, the stage production opens with an image omitted from the thirty-six-minute film. The performance begins in almost complete darkness. A video monitor downstage flashes on, showing a close-up of the face of the old native woman who sets the scene for the play. But there is something otherworldly, uncanny about this image: the face is a ghastly white with black lips. After the initial disorientation, the first impression one gets is that it is a black actor in whiteface – yet that is not it. Only when Valk appears speaking into a video camera in the dim light at the back of the stage, showing us a white actor in blackface, do we realize that the monitor is actually showing us a negative image. Yet the disorienting effect is not diminished but compounded, for the negative image does not serve simply to erase the black makeup on Valk's face, but instead creates a hybrid that neither melds the two races nor privileges one over the other. When we see Valk in blackface, we understand that the screen image is a video distortion of a black face – or is it? We are also instantly aware that Valk's black face is the product of blackface makeup, and that, in actuality, her face is white. Yet when we look back to the video image, half expecting to see the "white" Valk, we find a ghostly image that is racially indeterminate. If Valk in blackface alone produces a dialectical image, the sublation of face and mask, the simultaneous staging of its negative image through video multiplies the effect exponentially. The dialectical tension is now distributed among four nodal points: the white Valk, the blackface Valk, the white video image, and the imaginary, pre-processed blackface video image – for just as the phenomenological impact of seeing Valk in blackface causes us to imagine the white skin beneath the black makeup, the vision of the wraithlike white video image compels us to create an imaginary video image of Valk in blackface in order to conceptually process the actual video image. Moreover, if these four points exert the greatest gravitational effect in this matrix, nonetheless they are further compounded by the doubling effect of the video itself. In other words, a long series of dialectical combinations is also generated: live/mediated, real/virtual, natural/technological, etc.

This complex matrix, in its dialectically kinetic operation, is extremely suggestive of Adorno's concept of the "constellation." (1973 & 1977) For Adorno, knowledge of social forces and objects could be

gained by the arrangement of ideas and images in dialectical juxtapositions. Representation was problematic for Adorno insofar as it claims a
kind of specular truthfulness, or insofar as it performs its mimetic
function in isolation. However, when placed into a constellation of
relations with other representations, it generates a dialectical interaction
that can be epistemologically illuminating, so long as each point in the
constellation is conceived in its necessary historicity.

In the constellation created and arrayed by the negative image of
Valk in blackface, because the nodal points have doubled from two to at
least four, as dialectical antipodes they have become exceedingly
unstable. For example, Valk in blackface is now no longer solely the
dialectical opposite of the white Valk, but also of the white video image.
We cannot locate the white Valk without also being aware of the white
video image, which compels us to locate its opposite, and in searching
for that opposite we slip between the two blackface images, and so on. It
is crucial to note that this slippage will now occur at every nodal point
because of the synchronicity of the images *in performance*. What is
essential about performance as the mode of presentation is its temporal
dimension: the fact that these images can be deployed simultaneously
and therefore operate synchronically, and yet are diachronic insofar as
they are caught up in the narrative progression of the drama (as well as
the metatheatrical and metahistorical "drama" of the two downtown
theatre companies folded into the production) as it unfolds through the
temporal flow of its performance. Importantly, this allows us to have an
experience of time, and, at the same time, history.

While the Wooster Group's *Emperor Jones* relentlessly undermines
determinate representations of race, place, time, and, although I have not
mentioned it, gender, this is not to say that we lose all meaning in a
troubled sea of textualization or undecidability. We can, certainly, still
read the piece as an exposé of racism. But if, to use Elizabeth
LeCompte's words, a Wooster Group production is a locus for "many,
many meanings" (Savran, 1988: 53), perhaps it would be shortsighted to
end the reading there. If all the representations of race the piece provides
seem to deconstruct themselves, this warns us not only that representations of race are often misrepresentations, but that racism itself may be
equally mis-represented. Or perhaps the "mis-" here is mis-leading. For
what the Group demonstrates is that misrepresentations are not necessarily such because they are deliberately inaccurate, nor because all
representations are indeterminate, but that they are culturally constructed and thus historically contingent. Nowhere is this more apparent than
in the way the Group's *Emperor Jones* explores the complex constellation of race, history, and authorship.

The Author-Function of *The Emperor Jones*

It is useful here to examine for a moment what Foucault would call the "author-function" in a theatrical context. For Foucault, the author is a function of discourse, which is necessarily historically embedded. In other words, the larger social "text" actually writes the author; that is, the "legal and institutional systems that circumscribe, determine, and articulate the realm of discourses" construct the subject position indicated by the term "author" (1977: 130). Thinking in terms of author-function, we can locate with reasonable certainty the "author" of most literary and artistic works at any given historical moment. But in the case of theatrical production, contemporary culture is much more ambiguous about authorship precisely because its function is much more ambivalent. The terms "production" and "work," themselves a function of discourse, take on different connotations or valences: is theatrical production simply a medium for the "work" of literature (leaving its literary integrity intact), or does the theatre production become the "work" (the literary text becoming simply an element of the theatrical performance)? At what point does a stage production become an adaptation of a dramatic text rather than an interpretation? And at that point, to whom should authorship be attributed – the playwright, the director, or the collective company? While any cultural production may become a site of contestation with the dominant discourse, the instability of the author-function at the site of theatrical production provides a particularly open arena for such contestation, exposing, as Foucault notes, the ruptures and interstices in the discourse which the author-function is meant to elide.

What is initially striking about the current critical reception of *The Emperor Jones* cited earlier is its unabashed attack not on the racism of the play, but of the author. O'Neill is variously characterized as "insensitive" and "maladroit" in his treatment of black characters, as well as intent on "stressing" the opinion that blacks cannot live up to white standards. Yet, in the W.E.B. DuBois essay included in the Wooster Group and Provincetown programs, O'Neill is lauded not only for writing about African Americans, but for the truthfulness of his representations. DuBois even explicitly laments that O'Neill's motives and aims will receive "almost universal misinterpretation." How do we square this with the more recent critical allegations? Quite simply, we cannot – except by placing these conflicting assertions in their historical contexts. We can easily understand why DuBois would speak out against what he considered an unjust characterization of a contemporary colleague (with, perhaps, other political motives in mind as well). However, what is more curious is that Cooley, Turner, and others would use *The Emperor Jones* and other plays to brand O'Neill a racist some eighty years after the fact; obviously, for these critics, the death of the author has been greatly exaggerated. At the same time, we should not assume that such criticism is ignorant of or simply disavows poststructuralist imperatives or historicization. Instead, this criticism uses "authorship" to fulfill a political agenda; or, in other words, uses the author-function for political ends where using the literary work might be much less effective.

If we think of critical representations of a work, in this case *The Emperor Jones*, as existing within a field of play, we must also recognize the boundaries that define this field: for example, the object of inquiry is literary/fictional, the discourse is academic, etc. While the critical contestations which transpire within these boundaries may well be politicized, the political impact achieved may also be contained by these boundaries. Criticism which challenges *Jones* as racist would likely see its political impact dulled precisely because the play is textual – textual here both in a poststructuralist sense but also in the *Realpolitik* sense of lacking agency. Indeed, agency is what is gained, or attributed, by this evocation of the author-function. When one considers that agency is the boundary that marks a division between a 1920's expressionist play and the American literary lion that is its author, the political stakes are clear. If *The Emperor Jones* is accused of being racist, the agon will manifest itself on the field of literary interpretation; but if Eugene O'Neill is accused of being racist, the struggle will be over historical fact. I am not arguing that such a "fact" can ever be established or ever be more than an historiographic construction, but rather that the dominant discourse today still allows for the establishment of such "facticity" *vis-à-vis* authors and other public figures. This is precisely one important aspect of the author-function in contemporary culture: because authorship is imbued with agency, the author bears political responsibility for his or her own writing. In a very real sense, then, we can say that it is the text that "reads" or creates the author, or perhaps more accurately, it is the text that is *used* to create the author. The creation of the author becomes a political imperative in this scenario, for the author functions here to disguise the textuality of the text, to fill in its gaps and unify its discontinuities. At the same time, and just as important, the author-function occludes the reader and the agency involved in the act of reading, the politics of interpretation.

What the Wooster Group accomplishes in its *Emperor Jones* is to expose and historicize the workings of the author-function. Ironically, even though significant elements of the white community of the day were castigating O'Neill and the Provincetown for their racial progressiveness, DuBois was most concerned with the African American community, which he feared would object to O'Neill's representations as too negative. While DuBois found this understandable in light of the malignant history of such representations, he trusted in the progressive potential of realistic representation. Still, what DuBois's essay does not comment on or invite us to contemplate are the plays themselves – no text or character is specifically mentioned. Instead, the message we receive is that O'Neill, based on his writing, was not a racist.

Then we watch the Wooster Group performance. And we are forced to reconcile the tension between O'Neill the non-racist (at least as declared by DuBois), his play, and what we are witnessing on stage. On one level the DuBois essay seems a spurious inclusion into the event, a red herring, for obviously the connection between O'Neill and what we are watching is so attenuated that we could not possibly extrapolate racial motives from this production to O'Neill's character(s) or from O'Neill's character(s) to this production. But this is precisely the point. In the gesture of including the essay in the program, the Group has already begun to expose the author-function. When we remember that the essay first appeared in the program for the Provincetown Players, we can imagine the author-function operating in an antithetical and inverse manner from the way it has been manipulated by the recent critics of *The Emperor Jones*: if these critics use the plays to ascribe racism to their author, the Provincetown uses the author to absolve the plays of racism. In both instances, the author functions here as a way to view the play, to read the performed text.

In the context of the 1923 production of *Jones*, the immediacy of the DuBois essay to the performance would tend to make the author-function a fairly straightforward and transparent operation. But the historical mediation of seventy-five years between its appearance in the Provincetown program and the Wooster Group program serves to draw attention to its author-function, and contributes as well to the constellation of moments that develop the production's sense of historicity. Obviously, the Group's *Emperor Jones* is in no way intended to be a "faithful" rendering of O'Neill's play (if such a thing were even possible). Although it dispenses with much of its usual deconstructive layering, the work is still the idiosyncratic product of the Wooster Group's own unique style and aesthetic. The author of this *Jones*, we must conclude, is the Wooster Group (or Elizabeth LeCompte, but that is another problem).

There now exist at least three authorial moments in historical constellation: Eugene O'Neill as author in 1923, Eugene O'Neill as author in 1998, and the Wooster Group as author in 1998 (along with traces of the Provincetown Players and W.E.B. DuBois as authors in 1923). While we can and do conceive of these as historically positioned, at the same time we are acutely aware of the forces and energies which circulate among them in a transhistorical way – most prominently, the issue of race. The DuBois essay clues us in to the conflict surrounding O'Neill and race, and, if we know their *Route 1 & 9*, we inevitably recall the Wooster Group's own troubled history in this regard. To the constellation, then, we must add another moment: the Wooster Group as author in 1981.

At that time, the Group knew that the blackface Pigmeat Markham sequence was objectively racist, but they believed it simultaneously assumed a confrontational stance toward the audience's racism as well as their own, that it was an attack on self-congratulatory liberalism (Vawter, qtd. in Savran, 1988: 14). But at the time, only a few spectators read the performance as paradoxically both racist and non-racist, and the Group suffered the political and financial fallout. The performance itself, however, was not the only paradox in operation: critics, funders, and spectators alike had to wrestle with the perceived contradiction of what they took to be a racist performance and the theatre company they believed to be radical. Certainly the Wooster Group's resumé would appear unimpeachable in this regard: its previous production history, the life-style and reputation of its members, its "downtown" address, etc. Yet authorship here could not ultimately function as an umbrella against charges of racism, although critics' responses made it clear that it lessened the blows: as Mel Gussow noted in the *New York Times*, "were it not for the company's experimental credentials, the scene might appear to be racist" and, in the *Village Voice*, Eileen Blumenthal distinguished between the guilty act and the guilty intention in saying, "one takes for granted that the Wooster Group are not intentionally yahoos."

Admittedly, the Pigmeat Markham sketch in *Route 1 & 9* was more blatantly transgressive, more directly and energetically confrontational than any use the Group has made of blackface since. Still, following the uproar over *Route 1 & 9*, one would have expected more than the docile critical grumbling the blackface received in their 1984 production of *L.S.D.*, or the complete absence of any critical mention of it with *The Emperor Jones*. There are many reasons to explain this complete acceptance of a reviled theatrical convention in the short span of seventeen years, but one must be the continued evolution of the Group's author-function. Such an evolution is, of course, again a discursive function, the product of critical reception and explication as much or more than the product of the Group's own subsequent work, so that today, especially in the face of more subdued uses of blackface, the Group is granted authorial license.

At any rate, what is important here is that the reception of the Group has changed significantly in the last seventeen years: in 1981 they were publicly accused of and sanctioned for racism; in 1998 they could use blackface with impunity. Clearly the Wooster Group as author *functions* differently now than it did in the early 80's – its name serves as a kind of totem which affords it special privileges. Indeed, the Group's return to blackface with *The Emperor Jones*, when viewed as a self-reflexive gesture, comments on this historical change in status. What the Group points out is precisely this: they have not changed (much), cultural discourse has.

If we reexamine now the constellation of authorial moments, we find a surprising and ironic inverse parallelism. If O'Neill was acquitted of racism by DuBois in 1923, from the retrospective vantage point of some critics (and one potential reading of the Group's *Emperor Jones*), O'Neill stands guilty as charged. Quite the opposite dynamic applies to the Wooster Group: if in 1981 they were censured for racism, in 1998 history has absolved them (as has, again, one reading of their *Emperor Jones*). The effect of placing these parallel but inverse histories in kinetic play, as the Group's production of *The Emperor Jones* does, is to explode all notions of history as linear or progressive, as Eugene O'Neill, the Provincetown Players, *The Emperor Jones*, and the Wooster Group combine, separate, and recombine like strings of genetic material. To see the Group's *Emperor Jones*, however, is not just to understand discourse as historical and history as discursive, but to experience this history ontologically. With authorship and political effect arrayed in this historically galvanized constellation, we apprehend our own act of reading, apprehend our reading's radical spatial contingency – we are not just in the Performing Garage, we are located mere blocks from the "historical" Provincetown Playhouse. We apprehend our reading's radical temporal contingency – we are not just in the Performing Garage, we are in the Performing Garage in 1998. Most importantly, however, as we watch the Wooster Group's *Emperor Jones* unfold, as we experience the Group's performance of history, we apprehend that, in this moment, we, too, are historical actors.

Voice Masks

Subjectivity, America, and the Voice in the Theatre of the Wooster Group

Gerald SIEGMUND

Justus-Liebig-Universität, Giessen

Media

The theatre of the Wooster Group is famous for its use of media. In the German critical discourse it has almost exclusively been described as a media script, as a scenography staged with the help of new media (Petra Meyer, 1995). Film, video, and tape recorders are used as much as slides, microphones, or, more recently, computer programs to disrupt bodies and the dramatic text in order to create a rich performance text by layering audio and visual material and distributing it in space (Savran, 1988). This disintegration of material runs counter to a naturalist effect that homogenizes the reality of the stage and the life-world. It is a cinematic gaze that characterizes their use of material, a gaze that has thoroughly internalized the perceptive mechanisms of film by cutting images, speeding up or slowing down language, and separating the visible from the audible. By these means the Wooster Group also points towards the theatre's construction in the moment of its production, in order to throw a critical glance and a theoretical reflection on that which is shown in the moment of its showing and that which is said in the moment of its utterance. In what follows I would like to take this description of their working method one step further and ask what may be one of its possible results.

In his well-known essay "Toward a Concept of the Political in Postmodern Theatre" Philip Auslander describes the Wooster Group's as a "resistant" as opposed to a "transgressive" theatre practice that inhabits an economic structure and its cultural products such as the media while at the same time deconstructing and criticizing them. I take this argument as a starting point for my own inquiry into how this can be achieved. I will concentrate my attention on the use of the voice and its relationship to the body, because it is a relation that is central to the art of theatre. In the voice, as I will argue, the crucial notion of subjectivity both in the productions of the Wooster Group and in theatre in general manifests itself. Using Elizabeth LeCompte's production of Eugene O'Neill's *The Hairy Ape* as shown in Frankfurt am Main in 1997, I intend to demonstrate how the voice makes present those excluded social and cultural elements that otherwise remain absent in the space of the stage.

Subjectivity

Eugene O'Neill's play *The Hairy Ape*, written in 1921 and first performed in 1922, which forms the basis of the Wooster Group production, can be read as the allegory of a consciousness on the way to itself. The stoker Yank feels fine. In contrast to the Irishman Paddy, who longs nostalgically for pre-industrial times, and Long, who already possesses an awareness of his exploitation and alienation on board of the ship, Yank rests within himself as a Hegelian consciousness that has not yet achieved the full status of self-recognition. Yank, the Yankee as the typical American worker, still feels at one with the world and perceives himself as its engine, being a boilerman in the belly of a large ocean cruiser. The vessel that he keeps going through his physical strength functions as a microcosm of a hierarchically structured world. At its bottom is the boiler room that is as much a melting pot of American society as it represents a kind of early stage of humankind's evolution, since we find in it hairy creatures, Neanderthals on their way to becoming the human species. At the top of the order civilized society lethargically drifts back towards Europe. Below is the New World, above the Old one; below is hell, above heaven; below is the black soot of the workers, above the white clothes of the rich; below is a sexually heated atmosphere, above cool Puritanical purity; below is hard labor, above decadence and effeminacy; below are the men, above the women. Below is Tarzan, the ape man, who must guard himself against effeminate civilization in order to protect his masculinity, above is the white woman Jane who looks for a vital life, authenticity, strong arms, and her roots. *The Hairy Ape* is not merely an allegory of individual self-consciousness, but in its cultural references and stereotypes, such as the allusions to Edgar Rice Burroughs's early twentieth-century Tarzan stories, it is also an allegory of American masculinity and, as a corollary, of America's potent self-image in relation to the Old World, whose values and *noblesse* were considered decadent, yet copied at all times by the American *nouveaux riches*.

Into these fixed binary oppositions structuring the text a tension is introduced when the bored daughter of the steel magnate enters the engine room in order to see how the other half lives. A figure of light in her white dress, she cuts across the sooty darkness and thus severs Yank's world from itself. Their looks become entangled so intimately that Mildred needs to cover her face, mumbles "Oh, the filthy beast" (436), and faints. Her blackout is mirrored by a blackout on the side of Yank who apparently failed to hear her words. Thus Yank's Irish co-worker Paddy is forced to repeat what Mildred has supposedly said. His repetition, however, adds a crucial difference to her words: the "filthy beast" becomes a "hairy ape" (438) in Paddy's translation. In this double mistaking of the disapproving glance and the linguistic naming and labelling that makes the subjects drift lies the foundation of the theatre of self-consciousness. Out of not hearing, mistaken understanding, interpreting and wrongly repeating evolves a strange promise: Paddy's "hairy ape" promises Yank his future.

Yank's self-consciousness is, in Hegel's sense, one that originally knows itself as immediately given, yet without having recognized itself as such. The ghostly appearance of another consequently negates it, turning their relationship into a version of the old master and servant dialectic. The text consequently has him exclaim: "I thought she was a ghost" and describes her as "a white apparition" (438). Yank steps outside of himself, an act that is symbolized by his abandoning the ship and moving into the world of the others. Yet what fails here in Hegelian terms, is the re-acquisition of the subject as a subject that is aware of its "self" beyond the impasse of an unhappy consciousness. This final sublation, O'Neill's play makes clear, can only be achieved by the death of the subject. Wherever Yank, the Yankee, turns, he experiences rejection, until he eventually decides to adopt his falsely promised identity as a hairy ape in a zoo – only to be eventually crushed to death against the cage by one of his primate "brothers." The epithet becomes his epitaph, his obituary or post-*script* that has, however, preceded him. Finally being at one with himself, he is also dead. Subjectivity is given birth by a naming, a speech act, that here coincides with a second instance of subject-creation, namely the act of being looked at ("Hairy ape, huh? Sure! Dat's de way she looked at me, aw right" [438]). It is a doubly performative identity bestowed by word and gaze alike which, and here lies the irony of O'Neill's text, in both constitutive cases misses the identified object in the act of identification.

When O'Neill uses as the subtitle of his play "A Comedy of Ancient and Modern Life," he not only refers to the cultural implications of the Old and New World and their respective values. He also refers to the comedy of self-consciousness that it stages. The self-consciousness displayed by Yank lacks substance. It is a play with the mask of another, a mask given to him by Mildred via Paddy's falsifying repetition. The subject of speech constitutes itself via the masked speech of an Other. It speaks through the hairy ape, a mask that gives him a face in the first place, yet one that is not his own. It is always, as Werner Hamacher has stated in his analysis of Hegel's "Kunstreligion" (134) on its way to becoming absolute knowledge, a comedy, an essentially masked subject which, like Yank, can only merge with its mask in death. In comedy, the subject has accepted its lack of substance in its speech which ever only enables him or her to play with itself as a mask. As a consequence the subject is also an essentially comical subject, since, in contrast to epic and tragic speech which are according to Hegel lesser forms of linguistic articulation, it knows about its mask-likeness. But if Yank's is an essentially comical subject, that can only mean that it has no essence at all, apart from the impulse and the drive to play.

In Hegel's tripartite argument the epic as speech act still postulates a universal whole mediated by the unifying voice of a narrator. The world and the individual are still one. The objective epic is split apart by the subjective speech act of tragedy. If the subject of tragedy expressed itself for the first time as a speaking self in contrast to the narrated epic – it also moves in opposition to the powers of the divine world as an acting agent whose ambitions of self-knowledge are, as in the case of Oedipus, thwarted. According to Hamacher (126), this higher speech (compared with the language of the epic) is tragic because it fails both as act and as communication and therefore its attempt to constitute a self-consciousness in the shape of active speech founders. The consciousness does not yet know whereupon it acts – the gods are elusive and random. It exerts itself in contingent, necessarily unconscious acts, which will only be sublated in a subsequent third step, namely that towards comedy.

In *Phenomenology of the Spirit* Hegel makes art end with the irony of comedy that knows about the misconceptions of the subject in acting speech and deals with it easily and playfully. The subject is at ease with itself only in comedy, it is as self-consciousness "wie es sich außer dieser Komödie keines mehr findet." (544) This means that there is no self-consciousness outside of comedy, but it also implies that self-consciousness possesses the structure of a comedy, since the self plays with itself as a mask, as something taken off and cast aside, thus with its own death (Hamacher: 142). The linguistic label negated by Yank, that makes him an active force in the first place, therefore turns into the rhetorical figure of *prosopopoeia* in its etymological sense of *prosopon poien*: giving a mask, a face. In the performative figuration of subjectivity, however, the mask, in our case the "hairy ape," disfigures as much as it grants the stability of a face and a voice. It disfigures, as Paul de Man has shown (1984; Menke, 1993), since the previous old face is missing. Hegel distinguishes between self and person, i.e. the self wearing a mask only to merge the two in the course of his argument:

"das eigentliche Selbst des Schauspielers fällt mit seiner Person zusammen," the actual self of the actor merges with his persona (544), or: "das komische Bewußtsein [...] ist die vollkommene Entäußerung der Substanz," the comical self-consciousness is the complete depletion of substance (547). This general self, that has finally acknowledged itself, "hat durch seine Leerheit den Inhalt freigelassen" (546), has set its content free by being empty. If the comical self-consciousness plays with its masks that are itself, what lurks behind the mask is in Hegel's words, its own "Nacktheit und Gewöhnlichkeit" (542), its own nakedness and commonness, that can only know itself by using a mask. The mask restores the old face as a disfigured one. Yet since, according to Hegel, we can only know and recognize the old one through *prosopopoeia*, this can only mean that it simulates in the disfiguration a face that was never originally given in all senses of the term.

Voice

Hegel's idea of self-consciousness as masked and therefore as always comical has various implications for the work of the Wooster Group. Firstly, it draws attention to their onstage personas as rhetorical figures, speaking machines, rather than psychologically developed characters. This observation is underlined by the frequent use of frontality in their acting style that addresses the audience directly. It also draws attention to the deeply ironical structure and tone of their productions including their proximity to the bastard child of theatrical genres, namely that of farce. Farce empties the subject by laughter which is a physical act. The laughter therefore also stresses the importance of the body that Hegel wanted to get rid of by sublating it into the absolute of an ethical norm. Hegel can only do this, as Judith Butler (31-62) has pointed out in her reading of the passage, in an act of "absolute negation" that contradicts his previous attempts to control the body within the realm of life. If the bodily functions which the subject is engaged in, however, are kept very much alive as a negative reminder by the very rules that forbid them, they will inevitably re-appear in the comical subject as an act of transgression, very much to the chagrin of Hegel who in his whole discussion of physicality never once uses the word body, as if it were a dirty word. The comical subject will be free and at ease with itself, not as Hegel wants it, by sublating the body in a spiritual i.e. non-physical exercise, but because it also treats like masks the bodily functions Hegel calls "tierische Funktionen" (174), i.e. animal functions. The Wooster Group's insistence on scatological acts in *To You, The Birdie!* may stand as an example of this.

Secondly, the notion of self-consciousness as a continuous conflicting motion or movement that is forever re-configured by cast off masks may throw a light on the Wooster Group's forever evolving work-in-progress that performs its identity by momentarily putting on new masks for individual productions before it moves on. The fact that the Wooster Group frequently dons the mask of a theatre troupe on the road as in a road movie may serve as an allegory of their performance identity. Related to all of the above is, of course, the notion of dance as continuous movement. The precisely choreographed slapstick dances in *Route 1 & 9, L.S.D.* or *Frank Dell* are examples of this. In *To You, The Birdie!*, perhaps their most choreographed piece as a whole, the actors actually copy movement material from Martha Graham and Merce Cunningham who are visible on the screens directed towards the stage. In what follows, I will consider the importance of the body in the Wooster Group's production of *The Hairy Ape* as a result of its use of voice.

The irony of the subject as mask, as a serious figure of inauthenticity, becomes the crucial principle in LeCompte's production of O'Neill's play. In her staging of the play the figure of *prosopopoeia* that grants voice and face through language undergoes a crucial extension that is significant for what I shall call theatrical *prosopopoeia* as opposed to its literary counterpart. The device that LeCompte applies in her production is the disconnection of voice and body image, a strategy that certainly has its roots in the use of sound in film and, especially in the speeded-up section of the show, in video. The voice of the actors no longer has its seat, its starting point and thus its origin in their bodies. The voice consequently neither transports an inner essence of a subject to an outside nor does it guarantee the identity of its utterance. Instead the voice figures as a social mask that belongs neither to the self nor to the person of the actor or actress. The two sides of the mask, the self behind it who sounds through it and the face that it displays towards the viewer, thus become equally phantasmatic tropes or figurations, but also seductive deceptions that come into being through the mask as a work of art without essence. In this sense I understand "figuration" as a momentary, instantaneous fixing of a process that delimits the self towards an Other, the (kn)own towards the unknown. The hallucinatory unity of figure, role or character and self is exploded and exposed. It becomes visible and thus also conscious and capable of being analyzed as a principle of theatre as much as of a self-consciousness in general which is then shown to follow a theatrical structure.

This principle of the mask as a third entity between self and person or role becomes particularly evident in the second scene on the deck of the steam ship, where Mildred and her aunt quarrel about the propriety of taking a closer look at the boiler man, an act of social voyeurism with obvious sexual connotations. The frequencies of Kate Valk's and Peyton Smith's voices are electronically altered during the exchange. Valk's voice is speeded up, the frequency is turned higher until she talks in shrill squeaks. Smith's voice is lowered in contrast, so that she ends up sounding like a man with a nasal tone of speech. If one perceives language acquisition or learning to read as the coupling of a sound, an acoustic pattern, with a culturally determined concept or optical image which de Saussure understands as "psychic reality," their disconnection in the theatre makes the evocation of different images possible. Not only of different images, but, as in the case of Peyton Smith, of different bodies, too: that of a man, for example, even though the body from which the voice ostensibly originates is that of a woman. Thus her voice becomes the mask of an absent body which the voice grants a presence. Yet Smith not only speaks through the mask of a man. Her voice itself contains that of a man, since our voices, despite their uniqueness of frequency, rhythm, tone, and timbre, inevitably contain other alien or dumb voices that belong to our culture.

The acoustic image of our voice, as Helga Finter has repeatedly pointed out since the start of the 1980s, always also implies an image of ourselves. Our body image is thus not only constituted optically as Lacan's famous mirror stage would have it, but also – and often primarily – acoustically. Freud (1982: 293) already knew this when he gave the ego a "hearing cap" in *The Ego and the Id*, one that, much to the irritation of the subject, always fits badly. In psychoanalytic theory voice functions as the first instrument for the differentiation and segmentation of objects which start off and accompany the separation of psychic interior and objective exterior. The voice of the mother thus becomes an acoustic mirror, to borrow Kaja Silverman's famous phrase (72-100), that promises continuity on the way towards becoming a subject, but also an *archive* for affects and desires of childhood. Via the detour of the voice of the mother the voice is always already a figure, a symbolic, trans-individual mother-tongue; it is a voice mask that configures the subject as a process. The voice as psychic reality thus plays around one's own body limits which it helps to produce in the first place. At the same time, the voice is also a bodily reality that is shaped with the aid of larynx, vocal cords, throat, mouth, and breath. Because of its crucial role in the creation of a body image, it is capable of evoking bodies as psycho-bodies. Thus the different, altered voices that can be played out in the theatrical space imply other subjects and other concepts of subjects than that of a subject given to itself in its speech.

While I defined *prosopopoeia* in O'Neill's dramatic text with Paul de Man as the granting of voice and face through speech, it gains a further meaning here. In the theatre language, as a rule, is only given as spoken and audible and therefore transient, insubstantial, regardless of its being tampered with electronically or the role being read rather than acted. Yet, what characterizes *prosopopoeia* as a theatrical as opposed to a literary category is less its ability to grant a face and thus, in the metonymic sense, also a voice (Menke, 1997). It is the ability to grant a *body through a voice*. The voice calls up imaginary bodies, absent bodies that people the stage without ever being present on it. Theatrical *proso-popoeia* replaces in a metonymic strategy one body with another *without* making the visible or invisible body represent a role. For the text embodies itself not primarily in the bodies of the actors, a principle that even in traditional theatre makes the production irreducible to its written source. The text moreover embodies itself in the voices as an insubstantial body, as voices that make it heard and seen as an echo, yet without ever being able to represent it in its insubstantiality. In what follows I want to sketch briefly what this implies for the Wooster Group and *The Hairy Ape*.

America

At the start of the production the stokers sit with their backs to the audience on the lower level of the stage set, holding on to a metal bar above their heads. Their voices are captured with a microphone that moves above them on a dolly like that of a film set and are slowed down surreally and provided with an echo. The semantics of the words are eclipsed by their echoing spatiality, through which the words fill the room and thus exceed the individuality of the actors. Disconnected from their bodies they multiply until they have become the sound of an entire society, a *basso continuo* that grows louder and louder and creates the impression of slowly creeping towards us from the past. John Lurie's composition for saxophone and percussion adds a jazz element to it. The soundtrack becomes a track into the 1920s, the time of the emergence of jazz and the creation of the play. Yet the use of sound is more than an atmospheric one. The fact that it partly originates in the voices of the actors implies a specific idea of the function of the voice. The voices, despite being generated by the actors, also become alien voice-bodies that eventually mutate into the entire body of a society. This principle becomes especially evident when the actor playing Yank, Willem Dafoe, turns the "voices" that are already labelled as such and composed in O'Neill's text into a kind of singsong, a rap that grows faster and faster and eclipses that which is said in favor of its rhythmical presentation.

With this rhythmical distortion of the speaking voice the voice as mask as a third instance between self and person enters Elizabeth LeCompte's production. Dafoe's masked voice calls up one or more different cultural contexts: that of America's Afro-American population which, as German critics have remarked (Peitz, 1997: 12), have found in rap and hip-hop culture an expression of their social situation since the late 1970s, but also, as many native speakers have pointed out to me, the slang of the workers and immigrants of Brooklyn. Invented in the ghettos, rap as well as slang articulate an idea of the oppressed subject that empowers itself in occasionally megalomaniac fantasies of violence – a thought that is not alien to Yank, the stoker. By analogy Peyton Smith's nasal masculine voice with its implications of upper-class decadence and effeminacy can easily be read as a homosexual voice. The combination of masculinity and effeminacy which can be read as "gay" and which makes a masculine body appear besides the feminine one in Smith's voice continuum is, according to Alan Sinfield, a rather late cultural development that eventually becomes inscribed in the public consciousness with Oscar Wilde's trials for moral indecency in 1895 (Siegmund, 2000).

By contrast, the heightened frequency of Kate Valk's voice marks her as prototypically white. Her helium voice makes her sound like a slightly hysterical Mickey Mouse or a teenage peroxided bombshell (from the suburbs or American movies) who can barely sublimate its sexual curiosity with charity events. Immigrants, blacks, gays, gender relations and different concepts of masculinity – neither of these actually feature in O'Neill's play. What the rhythmical and frequency distortions of voices in the Wooster Group's production add to the text is that which it remains silent about, therefore that which literally lacks a voice in it, even though it forms part of its contemporaneous cultural context. While the text focuses on class struggle, behind which another conflict, that of the cultures of the New and Old World, only weakly shines through, the production lends an ear to other forms of oppression and cultural exclusion. The voice-masks are connected to a specific knowledge. They call forth certain connotations, since they are recognizable. This knowledge is shaped by a specific cultural constellation that is linked to a specific historical situation. The voice becomes a voice-mask hovering between self and role when the signature of a culture is audibly played out in it.

This work of the voice-masks is supported by the visual dimension of the production in which masks are also played with. Willem Dafoe and the stokers all wear black makeup. This does not merely refer to the soot of the engine-room. For the stokers all wear white gloves. In connection with rap these "physical masks," as Elizabeth LeCompte once called her use of "blackface" in other productions (Savran, 1988: 27), not merely point generally towards black culture, but specifically to a typical form of entertainment, that of popular vaudeville and minstrel shows. Needless to point out again that blackface was used in the mid-nineteenth century by white performers who painted their faces black in order to create the prototype of the servile, stupid, and submissive

negro.[1] Through the use of both voice and physical masks a reconfiguration of O'Neill's class struggle through gender and race
relations is effected in the performance.

To use another example: In *To You, The Birdie!* the voice masks do
not re-configure gender by means of race. The production of Racine's
Phèdre re-configures gender by means of the power relations in an
absolutist state. Kate Valk's voice is prompted by the actor Scott
Shepherd who sits in the back of the stage. Electronically distorted it
reaches Valk who lip synchs the words with a noticeable time lag,
thereby creating an absent third body which is that of a man. Elizabeth
LeCompte only uses the voice mask when Phèdre is exposed as a public
figure, framed by the movable devices that keep her image imprisoned
as an icon. Valk carries the psychic body of a man when she is supposed
to enact power as the queen because her husband Theseus is absent.
Masculinity and power here are equated over the ruled out body of the
woman "ghosted" as that of a man. On the other hand, Valk speaks in
her own voice when she is talking privately to Œnone to inquire about
Hippolyte. Standing close to Frances McDormand right in front of the
stage the couple is protected from the onstage public, the eavesdropping
court, by a glass panel behind their backs. Still, at their most intimate
they are also most exposed to the audience and their surveilling gazes.
The production thus draws attention to the theatre as an apparatus of
desiring gazes which reifies bodies and is also the driving force of
Racine's play.

What these voice masks, which ghost the actors by creating absent
bodies on top of their individual bodies, also bring into play is American
entertainment and popular culture together with its images of black,
white, feminine, and masculine – masks, that is, clichés or framed and
fixed gazes, which are originally nothing but masks behind which
something can be articulated in the first place, in the same way as masks
provide a form or figure for an utterance in order to express oneself
differently or to express oneself as different. What comes to the fore
behind the masks employed by the Wooster Group are ever more masks.
Mickey Mouse is among them as much as the ballet girl embodied by
Valk in knee-length skirt and oversized point shoes. They may include

---

[1] Since their 1981 production of *Route 1 & 9* the Wooster Group has repeatedly dealt
with this racist tradition of blackface in popular culture. The group had reconstructed
several routines of Pigmeat Markham, a black comedian who used blackface as a re-
appropriation of a white tradition to turn it against itself and play it back against its
origins. Blackface is subsequently used in *L.S.D. (...Just the High Points...)* where
Kate Valk plays Tituba in Arthur Miller's *The Crucible*, and in *Emporer Jones/Fish
Story*, where she acts with a similar rhythmic use of voice the runaway slave Jones
who plays king of an island. This can also be read as a masked self-appropriation of a
subject with a deadly result.

black rap and fake Irish accents as much as the boxing match that happens on the video screen center-stage. The eight scenes of *The Hairy Ape* are separated by shrill ringing sounds resembling those announcing a new boxing round.

Echo Theatre

In his *Metamorphoses* Ovid tells us of the nymph Echo who wastes away out of unrequited love for Narcissus, until she eventually disappears. What remains of her is her voice, a voice without body that can never be located anywhere as substantial. This voice is ever only capable of repeating the last words or syllables of someone else's speech. Echo can only become audible as an effect of doubling what has been said and therefore by spatializing it and throwing it back onto the speaker as something which is uncannily familiar. When Yank is called by the epithet "hairy ape," it is also Echo who throws it at him. Her voice carries the traces of another voice without which it could not manifest itself as an audible one.

Here another subversive model of the voice appears that can relativize the idea of an all-controlling logo- and phonocentrism, which was criticized by Jacques Derrida as early as 1967.[2] That the voices always convey the traces of other voices and, especially in the case of the Wooster Group's intertextuality, of other productions, explodes the closed semiotic and aesthetic system of the production. For the figure of theatrical *prosopopoeia* that grants a body through the voice cannot represent these bodies. They remain invisible, even though they are imagined and called forth. Present as absent they remain as mask-like figurations in the in-between space of the undead from which they communicate with the living as echoes. The "phenomenalization of a bodiless voice" as "echo or reverberation" of which Bettine Menke (Neumann, 1997: 239) writes in the context of Romantic poetry gains its ontologization in the theatre not as a substantial one, but as one without origin: audible as a (technological) effect and yet invisible. *Prosopopoeia* is not a figure of representation, but one of metonymic replacement that disfigures the body in the act of embodiment through speech.

The acoustic space generated by voices thus functions as an echo chamber for individual subjects and groups that lack a voice in dominant culture, who, as in the myth concerning the nymph Echo, cannot them-

---

2 Albrecht Koschorke (Neumann: 40-51) has argued that only the emergence of a culture of the written word has led to the concept of a pure bodiless *logos* of vocality in Plato's writings. Koschorke refers to the implicit passing of time while reading, a structural process that evokes presence out of absence without leading to the aporia of a supression of the "différance" that Derrida criticizes presence for.

selves achieve representation, not least because their "self" is ever only accessible in already alienated and framed forms, such as those of the entertainment industry. Through their reverberation or rebound, however, they are capable of destabilizing this cultural self and self-consciousness, in the same way as the Wooster Group production of *The Hairy Ape* confronts its literary source with that about which it remains quiet. The theatre of the Wooster Group is a theatre of voices that adds to the presence of the theatrical event moments of absence in which it repeats those who are absent, dead, or forgotten via voice-masks. The use of media in this context furthers an understanding of the media in the old sense of "medium," of a link with this spirit world. As a potential of the production, however, they exceed their codification, which would exhaust them in their legibility as signs. The voices without bodies, the missing bodies, which can therefore neither be legitimized in the system of the performance nor in any political system, open the theatre towards a history that is always also the history of the theatre. This is what the mask stands in for. Consequently the Wooster Group paradigmatically represents, in a metatheatrical move that is already implied in the thematization of excluded popular theatrical forms in its productions, that which has always constituted the *memory of theatre*: it grants ghosts – be they individual or socio-cultural in nature – potential bodies and voices.

South Pacific-North Atlantic

From Total War to Total Peace

Branislav JAKOVLJEVIĆ

University of Minnesota

On January 13, 2000, American national TV networks reported that Staff Sergeant Frank J. Ronghi of the 504th Parachute Infantry regiment stationed near the town of Vitina in Kosovo had been charged with the rape and murder of an eleven-year-old Albanian girl. The official military report of this gruesome act was read by a female officer filmed under a tent furnished with mobile, uniform furniture and equipment. The TV camera recording the event swept over avenues of tents pitched in the frozen fields of Kosovo, with U.S. Postal Service mailboxes scattered across the ephemeral city.

The news of the first *Pax Americana* rape in Kosovo came in the middle of the run of the Wooster Group's *North Atlantic*. The resonance between the two stories arises from their common concern with the unspectacular and almost invisible side of the war: maintaining and providing peace. *North Atlantic* is a performance about the life of military personnel aboard an aircraft carrier located in the North Sea off the Dutch coast, a floating community of professionals, an armed diaspora on a mission of "armed observation."

Based on James Strahs's text, *North Atlantic* was originally developed within the Wooster Group's 1984 project *L.S.D. (...Just the High Points...)*. According to David Savran's account in *Breaking the Rules* (1986), director Elizabeth LeCompte planned to use *North Atlantic* as a second part of *L.S.D.*, while Arthur Miller's play *The Crucible* would provide the "raw material" for the first part. *North Atlantic* was rehearsed during the group's 1983 European tour. After Miller denied the Wooster Group performing rights for *The Crucible*, the group developed three new parts for *L.S.D. North Atlantic*, says Savran, was "excised" and performed as a separate piece. It opened in February 1984, under Orwell's shadow, and was restaged in 1988 as the Warsaw Pact was disintegrating. *North Atlantic* does not comment directly on the NATO air war in Yugoslavia, or on any other armed conflict in which American troops have been engaged since the Cold War ended. Moreover, the Wooster Group insists on the original historical context of the production. In one of their rare gestures of public self-explanation, the information about this production on the group's Web site was accompanied by the following slogan: "The Cold War has ended, and nobody noticed the difference."

North Atlantic does not address war as an ideological question, or as an ethical abstraction, and least as a spectacle. It addresses war in its mode of production, which is not ideology but precisely the opposite: its emphasis on efficiency. The hubris of a tragic protagonist is replaced by a bureaucratic noncharacter. This mode of production is best represented by the figure of displacement, from the battlefield to the banality of the everyday.

Postmodern theatre of the last three decades of the twentieth century was repeatedly identified as apolitical. Arguing against this customary accusation, Philip Auslander recognized in *L.S.D.* a movement away from the "'transgressive' politics of [1960s] avant-gardism" toward a new "understanding of political art as 'resistant'." (1997: 60) To support his argument, Auslander relies heavily on Hal Foster's and Fredric Jameson's understanding of postmodern culture as a phenomenon characteristic of late capitalism in which the distinction between "the economic and cultural realms" has been erased and replaced by a "growing tendency to see political reality as theatre." (1997: 59-60) Apolitical theatre is not the same in the fascist state as it is in the late capitalist state. Or is it? Auslander argues that "the postmodern theatre of resistance must therefore expose the collusion of presence with authority and resist such collusion by refusing to establish itself as the charismatic Other." (1997: 63) According to Auslander, postmodern political theatre *must* find a way of stripping the authority of its secrecy and strategies of concealment. But in order to expose the general public's easy fascination with authority (which *is* the same in the fascist and late capitalist state) it has, so to speak, to "decharismatize" itself. Therefore, the main challenge of postmodern political theatre is how to distinguish itself from mainstream, explicitly apolitical, theatre. The question of political engagement in postmodern culture is problematic in a number of ways, and it remains wide open. One of the most pertinent questions, however, concerns the connection between war and postmodern theatre. If, as Paul Virilio argues in *Pure War* (1997), the war stepped outside of politics, how is theatre to respond to it? Does it require an apolitical response? What is the form, then, of an apolitical response to Pure War? Can theatre bring the Pure War back to the political sphere?

Virilio was not the first to note that Pure War turns territorial advance and external colonization into temporal and technological advance and endocolonization. This was the mantra of countercultures from the 1950s well into the 1970s. The one constant argument of the countercultures of this period was pointed against what Auslander calls the "collusion of presence with authority," or, in plain language, the conspiracy of the state against its own citizens. The discourse of conspiracy is often taken as a symptom of paranoia. LeCompte points out that she chose *The Crucible* because it was the most successful American modern classic to examine the euphoria and paranoia provoked by the House Un-American Activities Committee. The entire production that included Miller's play (and was supposed to encompass Strahs's *North Atlantic*) was named after Timothy Leary's LP *L.S.D.* It can be said that the Wooster Group's performance addresses the history of the erosion of the counterculture's potential and its drift into a catatonic state of paranoia. On the record that inspired the production, Leary talks about the danger that surrounds his "chemical commune": "The situation here is not completely serene at the moment because this quiet island is under siege, for the last two days, the last few weeks, the last few months, this peaceful surrounding has been surrounded by government agents, wiretappers, anxious and angry politicians." (Qtd. in Savran, 1986: 177) The Wooster Group's gesture of pointing to the Cold War as the original historical setting of *North Atlantic* also points toward *L.S.D. (...Just the High Points...)* as the creative starting point of this production. If *L.S.D.* represents an account of the paranoia that crashed attempts to oppose the state apparatus, then *North Atlantic* is an analysis of that apparatus, itself fueled by paranoia. If *L.S.D.* offers an unsparing account of the historical mutations of this sense of besiegement, then *North Atlantic* poses the question of its ultimate consequences.

According to Gilles Deleuze and Felix Guattari, one of the crucial points in "universal history" is the moment of appropriation of the idea of war ("War Machine") by the state ("State Apparatus"). Insisting on the difference between the War Machine and the war itself, they assert that "what we call a military institution, or army, is not at all the war machine in itself, but the form under which it is appropriated by the state." (113) Following this distinction, Virilio concludes that the military class is much more diffused and less definable than the warrior caste ever was (1983: 24). In premodern warfare, the warrior caste engaged in battle, leaving to nonwarriors the role of observer (hence the military-science phrase *theatre of war*). The military class blurs this distinction between military and civilians: it is a vast bureaucracy engaged in Pure War without necessarily participating in its battles (if and when they occur). The protagonists of *North Atlantic* – Captain Roscoe Chizzum, General Benders, Colonel Lud, and word processor

Ann Pussey – are not warriors. They are members of the military class on a rampage: they are spying on the enemy, interrogating the natives, telling bad jokes, engaging in murky business operations in order to make some retirement money, and, above all, struggling to achieve promotion, that ultimate goal of any bureaucrat, anywhere. The military class, like any other bureaucracy, does not recognize aesthetic values of performance. Its sole concern is the efficiency of performance. Bureaucrats do not live; they perform. This efficiency may be mindless, but it is not absurd. It is intelligent and deadly.

In his account of *L.S.D. (...Just the High Points...)*, Arnold Aronson correctly observed that from the very beginning "the [Wooster] Group's pieces have been 'about' performance itself." (1985: 75) *North Atlantic* is, in this sense, not "about" war and its perils but about the military class's performance that constitutes the mechanics of the war. In this piece, the Wooster Group investigates military "performance" in at least two ways. First, gender relations are posited not only as a metaphor of military hierarchy but also as a questioning of the general militarization of culture. LeCompte remarked on several occasions that in *L.S.D.* "the men got the mics" and "the women got the costumes." (Qtd. in Aronson, 1985: 72) In *North Atlantic*, however, while both men and women are costumed in military attire, the men keep the microphones and the women lose their voices. The impersonality of the female voice is emphasized by the high pitch and choral delivery of the female characters' lines. Individual and singular voice belongs to the male officers, who issue orders and engage in verbal duels. Female consigns[1] only provide information, responding without engagement and answering to orders and inquiries diligently and dutifully. The "eternal couple" of a strong soldier and an airhead blond is the paradigmatical image produced by Broadway and Hollywood, and it has been drilled deeply into the audience's consciousness. The question of "drill" and rehearsal of cultural stereotypes brings up a second point in the Wooster Group's investigation of bureaucratic performance. The performers' actions often seem halfway between military exercise and rigorous theatrical performance. This tension between military drill and theatrical flair is revealed in their use of the force of gravity (vigorous sliding down the steep platform, dance as spectacle of legs dangling behind the table), in their performance of standardized military gestures, in their use of more personalized but still highly quotable tics and eccentricities, and in the manipulation and distortion of voice (microphones, choral speech, military orders and greetings in formal address, vulgarities in private

---

[1] In this general division according to gender and rank, the two male privates are clearly marked as homosexuals.

conversations). The Wooster Group simultaneously appropriates certain aspects of military behavior and offers its critique.

The most important aspect of this double gesture toward military bureaucracy is an emphasis on the interchangeability of roles, lines, and personalities. This sense of interchangeability of individuals in the bureaucratic structure comes from the complete reduction of horizontal relations (camaraderie, *esprit de corps*) in favor of a vertical chain of command. But it also emerges from a general interchangeability of places, or, in other words, in the deterritorialization of the military. War as the objective of the State Apparatus is not oriented anymore toward conquest of lands and territorial expansion. Instead, it is oriented toward control as pure potentiality of action that requires highly mobile military power. In this sense "North Atlantic" is interchangeable with, say, "South Pacific." Events depicted in *North Atlantic* are not geographically specific: the play can take place "12 miles off the Dutch coast," as Strahs's script suggests, but also in the Persian Gulf, the Mediterranean, or the Adriatic Sea. The general principle of interchangeability can be further extended to the creation of roles in different stagings of *North Atlantic*. Only two members of the original cast, Willem Dafoe and Kate Valk, appeared in the latest staging of the piece. Out of the two, only Valk kept her role from the first staging. Dafoe took over the role of Captain Chizzum from Ron Vawter, who, as the only Wooster Group member with extensive military experience, developed this remarkable role.[2] Dafoe's role was subsequently taken over by Steve Buscemi, who did not appear in the first production of *North Atlantic* but did participate in the work on *L.S.D.* While the network of intersections between roles, performances, and performers in *North Atlantic* is extremely complex, it underlines interchangeability as the basic principle of bureaucratic performance.

In order to examine this aspect of *North Atlantic*, it is necessary to make a clear distinction between two cultures of performance, artistic (or theatrical) and bureaucratic (or industrial). While performance in theatre and visual arts is the object of representation and therefore complete and done, performance in the bureaucratic context is always related to permanence, incompleteness, and instrumentality.[3] The effect of this distinction between two cultures (species) of performance in

---

[2]   Before he joined the Performance Group in 1972, Vawter was working in the U.S. Army recruiting office on Centre Street in New York City. For more on his work with the Performance Group and the Wooster Group, see his 1993 interview with Schechner.

[3]   Examples of the nonartistic use of the concept of performance are legion: from performance of stocks on the market to recurring use of this catchy word in advertisement campaigns, such as Old Navy's "performance fleece."

North Atlantic is twofold: first, movements, gestures, and other elements of the actors' performance are highly quotable because of their efficiency and simplicity; second, *North Atlantic* as a theatrical production is nothing finished and complete. This incompleteness points towards the technique of quotation, which, while always present in the Wooster Group's work, emerges in *North Atlantic* as the main organizing principle of the entire production.

Savran compares LeCompte's directing style with a visual collage of found objects and fragments that form a network whose structure is firm but whose meaning is unstable and arbitrary.[4] He notes that "the textual network of which every Wooster Group piece is composed is never simply an elaboration of a single pretext, since none of the *floating fragments*, regardless of its size or prestige, ever becomes a fixed center around which a piece is built" (1986: 52; emphasis mine). *North Atlantic*, the "excised" second part of *L.S.D.*, can be seen precisely as such a detached and floating fragment. The two "returns" of *North Atlantic* separated by more than a decade (1988, 1999-2000) are neither restagings nor revivals of the 1984 production. In theatre, revival and restaging always involve a certain amount of adaptation of the original material to new circumstances. Revival always has, to a certain extent, qualities of a version and a sequel. What is curious about *North Atlantic* is the absence of this kind of actualization and the use of the previous production of the same piece as the only point of reference. While other Wooster Group pieces have been seemingly endless works-in-progress, in the case of *North Atlantic* the "progression" of the piece has been severely limited: its most recent staging (1999-2000) can be seen as a quotation of the 1988 production, itself a quotation of the 1984 "original."

"A quote brings the past closer to us," says Mikhail Iampolski, "but cannot make it part of the present. The present is in fact further distanced from us by quotation." (257) *North Atlantic* has the look of a film quote as described by Iampolski. It looks old-fashioned and antiquated primarily because the Wooster Group refuses to update the military equipment used in this performance. Over the two and a half decades of its existence, the Wooster Group has maintained a certain notoriety for their revolutionary use of new technologies in theatre, from video in the late 1970s to digital technology in the 1990s. Use of outdated technology in *North Atlantic* seems all but accidental: it shows the aging of the piece without turning it into museum theatre. On the ramp that faces the

---

4   For example, in *L.S.D. (...Just the High Points...)*, the "raw material" of "found objects" ranged from excerpts from books by Beat Generation writers and Miller's *The Crucible* to Leary's record *L.S.D.* and his videotaped debates with Watergate veteran Gordon Liddy.

audience there are pieces of electronic equipment operated by female consigns: corded telephones, huge headphones, reels of magnetic audio tapes, recording equipment, even a turntable with an LP on it.[5] This technology pointedly lags behind the image of the high-tech military portrayed in television ads and in television reports from the Gulf War and the air campaign in Yugoslavia. Here, the front lines of the classical war are clearly replaced by the technological "cutting edge." The experience of this new species of high-tech warfare was accurately described by a British combat pilot, who, during the Falkland War, sent a brief message to his base: "Fire and forget." The military class, according to Virilio, is defined by its adherence to the latest technologies. It is, he says, "that kind of unbridled intelligence which gets its absence of limits from technology, from science." (1983: 27) The limits Virilio mentions are not only spatial and temporal but also scientific and ethical. During the Cold War as well as in its aftermath, the Pure War driven by technology abolishes all limits and levels all boundaries.

The outmoded technology of *North Atlantic*, like Miller's *The Crucible* in *L.S.D.*, has the quality of "instant recognizability" (Aronson, 1985: 71). Unlike the latest digital recording technology, messy magnetic tapes are technology displaced in time and therefore defamiliarized. Technology used by military intelligence in *North Atlantic* is not old enough to become nostalgic exotica, nor is it advanced enough to produce a science fiction-like effect of amusement. By not being the most advanced technology of the day, which is always referred to as "technology of the future," it speaks of technology as precisely what it is: junk in progress. It is not only technology made strange but also, more importantly, technology dethroned and stripped of its seductiveness. In *North Atlantic*, the Wooster Group poses the question of war as a question concerning technology. They also hint toward a response to this question. The main dramatic conflict in the play evolves between the naval intelligence Captain Chizzum and an army air corps intelligence colonel whom Captain Chizzum shoots and kills in the end. The colonel's name is Lloyd "Ned" Lud."[6]

With *North Atlantic*, the Wooster Group addresses the war without falling into the traps of twentieth-century political theatre. In other

---

[5] Most of these objects are quotes taken from other Wooster Group productions, from *Sakonnet Point* to *L.S.D. (...Just the High Points...)*.

[6] Ned Lud was a semifictional personality who in late eighteenth-century England became known for destroying knitting machines. In the early nineteenth century, a group of proto-anarchists who called themselves "Luddites" gained notoriety for their attacks on machines, mostly in textile factories. Scientific Marxism dismisses Luddites as an early example of spontaneous and ill-directed proletarian struggle. Over the past two centuries the names of Ned Lud and the Luddites have commonly been associated with any kind of antitechnological sentiment.

words, *North Atlantic* is not a didactic performance but instead a diagnostic performance. Walter Benjamin said that epic theatre, that most recognizable form of twentieth-century political theatre, is based on "the dialectic of recognition and education." (1973: 25) Action itself is the third element, the synthesis, in this dialectical process, and it is quite interesting that Benjamin paid special attention to Brecht's theory of quotable gesture (performer's action). The Wooster Group's practice of quotation in theatre is more reminiscent of another theory of citation offered by Benjamin. In his essay on Karl Kraus he calls citation the "basic polemical principle." (1999: 453) Polemicists quote each other in order to make an argument. Quotation is not only the instrument of instruction but also an instrument of confrontation and clarification. "In citation," said Benjamin, "two realms – origin and destruction – justify themselves before language." (1999: 454) Citation, like polemic, destroys the original context and at the same time preserves a fragment of the original. This openness of polemics belongs to *North Atlantic*. The argument of this performance is not scripted in Strahs's text and then delivered on stage. It has been developed over years of performance. Each of the three stagings – the original and the two total quotations – represents only one half of the polemic. The other half belongs to the audience.

The permanence of the Wooster Group's argument was confirmed by a telling constancy in critical responses. In his review published in the February 18, 2000, issue of the *New York Times*, Ben Brantley asks his readers to remember "those classical musicals that seemed to mirror the strapping, restless soul of the United States – Rodgers and Hammerstein shows like *Oklahoma* and *South Pacific*." He then announces that the Wooster Group's new piece is "a robust song-and-dance spectacle with the contrarian name of *North Atlantic* that does indeed bring to mind the keystone works of the American musical theater." Sixteen years earlier, Frank Rich concluded his review of *North Atlantic* on the pages of the same influential daily: "But it's unlikely that even the most spirited musical numbers in *North Atlantic* will make anyone forget *South Pacific*." North and South, Pacific and Atlantic, fire and forget. In the year 2000 as in 1984, theatre critics forgot that the phrase "North Atlantic" is not only a "contrarian" reference to a musical about marines who desire Polynesian women. It also represents half of the name of the most powerful planetary war apparatus, the North Atlantic Treaty Organization (NATO). In 1984, critics expressed shocking insensitivity to the Cold War and the fact that *North Atlantic* was conceived and developed during the peak of pacifist protests that opposed installation of middle-range nuclear warheads across Europe. In 2000, they were equally insensitive to the NATO air war that had occurred across the Atlantic less than a year earlier. Over a period of almost two decades, they kept forgetting that *South Pacific* is not only "the keystone work of American musical theater." It is part of a complex cultural code. If we move from James Michener's novel, *Tales of the South Pacific*, to Rodgers and Hammerstein's Broadway musical based on the novel, to the 1959 film version of the musical, we will see that this code belongs to a complex culture that is all but dead.

In the first decades after World War II, when this culture emerged, *South Pacific* imagined an island that could be a peaceful oasis in the midst of Total War. Precisely in order to confirm its totality, the war establishes within itself its own negation, an exception, an island of peace. At the far end of this dialectical procedure there is *North Atlantic*, which depicts the floating islands of war in the civilization of Total Peace.

The Wooster Group's
House/Lights

Ric KNOWLES

Guelph University

The work of the Wooster Group is known as the ultimate in deconstructive theatre, responsive with a complex postmodern blend of critique and complicity to the mediatization and brutalization of contemporary urban life. This reputation is based on a 1980s staged series of interrogations of classic realist plays, mostly American, that worked to expose those works' compulsory normativity in the construction of American national identity. Through the criticism of David Savran, Philip Auslander, Baz Kershaw, and others, this work has become a key site for debates about the politics of postmodern performance. It seems perverse, then, to read it as pastoral and elegaic, as Elinor Fuchs does in an essay that anticipates the Group's turn to Gertrude Stein in *House/Lights*, first developed in the company's 1996-97 season (1996: 92-107). But a reading of *House/Lights* in the context of the work and reputation of Stein, of the Group's earlier work, and particularly of the cultural geography of their performance location, positions it not only as pastoral and elegaic, but, in its home location, fundamentally nostalgic. Such a reading highlights a nostalgia that has always been part of the Group's work, and argues that the cultural work it performs is recuperative: as Susan Bennett says, nostalgia is, "in its praxis, conservative (in [both] its political alignment and its motive to keep things [...] unchanged)." This is so, she says, because "the optic of nostalgia insists [...] upon a stable referent" and "works to downplay or [...] disregard divisive positionalities" in promoting "a false and likely dangerous sense of 'we'."[1] (5)

In an unlocated, formalist reading, *House/Lights* does seem continuous with the Group's politically interrogative deconstructions of Ameri-

---

[1] Bennett acknowledges, quoting Lowenthal 27, that "the left no less than the right espouses nostalgia," but she argues convincingly that even in its left-wing manifestations the cultural work nostalgia performs is, in both her senses, conservative. To this effect she also cites Davis 112.

can classic drama: it brings a 1964 cult lesbian bondage flick, *Olga's House of Shame*, directed by Joseph Mawra, into productive contact with an American avant-garde classic, Stein's *Doctor Faustus Lights the Lights*. Tossed disruptively into the mix are bodies distorted by prosthetics; voices filtered through sound chambers, supplemented by blips, squawks, and quacks; dancing outsized lightbulbs and a hand-puppet viper-mic; and sound, video, and performance bites ranging from *I Love Lucy, Young Frankenstein*, and Esther Williams to Yiddish Theatre, classical ballet, and Cantonese Opera. Most reviewers indeed described the show as deconstructive – some as neo-cubist (Brantley, 1999), some as interrogative (Guay), and some as incomprehensible (Kaufman), but most, citing earlier "explosive multimedia deconstructions" (Kalb), as postmodern. But some, noting director Elizabeth LeCompte's ability to "lay bare what was essential and enduring in the original," also saw the show as oddly faithful to Stein, or as a confirmation of the Group's continuity with "the age of Picasso." (Brantley, 1999) Far from merely deconstructing its source, *House/Lights* reinforced for many Stein's own deconstructive reading of the Faust legend, her metatheatrical focus on representation, and her understanding of performance as a landscape. Like its source, and for all its frenetic activity, *House/Lights* could work, particularly when performed at the company's home base in New York's SoHo district, as a curiously contemplative exploration of time, art, and nature – the classic concerns of the classical pastoral.

But pastoral landscapes were not new to the Wooster Group in the late 1990s; indeed, most of its work has evoked an idealized past, usually in the form of a "natural" and/or childhood landscape. Even the archetypally deconstructive *L.S.D. (...Just the High Points...)*, Savran notes, "conjures up the dynamics of memory in the tension between the absent 'real thing' and the substitute at hand" (1986: 170) in a way that is perhaps definitive of nostalgia. And, significantly, the longing, explicitly in this case, was for a 1960s version of the American avant-garde that the belated 1980 founding of the Group almost inevitably positions as a golden age. And in spite of their (anti-) canonical reputation, the Woosters have a more recent history of treating avant-garde (vs. realist) source texts *re-* (rather than de-) constructively. As their SoHo neighbors renovated their classic ironwork lofts, the Woosters in the late 1990s were renovating classics of the American avant-garde, such as those of the expressionist O'Neill, more honored in the academy than in performance. Does this recuperative tendency at the archetypal American postmodern theatre suggest an amplification of the still unrealized disruptive potential of these texts? Or is it an attempted return to the halcyon days of the American avant-garde, when that military metaphor seemed less disjunctive than it does now, and its alignment with national myths of progress – including technological progress – continued to hold sway? The invocation of Stein certainly links the Group with the great American chronotope of Paris in the 1920s, and also with key avant-garde moments of earlier productions of *Doctor Faustus Lights the Lights*. After all, the play has become something of a right of passage for American experimental theatres since it was chosen for the inaugural Living Theater season in 1951.[2]

In 1990 Richard Kostelanetz called Stein "the greatest experimental writer in American literature, an inventor whose achievements are [...] scarcely understood, even today, more than four decades after her death." (xi) But what does it mean to stage a "classic" of the "avant-garde" that, fifty years later, is still ahead of its time? At the very least, to do so drains the term of temporal significance – perhaps especially for the Woosters, who belatedly set up shop in the legendary Performing Garage a decade after the moment Philip Auslander identifies as the onset of postmodernism (1997: 59). Perhaps *House/Lights* marks the Group's nostalgia as less longing for a simpler past than postmodernist longing for time itself – for a time when (in several senses) there *was* time. Stein is widely honored as the "patron saint of the avant-garde," in Bonnie Marranca's phrase, "hovering over the artistic landscape, radiating a grandiose personal freedom, delight in invention, and intellectual courage" (Stein xxi) – all notably mainstream American ideals. As such, Stein evokes nostalgia for a golden age of American avant-garde (as opposed to alternative) art (Usmiani 1-2), poised to take its place within, and to renew rather than overthrow, the mainstream. But as Kate Valk, the dramaturg and lead performer for *House/Lights*, asked, "how much have you read of Gertrude Stein?" The work "itself" is largely unread, unseen, and relatively unmarked, positioned to function as both cultural authority and empty landscape. "Its landscape is as abstract as the landscapes we make" says Valk (qtd. in Conti). It is the very abstraction of Stein's landscapes – their lack of social referent – that has made her work recruitable for high-modernist formalism. Thus William Carlos Williams can say "It is simply the skeleton, the 'formal' parts of writing [...] that she has to do with, apart from the 'burden' which they carry." (Qtd. in Kostelanetz 20) But Stein has more recently been celebrated less for her construction of socially inscrutable modernist artifacts than for her commitment to process, her concentration on the materiality of language, and her role as a proto-feminist. The Wooster Group has similarly conflicted relationships to modernism, politics, and particularly feminism that can seem from outside the country to be characteristically American: LeCompte describes the Group's apparently confron-

---

2   *Doctor Faustus Lights the Lights* has since been staged by, among others, the Judson Poet's Theatre in 1978 , Richard Foreman in 1982 , and Robert Wilson in 1992. See Ryan 165-89 for a chronological listing, and 191 for reviews of productions.

tational politic as unintentional, "an inevitable outcome" – "a *result*, but not the *object*" – of their working process (qtd. in Auslander, 1997: 71-2; Savran, 1986: 39). And yet *House/Lights*, casting women as Faust and Mephisto and staging the objectification of women in *Olga's House of Shame*, is easily read as an interrogation of the construction of gender in America; indeed the show on tour was frequently reviewed this way, though not, significantly, in New York.

One way to approach the apparent tension between the Group's lack of political intent and the frequent reception of their work (particularly outside New York) as politically confrontational is to examine Stein's concept of theatre as landscape,[3] which Fuchs calls "a signature style of contemporary experimental theater" in America, citing "the multifocal scene and the diffused spectatorship it calls for" as "central." (1996: 92) But like the American academy's embrace of Bakhtinian dialogism in the 1980s, and like its more recent turn to chaos theory for dramaturgical or analytical models (both of which tend to skirt the issue of existing power relationships within apparently empty spaces), the American avant-garde theatre's embrace of theatre-as-landscape can be read as politically naive. Stein's search was for a peculiarly American *balance* within "a given space," balance which she herself called "a definitely American thing." (Qtd. in Ryan: 22-3) "Nothing really moves in a landscape but things are there" (qtd. in Ryan: 1), she says, "always in relation." (Qtd. in Ryan: xlvii) Stein compared herself to Einstein (xxvi-xxvii), and it is clear, as Marranca argues, that her technique "has affinities" with post-Newtonian physics "in its development of composition as a field of innumerable centers." (xxvi-xxvii)

All of this sorts well with the work of the Wooster Group, suggests a parallel between the "chaos" of *House/Lights* and the Steinian theatrical landscape, and serves a familiar American liberal-individualist politic. LeCompte talks of wanting "as many interpretations as possible to coexist in the same time and same space" (qtd. in Savran, 1986: 53), and Savran argues that the "reagent" in her work is the empowered individual spectator: "the Wooster Group initiates," he says "an Einsteinian project that celebrates the multiplicity of perspectives and only one certainty: that the phenomenon will be different for each member of the

---

[3]   It must be acknowledged that *Doctor Faustus Lights the Lights* is not normally considered to be one of Stein's "landscape plays" (which Ryan considers to be the plays of her "second period of playwriting" [51]; she groups *Doctor Faustus* with other plays written after 1932 as her "last period," comprising "plays as narratives" [55]). The play nevertheless evolves out of the earlier work and shares many dramaturgical features with it. It may be worth noting that, whether consciously or not invoking Stein, LeCompte explains the appeal to her of a famous acid-assisted rehearsal for *L.S.D. (...Just the High Points...)* by saying "I just knew there was something about landscapes" (qtd. in Savran, 1986: 196).

audience." (1986: 54) Stein herself said that "to me one human being is as important as another human being, and you might say that the landscape has the same values, a blade of grass has the same value as a tree." (Qtd. in Ryan: 25) This fundamentally sentimental politic resonates with the liberal pluralism of the current humanist embrace of chaos theory in such works as William Demastes's *Theatre of Chaos* and Tom Stoppard's appropriately named play, *Arcadia*, a post-Newtonian play about a pastoral landscape.

Fuchs also notes Stein's tendency to slip from an understanding of landscape as "spatial and static as opposed to temporal and progressive" (1996: 95) to an idealized vision of the "natural." In an analysis that echoes the American avant-garde director Peter Sellars's discovery of "a lyricism and classical repose [...] beneath the busy surface level" of the Wooster Group's work (Savran, 1996: xv), Fuchs suggests that "landscape to Stein was wholly present to itself, simple and un-anxiety-provoking to the spectator." (1996: 95) But in her brief treatment of LeCompte's "edenic dream of returning the earth to the way it 'might have been naturally'," Fuchs also argues that, "for LeCompte, artistic endeavor itself represents (both stands for and depicts) a kind of original sin, a fall from the whole of nature." (1996: 103) Contemporary theatre as "art" and technology, I suggest, constructs a contradiction for LeCompte: her own technological urban pastoral and the traditional American dream of progress struggle against an inherited generic vision of technology, and art, as the *death* of the natural – or of the nostalgic belief that the natural has ever existed. In staging a technologically sophisticated performance that "links the [already nostalgic] Faust myth with American history" by linking loss of innocence with technological progress through the invention of electricity, LeCompte stages a tension at the heart of her work. In staging a late play by a modernist artist of the perpetual present that *portrays* an artist's – Faust's – realization "that the perpetual present for which he has bargained has deprived him of hope," (Bowers: 102) LeCompte evokes postmodern nostalgia for time itself, and for an (American) avant-garde as a temporal concept positing a (better) future, as well as an originary past.

*

Both *Doctor Faustus Lights the Lights* and *House/Lights*, in their "ideal" forms, can be read as contestable terrains, alternately legible as interrogations of the representation of women, as liberatingly open fields, and as sites of nostalgic longing. But performance never exists in ideal forms, and as Kershaw says, location is key to assessing "the political impact of theatre." A located reading of *House/Lights* produces significantly different meanings than does the formalist one I began with. In the literal sense, as far as initial production and reception are concerned, location for the Wooster Group is SoHo ("South of Houston" [St.]), the 43-block area of downtown Manhattan founded as an ersatz "neighborhood" between 1968 and 71, when the art market was thriving, small industry dying, and artists found cheap housing and studio space in vacated industrial lofts (Simpson: 1-5). But Sharon Zutkin makes clear in *Loft Living: Culture and Capital in Urban Change* that by 1979, a year before the official founding of the Wooster Group, SoHo was already an urban-pastoral landscape of renovated lofts inhabited by neither industry nor artistry but by what Barbara and John Ehrenreich call an emerging "professional-managerial class" – children of the 1960s with a (consumer) interest in the arts who returned to the city driving up rent and driving out the previous inhabitants. Zutkin demonstrates that "Far from being [...] a spontaneous artists' community, SoHo was really a creation of [investment capital]" (16): developers used "first-wave" artist residents as a "wedge" (4), effecting changes in zoning bylaws and ousting small industry before they were themselves ousted as "loft-living" became trendy, rents rocketed, and the fleeting, pastoral, SoHo moment was created retrospectively as a product of carefully orchestrated collective memory. Zutkin quotes (from Stratton), and refutes, the manufactured and widely circulated image of "first generation" loft dwellers – "artists and other adventurous souls" – as "urban homesteaders," "loftsteaders" (17), and "pioneers in the urban wilderness." It's not without (economic) consequence that Charles R. Simpson (1) and others construct the district as a pastoral "valley" between the financial high "court" of the southern tip of the island and the skyscrapers of mid-town. And of course the renovated living areas of the valley, using "real" materials – brick, iron, and oak (the loft equivalents of natural fabrics) – carve out spacious, open areas that, like all pastoral landscapes, bring art and nature together in contemplative, recreative spaces, retreats from the cramped and hectic life of the city.

This is the SoHo constructed by LeCompte, Spalding Gray, and other members of the Group when discussing the living/performing space at the Performing Garage out of which all the Wooster Group's work has been created. Distinguishing themselves from "most people," who are "dislocated," they talk of their space early on as a "clubhouse" (qtd. in Savran, 1986: 50) out of which, shepherd/artists in an urban-pastoral landscape rich with raw material, "we were just trying to make scenes out of who we were in the room." (LeCompte qtd. in Coe) And this is also the SoHo *re*created for cultural tourists in the 1980s, 1990s, and beyond, its cast-iron buildings now housing trendy galleries, upscale boutiques, cafés, and still, after all these years, the Performing Garage on Wooster Street, home of the legendary avant-garde Performance Group in its halcyon days, and now the fashionably downscale venue for the movie stars and others that constitute the Wooster Group. Here postmodernism meets late capitalism, as "mainstream" and "avant-garde" work less as developmental designations than as marketing labels – Stein's "continuous present" realized as SoHo takes its place with rue de Fleurus and Greenwich Village, not as Bakhtinian chronotopes, but as commodity theme parks: as at Disney, all is now, the avant-garde and mainstream coexisting as alternative consumer choices. Thus tourist guides recommend SoHo as a place where "industrious artists mix with industrial workers" and "white-walled, sun-drenched restaurants fill dingy commercial loft buildings." (Levine: 5) They market the Wooster Group – "a cult among its adherents," "too experimental for mainstream audiences" ("if *Phantom of the Opera* is what you're looking for, don't even *think* of making the pilgrimage to SoHo") – but nevertheless on "the cutting edge of the theatre." (Leon: 92) "A spirit of adventure is basic equipment for a SoHo theatre outing," one guide warns. "So is an open mind. Bring them and you will be rewarded." (Lawliss: 246)

Another way to approach the politics of location, to revisit my initial reading of *House/Lights*, and to tease out the cultural work it performs *in situ*, is to focus on the way the show has worked for an individual audience member, in this case a Canadian postcolonial subject who grew up in the 1960s, for whom New York is both a mythical theatrical testing ground and a prime tourist destination, and for whom the Performing Garage is legendary: I first saw *House/Lights* in preview at the Performing Garage in the fall of 1998. I walked south to SoHo from Penn Station on a late October afternoon, making my way down 5th Avenue, through Washington Square and the NYU campus, past the boutiques, cigar shops, cafés and Qigong masseurs of West Broadway, and across Broome, with its trendy store-front galleries, to Wooster St. I stopped at a chic wine bar of brick walls and cast iron hardware, slipped into a specialty shop for art books and old movies, and took my place in the ticket line – cash only, no plastic – that snaked north from the graffiti-covered shipping-dock door that is the streetfront of the Performing Garage. I stood beneath a plaque about the "SoHo Cast Iron Historical District" and its small-industry past looking across the street at an arched, poster-plastered wall beneath which a homeless man slept on a pile of newspapers. At 7:45 I entered through the narrow south door, squeezed around the corner and found a place among the 80 or so seats at the east end of the tiny "brick-box" space that constitutes the interior of what one reviewer had called "one of the last theatres around doing truly experimental theatre." (Steele)

Above my head in house center was a phalanx of technicians, equipment, and video monitors. Behind me to my right was the legendary "Liz" LeCompte, and before me a fabulous chaos of ramps, lamps, metal rails, and angled footrests suspended chest-level from the railings; two banks of fluorescent footlights facing forward; video monitors up-

left, up-right, and down-center; a lap-top computer mounted onstage down-right on an angled platform; and untold microphones, sliding stools, and see-saw metal platforms. I was enthralled.

First, there were the pleasures of sheer technical brilliance – in the acting, direction, conception, execution, and perhaps most notably the cutting edge work in live video technology – the pleasures, perhaps, of revisiting the (American) myth of technological progress. Next, there were the pleasures of democratic empowerment in sheer excess of energy and signification: the show meant everything and anything, and the choice, the show seemed to suggest, was up to me. Then there were the self-congratulatory pleasures of recognized revisionism – of seeing new and progressive things done with the Faust story, together with the superior, nostalgic pleasures of viewing from a 35-year distance the chaste leers and gropes that passed for eroticism in *Olga's House of Shame*; the simple pleasures of revisiting clips, sound bites, and re-enactments from the pop culture of more innocent times ("I Love Lucy," "Ring of Fire," Esther Williams, and so on); and the surprising pleasures of recognizing the grotesque prosthetic production of "ideal" 1950s and early 1960s female bodies–all of these allied with the pleasure of Kate Valk's brilliant "Betty-Boop" delivery of Stein. Finally, there were the vaguely pleasurable ironies that accompanied all this, ironies that positioned the present as both superior (in knowledge and experience) and debased. But of course irony, the signature tone of the Woosters, is a staple of the pastoral, which inevitably contains its temporary sojourn in the simple, natural (but clearly escapist and therefore "artificial") countryside, within a prescribed return, refreshed, to the reified and "naturalized" civilities of court and city life.

I left the show, walking up Wooster St., with "calm of mind, all passion spent" (to invoke Milton's encapsulation of the comforting effects of catharsis), buoyed by the revisionist and renovationist pleasures of the neighborhood, the fable, and its skillful and progressive treatment. As one New York reviewer said "the world that 'House/Lights' portrays may be in atomistic shards, but there's a strangely comforting wholeness in this century-enfolding symmetry." (Brantley, 1999) But as I flew out over the industrial wasteland of Newark to return to my work-day world in Southern Ontario, I began to wonder whether my enjoyment of *House/Lights* had primarily to do with nostalgia for an avant-garde theatre in renovated factories that held hope for political change. My sense of repose began to unravel as I sensed in my response a nostalgia – for (political) *progress*, for the 1920s, the 1960s, the lost days of the avant-garde, and the hope it used to bring. I began to share Savran's discomfort with "giddy undecidability" (Savran, 1991: 53), as I have long felt impatience with the pleasantly knowing but fundamentally recuperative critique mounted in pastoral dramas from *As You Like It* to

Our Town[4] – landscape plays that "explore the issues" in playful and balanced ways, but leave power *im*balances intact, uninterrogated, and reinvigorated when the pastoral sojourn ends.

Savran's book on the Woosters opens with an epigraph from Nietzsche that articulates, in spite of its origin, a peculiarly American desire for originality *über alles* (including political change), and encapsulates what I fear, in the end, *House/Lights*, in SoHo, in October 1998, for me, was about:

> Perhaps [...] we shall still discover the realm of our invention, that realm in which we, too, can still be original." (Nietzsche qtd. in Savran, 1986: vii)

*

The reputation and interpretation of the Wooster Group are very different when the company tours, as it frequently does. At a meet-the-artists "rencontre" in Montreal in May, 1999, when *House/Lights* was performed as part of the Theatre Festival of the Americas, I asked Elizabeth LeCompte and Kate Valk what it meant to tour shows that, throughout the company's history, have so often seemed iconically American. They replied that they did not think of themselves as having a national, or even a New York orientation, but thought of themselves as quite specifically located in Manhattan, and more particularly lower Manhattan, part of a local scene from which their work has emerged and where it has produced its primary meanings.[5] Indeed, in New York, the company is read as Off-Off-Broadway, a company with a very specific, indeed very narrow interpretative community, not particularly representative of anything beyond themselves. Meanwhile, however, they tend to be read internationally as one of the United States' most important theatres, a leading representative of the American avant-garde. Scottish theatre critic Mark Fisher, profiling the company in advance of their performances of *House/Lights* in Glasgow, traveled to New York and was puzzled to find that his New York colleagues, "theatre insiders," were surprised by his plan to take in a Wooster Group performance. What puzzled him "wasn't only that *House/Lights* was easily the most extraordinary thing I saw in a week of theatre-going, it was the idea that the New York theatre establishment hadn't noticed that one of the world's most significant ensembles was on its very doorstep."

Beyond New York the Wooster Group is invariably described as a New York Company, and is seen as in various ways representative of

---

[4] Thornton Wilder was a friend of Gertrude Stein and acknowledged her influence in the composition for *Our Town*, a play that was also subject early on to Wooster Group deconstruction in *Route 1 & 9*.

[5] Kate Valk, at the "Café des artistes du Monument-National," Theatre Festival of the Americas, 28 May 1999.

"what's happening" there. On tour within the U.S., this can render them
the object of critique or resentment rather than praise. In the case of
House/Lights, for example, early performances of the play in development in Columbus, Ohio, and in Chicago, were greeted with something
less than awe. Richard Ades, the reviewer for *The Other Paper* in
Columbus quoted the company's program notes to the show concerning
the juxtaposition of Stein with 1960s S&M producing "a shared kitsch-
cultural view of female power struggles." The reviewer then commented, "Sounds like the work of a deep mind, doesn't it? Namely, a
mind that's spinning its wheels in a meaningless hole of its own making." Describing the erotically charged performance of Kate Valk and
the 1960s eroticism of *Olga's House of Shame*, however, and citing a
line from the popular American television program, *Cheers* – "this
egghead stuff is making me hot!" – the reviewer went on ironically to
praise the show's capacity to give Columbus audiences "a rare gift:
guilt-free titillation." Even more explicitly, Achy Obejas, the reviewer
for the *Chicago Tribune*, felt that "What Chicago gave away is what
New York could not – 'HOUSE/LIGHTS,' the Woosters' new piece, is
a marvel of technology, a bravura performance, and pretty much inco-
herent." The emperor, apparently, had no clothes. Insofar as the show
was felt to be "about" anything in its American excursions beyond
Manhattan, it was about "destiny, about good and evil, about avoidance
of the self, about obsession, about love and dominance and submission,"
but fundamentally about the equal-opportunity chance "to create your
own story." (Obejas) With the exception of dominance and submission,
none of these themes was mentioned in reviews of the show in New
York or on its international tours.

On tour beyond the U.S., in fact, the Woosters tend to be read very
much and very positively as a trendy, hip, and postmodern New York
theatre company, leading exponents (cited almost inevitably in the same
breath as the experimental American theatre directors Robert Wilson
and Richard Foreman) of what is called the American avant-garde.
Within the U.S., LeCompte comments wryly, "avant-garde is a European joke. There's nothing avant-garde in America. Isn't it a French
word?" (Qtd. in Fisher) *In* France, or more specifically at the Festival
d'Automne in Paris, in performance at the semiotically rich site of Le
Théâtre de la Bastille near the site of the former Bastille prison, the
storming of which kicked off the French Revolution in July 1789,
House/Lights seemed at once both very American and very European.
Rue de la Roquette, on which the theatre is situated, is a narrow street
with a blend of small neighborhood shops and a more recent cluster of
galleries, cafés, clubs, and bars that sprang up in the wake of the building of the nearby Opéra de la Bastille in 1989. On the December Satur-
day evening in 1999 when I saw the show, the short walk from the

Bastille métro station took me through a throng of pedestrian traffic. The theatre itself, relatively nondescript, was filled to its capacity of about three hundred, with seats sloping slightly toward the stage. The theatre's small entrance area made available season brochures featuring fine art photography and line drawings, and placing *House/Lights* within the season's context of international contemporary experimental theatre and, especially, dance – *House/Lights* itself being categorized there as both, thereby inviting, as did the rest of the brochure, formalist readings. Reviews of the show (performed in English) placed it most frequently within the contexts of experimental American theatre (particularly the work of Wilson and Foreman), the writing, ideas, and Paris life of Stein, and the Woosters' reputation as "le cap de l'avant-garde sophistiquée." (Perrier) For me, the immediate context was the congruent one of having earlier in the day seen a matinée performance of Can Themba's *Le costume*, directed by the legendary experimental director Peter Brook at his Paris base, the Théâtre Des Bouffes du Nord.

Most Paris reviewers judged *House/Lights* to be "le meilleur spectacle d'avant-garde de ce Festival d'Automne" (Bourcier, 1999), and Paris audiences, according to a report in *The Guardian* that sorts well with my own experience, "howled with laughter." (Mahoney, 2000b) The show bristled with energy and intelligence in its Paris performances, as if charged by the atmosphere and invigorated by the context. There was little sense of the urban pastoral, or of nostalgia, and no sense of incoherence; rather *House/Lights* seemed to live, as Molly Grogan, the reviewer for the *Paris Free Voice* observed, in Stein's continuous present, and to evoke "Steinian concepts" such as "syncopation and the nature of language being sound and rhythm." For some, the show evoked what seemed to be peculiarly Parisian existentialist concerns about "la réalité de l'être," (R.S.) while for others it constituted "une magistrale démonstration sur la dualité de nos sens: entre le vrai et le faux, le passé et le présent, l'amour et la haine." (Bourcier, 1999) For most, however, viewing or reviewing the show in the final weeks of the millennium and at the height of the Y2K scare about global technological failure, it was understood to be a chilling invocation and playing out of Stein's own fascination with and fear of technological progress.

House/Lights returned to Europe in June of 2000 when it was selected to re-open the cavernous Tramway theatre on Albert Drive in South Glasgow, one of Europe's trendiest venues for the performing and visual arts, after it had been closed for two years to undergo a £3.6 million rehabilitation. The building had been a tramshed in the 19th century, stabling many of the 3000 horses used to pull the city's trams until the system was electrified in 1910. It remained the Coplawhill Tram Depot until the coming of trolley cars in 1962, after which it was transformed into a Museum of Transport (Thomson and

Cameron). The building eventually went to seed, matching the decay of much of the area south of the river in which it was situated. Indeed the environs of the Tramway, which have recently begun to emerge as a mixed and more lively intercultural neighborhood, had become for a time one of Britain's most desperate victims of industrialization and urban blight, the traces of which remain very much in evidence. The building itself, constructed on a large scale to accommodate tramcars and retaining the old steel tracks embedded within its uneven floor, was inaugurated as a theatre space in 1990 to house Peter Brook's epic show *The Mahabharata* in Glasgow when no suitable space could be found for it in London. Almost immediately, as Jackie McGlone wrote in *Scotland on Sunday*, "[t]he once derelict Glasgow Transport Museum became one of the most exciting theatrical spaces in the world. [...] Everyone was making tracks for the Tramway to produce and witness the sort of ground-breaking theatre that used to be shoe-horned into tiny studio spaces the size of a small wardrobe." "There was no question," wrote McGlone, quoting Brook's reference to the space as "an industrial cathedral," "here was a beautiful, rambling space, a space that had its own character, its own nobility, its own background and associations, free from all our old-fashioned notions of theatres with proscenium arches and velvety seats." Over the years the space hosted a checklist of the international avant-garde, including Brook, Robert Lepage, Brith Gof, Silviu Puracaret, the Maly Theatre of St. Petersburg, La Fura dels Baus, Wim Vandekeybus, Alain Patel, Michael Clark, Crush, and DV8, not to mention a phalanx of other Scottish companies, nor the work in television, video, and the visual arts that has been hosted there. The vast, high-ceilinged brick-built barn has been, indeed, Glasgow's "funkiest contemporary arts venue," (Thomson), and the renovations seem simply to have made things better, removing obtrusive columns from the Tramway 1 (the main theatre space), evening out the floors, and adding an x-shaped metal staircase leading up to a new bar and restaurant in what had been the old stables, but preserving from the original its industrial scale and unpretentious character – as well as, in spite of the re-roofing, the somewhat forbidding, graffiti-encrusted decay of its exterior.

The programming, too, retained its character, the summer season in which the space reopened featuring, along with the Woosters: *Gravity*, a music and theatre collaboration between a hot young playwright, Zinnie Harris, and composer Marina Adamia; *Desert Rain*, a show that notably featured Nottingham University's "Massive 2" computer among the cast; and *True*, a collaborative international project. In the gallery space of the Tramway 2, running concurrently with *House/Lights,* were three new art exhibitions, one international showcase that included the work of Turner Prize winner Tacita Dean, a group exhibition by five artists from Nantes, France, and one solo exhibition by Sally Osborn, then a recent graduate of the Glasgow School of Art.

All this seemed to sort well with the resonances of the show's Paris performances and its performance venue, though on a physically amplified scale. But to get to *House/Lights* in Glasgow – and few residents of the predominantly South Asian immediate neighborhood frequent the Tramway – it was necessary to drive through labyrinthine and unwelcoming streets, to take a cab or bus, or to board a commuter train from Central Station on Argyle Street at the heart of the city beneath the river to a somewhat forbidding (and largely deserted) outdoor stop at Pollokshields (East). From there, the commuter had to venture up a long flight of deserted stairs and along a street devoid of theatre-district-style restaurants or pubs to the nondescript main doorway of the theatre. This, clearly, was neither SoHo's retro-chic nor Paris's urban bustle. And again, the show read differently here. The Glasgow audience, according to a review in *The Scotsman*, found itself "caught [...] somewhere between explosive laugher and sheer slack-jawed amazement." (McMillan) Without the supercharged energy of Paris audiences, these felt more actively focused and intellectually engaged with the production's contemporary resonances than were audiences elsewhere, as is suggested by the headline of the *Scotsman* review: "Lights, Camera, Interaction: The Wooster Group are in exhilarating tune with the times." Reviewers – with one notable and apparently ill-tempered exception that proved the rule[6] – repeated the familiar-in-Europe welcome of the Wooster Group as "the cream of New York's theatrical avant-garde," celebrated their "achingly hip po-mo credentials," and placed them in the context of, as in Paris, the work of Wilson and Foreman, as well as that of Brook and other Tramway predecessors, including their own earlier work (Agate and Gibb). But they also welcomed the show with some of its most intelligent analysis. This largely working class city, home of a People's Palace museum celebrating the histories of working people, whose lively arts scene exists primarily to address a local rather than a tourist audience (as is often the case in Edinburgh), seemed prepared to see the show as a serious political work engaging with contemporary social issues. The reviewer for the *Sunday Herald* found it to be "an alarmingly sad rendition of modern day alienation and social schizophrenia" (Agate), in a positive review that nevertheless reflected the *Scotland on Sunday* attack on it as "the art of pessimism." (Brown) *The Times* (London) astutely reviewed

---

[6] Contradicting "a willingly enraptured press corps" who welcomed the Wooster Group as the ideal way of reopening the Tramway, Mark Brown wrote: "I'm sorry to rain on a long and eagerly awaited parade, but I just don't buy the promotion of sexy technology over theatrical purpose which characterizes this work from intriguing beginning to exasperatingly unfulfilling end."

the Glasgow performances in Brechtian terms as "just one great big distancing device, a highly charged mirror image that confronts and subverts the audience's passivity." (Cooper) But perhaps the most acute reviews of the Glasgow performances came from women, who had perhaps had to negotiate the unforgiving neighborhoods of South Glasgow in a different way than had their male colleagues. Only in Montreal, where the show had played at L'Espace Go, the former home of the city's most prominent feminist theatre, had *House/Lights'* feminist resonances been so clearly in evidence as at the Tramway, where it was held by Elisabeth Mahoney in the *Guardian* (2000a), focusing on the show's disruptively carnivalesque energies and its central female characters, to be in large part "about power and corruption, and more specifically about women and power." Joyce McMillan, in *The Scotsman*, who rightly located Kate Valk's multi-faceted performance of Faust, Elaine, and "Marguerite Ida and Helena Annabel" as central, found that the show had to do with "something [...] about the relationship between scientific curiosity, technological arrogance, and moral decadence," "something about theatre, as a free arena in which actors can finally shape their own relationship with the audience," and "something about women as subjects of their own stories rather than as objects." It is little wonder that Elizabeth LeCompte, complaining that New Yorkers do not really understand the work of the company, has commented that "In Europe it isn't the same. My favourite audiences are the British because they get every nuance." (Qtd. in Fisher) The differences, however, may have less to do with American, European, or British character or intelligence than with the complex geographies of the cities, neighborhoods, and theatrical spaces in which the Wooster Group performs.

A Case of Belated Recognition

The Wooster Group in France

Frédéric MAURIN

Université du Québec à Montréal

In 1997, a French critic writing from New York considered it her duty to make up for what she thought was an unfair oblivion. Pleading for the crucial importance of the Wooster Group, she concluded an enthusiastic essay about *Brace Up!* on a bitter note, bluntly stating that "the French audience knows nothing about this theatrical phenomenon" and that "it would be a shame to ignore it any longer" (Leich-Galland: 37). Indeed, in a country that has played host to so many foreign avant-garde artists and, in particular, has given American experimental theatre a level of appreciation and support, both critical and financial, that it does not always find in the US, the Wooster Group has received little attention until a couple of years ago.[1]

However, Leich-Galland's remark was overstated. The Wooster Group came to perform *Route 1 & 9* at Théâtre de la Bastille in Paris in June 1985, *Brace Up!* at the Sigma Festival in Bordeaux in November 1992, and *Fish Story* at Créteil's Exit Festival, on the outskirts of Paris, in May 1994 (see appendix). With those three productions, the "French audience" (a loose entity if ever there was one) had surely had the opportunity to know "something" about the Wooster Group before 1997. But Leich-Galland's inaccuracy may be more telling than it seems and her own oversight, ironically mirroring the French "shameful ignorance" of the Wooster Group, may prove more revealing of a reception weakness than detrimental to her argument.

---

[1] As opposed to the situation in Belgium, the Netherlands or Germany, for instance, where the association of the Kaaitheater in Brussels, the Mickery Theater in Amsterdam and the Hebbel Theater in Berlin made it possible to invite the Wooster Group early on. As a matter of fact, *North Atlantic*, originally conceived as part of *L.S.D. (...Just the High Points...)*, was first developed as a collaboration with the Globe Theater Company in Eindhoven in 1983, incorporating segments from a classic Dutch play, *The Good Hope*.

As a matter of fact, the productions in question did not take place within an institutional framework likely to provide exposure and promote recognition. *Route 1 & 9* was part of a short-lived theatrical competition called "Le printemps du théâtre," but it was performed outside of it, on its margins, at a time of the year when theatre-going is not a major activity in Paris. The now-defunct Sigma Festival, a late instance of the French decentralization policy, did not quite happen on a national scale and it attracted primarily a local audience. However, several Parisian critics made the trip to Bordeaux and one, in particular, blamed other programmers for their "short-sighted or lazy attitude" in his highly favorable review of *Brace Up!* (Solis, 1992). With a reminder of the company's history and the *Route 1 & 9* precedent, he went on to claim that "it is an urgent matter to (re)discover the Wooster Group." Lastly, 1994 was the year when the Exit Festival was founded and it could not therefore have the reputation for boldness and risk-taking that it has acquired since. At the time though, the same *Libération* critic spoke of "the return of a company to France, where it would have deserved to be invited more often" (Solis and Vernay).

Such was the situation in 1997. The Wooster Group had not been absent from the French scene, but access to its work had remained limited to a small number of spectators. If not entirely unknown, it had failed to be properly acknowledged. Did it come to the wrong places and at the wrong times? Was it not given a proper chance? Or rather, was it not the victim of other American artists' successes, of a certain weariness facing experimental theatre from New York?

Indeed, the recurring presence of earlier American artists in France may have cast a shadow on the younger generation. For the most part, French audiences were accustomed to the standards that Robert Wilson, Richard Foreman, Meredith Monk, and later Peter Sellars had set after The Living Theater and, to a lesser degree, the Open Theater. That is why, not unlike the 1980 Nancy Festival directed by Françoise Kourilsky, the Exit Festival purported to challenge, or complete, the image of American theatre in France by showcasing the latest alternative artists. The aim was clearly to move beyond those values that were by then so well-established on the international circuit that they could hardly be seen as representatives of either the avant-garde or the United States. Just as Kourilsky tried to present "a multifaceted America where cultures intersect, take over, mix or clash" (qtd. in Grünberg and Demerson, 1984: 213-214), the Exit Festival director, Didier Fusillier, endeavored to introduce "an America of contrasts as seen by Americans." (Fusillier, 1994) Under the motto "Destruction, Decomposition, Reconstruction" – three terms not wholly inappropriate to describe the Wooster Group's aesthetics – he offered an all-American program combining dance, theatre, performance art and music, and featuring, aside from the Wooster Group, Reza Abdoh, Richard Move, Rinde Eckert, magician Patrick Martin, choreographers Bill T. Jones and Donald Byrd, dancer Sean Curran, the Movin' Spirits Dance Theater, Chico Macmurtrie, the Anthony Braxton Quartet, and Sugar Blue from Chicago. Whereas a director like Wilson stands as an artist in his own rights, with no need to be referred to America (although America does influence his work), the Wooster Group was fettered to its roots and presented as an expression of American (counter-)culture.[2] Going against the grain, running off the beaten track, it remained in the shadows whence it came.

The Ambiguous Need for an Institutional Seal

Hardly any institution other than the Festival d'Automne could have ensured the Wooster Group the visibility it lacked. Since its inception, the Festival d'Automne has been responsible for bringing over most American artists, from Merce Cunningham to Richard Maxwell, and giving them a central place in France, however marginal their position might be in the US. It aims to "welcome landmark works as yet unper-formed in France, or in Europe" and to "present and encourage experi-mental undertakings" – two goals that were undoubtedly fulfilled with Wilson, Foreman and others in the 1970s and 1980s (see Carmody, 2002). Did the Wooster Group's productions then fail to be seen as "landmark works"? Did its undertakings seem not "experimental" enough?

Such an assumption is doubtful, despite Colette Godard's jaded criticism of *Brace Up!*, which she considered "outdated," with "as if galore," smacking of "a cold perfection verging on boredom because everything is being said and given with not an ounce of ambiguity" (Godard, 1992). The reasons the Festival d'Automne did not invite the Wooster Group earlier surely lie elsewhere. Firstly, as there exist national idiosyncratic tastes which have accounted, conversely, for Foreman's misfortunes in Germany, there was a certain reluctance in France to a living art that was overtly technological until the Exit Festival specialized in multimedia works and Peter Brook himself, the advocate of "poor theatre," used video in *The Man Who...* (1993). Furthermore, the interest in American theatre had gradually dwindled since the late 1970s and the Festival d'Automne programmers preferred

---

[2]   Such was also the case with the two previous productions: in 1985, *Route 1 & 9* ran parallel to John Jesurun's *Red House* and in 1992, *Brace Up!* was "pitched" against Reza Abdoh's *The Hip Hop Waltz of Eurydice* as an example of East Coast art versus Californian art. At Créteil, in 1994, Abdoh's company Dar A Luz performed *Tight White Right* and just as in 1992 the comparison with the Wooster Group, however far-fetched or illicit, was in Abdoh's favor in the eyes of most critics.

to tighten their links with those talents discovered early on rather than to foster new emerging artists. In the early 1990s, just before his untimely death, Reza Abdoh was one of the very few exceptions to the rule, while the presence of other directors was primarily due to individual initiatives: Peter Sellars, for instance, started out in Paris thanks to Patrice Chéreau at Nanterre's Théâtre des Amandiers and was then supported by Ariel Goldenberg at MC93 Bobigny before the Festival d'Automne began coproducing his work (Maurin, 2002). But apart from that, the Festival d'Automne's policy of privileged partnership continued unabated, benefiting the same artists as before, like Wilson or Foreman. Year after year, they have become stalwarts of the Paris scene. Of course, it might be argued that those who came after the heyday of the American avant-garde, performance artists like Holly Hughes, Tim Miller or Rachel Rosenthal, did not prove attractive or marketable enough in France, but the Wooster Group was already active in the late 1970s. Besides, from the mid-1980s onward, the Festival d'Automne tended to emphasize another goal of its mission, namely "to present non-Western cultures." It invited African, Russian, Asian and Latin American companies alongside other European directors such as Tadeusz Kantor or Klaus Michael Grüber. As the world was opening up, the Americanophile stance for which it had been criticized slightly dampened, and hardly any American "discovery" as resounding as *Deafman Glance* was made with its assistance.

However, in the past few years, the winds seem to have shifted in the curatorial concerns of the Festival d'Automne. The Wooster Group was placed in the spotlight twice to the point of becoming a must-see. *House/Lights* was performed to great acclaim at Théâtre de la Bastille in 1999 and it was called "the best avant-garde production" of the season by one critic (Bourcier, 1999) and a fine example of "sophisticated avant-garde work" by another (Perrier, 1999). Partly based on Gertrude Stein's play *Doctor Faustus Lights the Lights* (almost a rite of passage for American directors in Paris[3]), it served as a testing ground, a try-out or a trial for the Wooster Group's triple bill presented in the fall of 2001 at the Centre Pompidou: *North Atlantic*, *The Hairy Ape*, and *To You, The Birdie!* It was as if the comparatively late programming of the Wooster Group came as remorseful compensation for previous neglect. But it was justly rewarded, as nearly all performances were sold out and met with enormous critical success. However, the redemption process could not avoid the double-bind that accompanies an official boost. In other words, just as it was salvaged from relative ignorance and given full recognition, the Wooster Group was taken over, almost highjacked,

---

[3]   Foreman staged it with French actors in 1982 and Wilson brought his own version
with German actors in 1992 – two coproductions of the Festival d'Automne.

by the Establishment. Coming from limbo, it was recentered and suddenly canonized. For such is the paradox of politics in the arts that hardly any radical aesthetic style can now emerge unless the artist or the company agrees to forego their marginalized cultural status. As the Wooster Group became the talk of the town, previous invisibility threatened to turn into blind consensus.

The 2001 Triptych

At the Centre Pompidou in 2001, the three productions made up an odd triptych comprising the work of a completely unknown playwright (James Strahs), an American classic seldom read, let alone staged, in France (*The Hairy Ape* by Eugene O'Neill), and a "version" of the French tragedy *par excellence*, *Phèdre*. Perhaps they could be considered to form a trilogy of sorts, the Wooster Group's "Parisian" trilogy so to speak, after the two trilogies intended as such: *Three Places in Rhode Island* and *The Road to Immortality*. Unwittingly or not, they were linked by the boat as a common, albeit loose, theme or image: the aircraft carrier cruising off the Dutch coast in *North Atlantic* served as the setting of the performance; a good part of the action takes place on an ocean liner in *The Hairy Ape*; and a small inflatable canoe lay flat on the set of *To You, The Birdie!* Or, rather than a trilogy, it was perhaps more of an anthology, a partial retrospective of the Wooster Group's work, with the attendant risk of artificially bringing back to life vestigial traces of an art that otherwise exists essentially in the present. Each piece had originally been created in one of the past three decades, which was ironically fitting as the Festival d'Automne was celebrating its own 30th anniversary. Seen one after the other, referred to one another, they made up not only a body of work, but also a genuinely new work: a collage in three acts. Each deepened, displaced and diffracted the two others, thus enabling the audience to assess the Wooster Group's vocabulary by testing it against its own development. Perhaps not all three works were equally typical of the main features and working processes most commonly associated with the company (deconstructing the classics and dismembering textual sources, juxtaposing fragments of popular culture, inserting political and social comments) but the diversity of directions revealed the complexity of a coherent aesthetic universe while preventing any fixed conception of a style.

Entering a Universe

When dealing with foreign pieces, even if they are coproduced by an institutional agency boasting a number of subscribers and regular followers, the first question to be addressed is one of marketing. Despite the critical success of *House/Lights*, the Festival d'Automne and the media still seemed quite unsure of how to publicize the Wooster Group in 2001. Following the example of *Le Monde*, which ran a full portrait of Willem Dafoe on the first page of its annual Festival d'Automne supplement (Sotinel), the press often stressed the live presence of Dafoe in Paris (Mennessier) – and to a lesser degree that of Frances McDormand (de Baecque and Solis). The audience would have the opportunity to see one, even two well-known movie actors in the flesh. And Willem Dafoe would undoubtedly be very much in the flesh, as he moved from a stiff depiction of Captain Roscoe in military uniform to a raunchy embodiment of Yank covered with soot, and finally to a plastic performance of Theseus, sticking out his bare torso, impressively muscular through yoga training. Putting forward the name and fame of Dafoe was of course a promotional argument banking on international and commercial stardom. And even though the media quoted him saying that his commitment to the Wooster Group prevailed over his Holly-wood engagements, this publicity strategy was likely to play down the importance of the collective/collaborative aspect of the Group's working process.

Another crucial question regarding a travelling work deals with the way it is perceived as it moves to another culture. Can it resist the double pitfall of vapid internationalism and exotic otherness? To what extent does the meaning of the work shift as the change of cultural framework not only highlights certain contours and makes others opaque, but also brings out unsuspected interpretations? Of course, there are strategies to facilitate the cognitive approach to any theatrical event: for instance a detailed synopsis included in the program (as was the case with *North Atlantic*) or supertitles projected above the stage (as in *The Hairy Ape*). But above all, the transformations in the perception of a foreign work is an unpredictable matter of losses and gains.

In the case of the Wooster Group, a cognitive approach is actually of lesser importance than a sensory immersion. That is why *North Atlantic* (the first offering of the triptych) was as good an introduction to their work as any other piece. Many spectators were bewildered and several critics stated that the plot was drowned in an ocean of words that made it "impossible to follow the action" (Solis, 2001) or "hard to know what was going on" (Bourcier, 2001). Perhaps one could be relieved to find similar comments in American reviews when the original produc-tion premiered: "Language is garbled (deliberately) or overlapped" (Feingold); "everybody speaks at a fast clip in a private incomprehen-sible lingo" (Stasio). But surely, much more was missed in France. The scatological puns went largely unnoticed, like the recurring *double entendre* gags with such words as "debriefing" in the context of military operations and male-female interactions. So did many references to American cultural icons. Judging from the absence of any mention of

South Pacific in the press, it is likely that few caught the reversed allusion to the musical in the title; and the twisted interpretation of several songs, the deadpan rendition of "Back in the Saddle" or "Git Along Little Doggies" probably failed to be perceived in all their parodic intent. But "Dominique," a well-known song in France here sung with fake coquettish delight by the women dressed as nuns, ogling and winking at the audience, contained enough cheek-in-tongue humor to help one tune in to the romp and grasp the overall method of recycling genres, integrating heterogeneous bits and pieces with abrupt changes in tone, from fierce caricature to sheer fun. The audience probably understood the satire of the army through the complex coding and decoding activities, the threat of surveillance and the perils of power politics, the imbalance of men and women's relationships in the Miss Wet Uniform contest, but the general meaning was primarily conveyed through the physicality of the production. What was most striking was the breakneck pacing of the whole, the engagement of the actors alternating between virtuoso performance and mock casualness, the level of tension and discipline with very little left to chance in the midst of an apparent chaos. Though partly incomprehensible, action was everywhere. Not only did it intertwine, live, with prerecorded and amplified sounds, but electronic devices became objects of manipulation, as when the girls got tired of winding the tapes and used them as lassos. Entertainment lightened up indictment, so much so that it may have taken the upper hand for the French. Comic effects deflected serious blows as they probably attracted the attention more than they were originally meant to. Likewise, the dense layering of visual and aural stimuli may have relegated the trial of America to the background, and the intense overload of signs and signals may have blunted the debunking process at work. But at least it showed that *North Atlantic* could be experienced in formal terms without losing its impact.

The perception of *The Hairy Ape*, though more linear in structure, followed suit, giving space to an aesthetics of undercutting irony within O'Neill's plot of an impossibly savage love. As opposed to Yank's rough accent and tough appearance, the polished delivery of Kate Valk in the role of Mildred was simultaneously belied by her digitally sped-up, high-pitched voice turning her into a cartoon character, and moments later by the disproportionate toe-shoes which she exhibited almost off-handedly on the ship deck. As everything was thrown in the face of the audience and turned round and back against itself, nothing could be taken at face value. But in order to avoid any misunderstanding, a program note explicitly mentioned that the production respected every single word of O'Neill's play. However unorthodox the directorial choices might look, they did not meddle with the original but imbued it with a genuine theatrical thinking that produced a new image of it.

On the contrary, no one could ignore that *To You, The Birdie!* played freely with *Phèdre*. It was the only production of the three to be presented with a French title and an explicit undertitle: *À vous, volant! ou* Phèdre *revisitée*. No supertitles were therefore needed to make it clear that Paul Schmidt had cut Racine's text and adapted it into modern American English, and that Elizabeth LeCompte had further interspersed this version with other words of her invention, sighs, exclamations, and shreds of Phaedra's purely fictional inner monologue. She had also set the action by a badminton court, with Venus cast in the role of referee as much as she was the agent of fate, counting the winning points like so many successful lines in a verbal exchange. The phrase *À vous, volant!*, "borrowed from the precious etiquette of badminton games as practiced in the seventeenth century" (program note), was sometimes heard in the original language, too. Thus, the production became a perfect example for the French of the Wooster Group's much-trumpeted deconstruction of classics – say, the equivalent of what *Route 1 & 9* was to *Our Town* or *L.S.D. (...Just the High Points...)* to *The Crucible* for American audiences.

Although it might have seemed an unmotivated take on the play, the twist was nevertheless grounded from both a historical and dramaturgic point of view. The badminton court, where Hippolytos and Theramenes fiercely competed in highly choreographed games and Phaedra utterly failed versus Œnone as soon as she came on stage, served as a reminder, perhaps more easily caught by French spectators, that theatre, in the seventeenth century, first took place in former *jeux de paume* before the first permanent houses were built. A fault in the match was a derisive equivalent of the tragic flaw. The birdie served as the symbolic vehicle for exchanges, both physical *and* verbal. To catch it or to miss it was to voice one's strength or one's weakness; to play "he-loves-me, he-loves-me not" with it, as Phaedra did at one point, was to express one's uncertainties. Reversing d'Aubignac's famous precept that "to speak is to act," action could easily substitute for words: to act or not to act was to admit or to hide one's feelings. And so the body, hardly present in Racine's play except as a surface of inscription for desire, came to play a prominent role. Scatological allusions, which turned Phaedra's devouring passion into a serious eating disorder, were more easily perceived than in *North Atlantic*, as they were visually and aurally conveyed by suction instruments, acts of douching and the attendant amplified noises.

Most of the text was spoken by Scott Shepherd into one or two microphones – one for the monologues, two for the dialogues. The device contributed to severing his distorted voice from the speaking character(s), perhaps with a neo-Brechtian alienation effect,[4] but it also extended the much-debated use of narration in classical drama. As he sat at a long table at the rear of the playing area, Scott Shepherd stepped out of his role as Theramenes and was identified with "the reader." But in so doing, he also fulfilled Theramenes' function as narrator in *Phèdre* – especially in his famous report of Hippolytos' death, running close to 100 lines in the original (V.6, ll. 1498-1593), and only 13 in Paul Schmidt's version (1993: 29). Œnone also happened to act as narrator, or chorus, for instance when she imparted Phaedra's initial state of mind to the audience: "She says she wants to die," she could be heard saying when the weak queen entered silently. More generally, Racine's text was heard on another level of discourse. It was voiced and yet not fully represented, less embodied than quoted as commentary. It seemed grafted onto the stage action rather than entailing it logically, while the stage action, on the contrary, did not seem unduly tacked onto the play. As invention combined with cynical rendition, and witty adaptations of seventeenth-century conventions with forceful rejections of decorum, the production took on a metatheatrical dimension that was subversively respectful of the source material.

Evolution on View

The triple bill raised the question of aesthetic identity and stylistic unity in the work of a long-standing company. It was a matter of variation and evolution. Seen in sequence, the productions emphasized the characteristic features of the Wooster Group, the different directions it took and its development over the years. In that regard, no device was more revealing than the use of technology. Unsurprisingly, it was relatively low-key in the earliest piece, *North Atlantic*, with just an array of microphones and video monitors unifying the set like luminous frames; more prominent in *The Hairy Ape*, with a soundtrack of gongs and clatters, and archival footage of a boxing match or men showering in the haze; and much more elaborate in *To You, The Birdie!*

On a screen placed above the stage, moving her eyes as if following the badminton games below, Venus's face appeared as a young red-haired woman with two wing-like clouds shot against a blue sky: an innocent angel as much as a ruthless goddess. Downstage, other images were shown on a large sliding flat screen monitor. In the opening scene, Theramenes and Hippolytos sat facing the audience, wearing kilts. But the lower halves of their bodies were only visible on this screen, with their hands touching their bare genitals both when Hippolytos admitted

---

[4]   In that regard, it might be noted that Kate Valk lip-synched her words more in Paris than she seemed to do later in Brooklyn.

his love for Aricia and at other times. The image was of an ambiguous relationship between the virgin prince and his tutor, a juvenile masturbatory fantasy, or almost an homoerotic image in keeping with a valid reading of Racine's play. Moments later, Phaedra's feet were seen trying on different pairs of shoes on that same screen: "I hate these clothes. Pointless elegance," said Scott Shepherd in a deep voice (Schmidt, 1993: 6). But Phaedra could not find any shoes that fitted her mood: "I don't actually wear shoes. I just like to try them on," Shepherd said in a softer voice as if expressing her inner thoughts. "Everything ruins me, conspires against me," Kate Valk then said, speaking a more faithfully translated line from Racine (Schmidt, 1993: 6), and diverting the spectators' gaze from the screen to attract it back to her own live presence.

As a matter of fact, all those images were prerecorded and the performers moved in and out of synch with them. Just as in those children's books where different faces may be matched, or ill-matched, with different torsos and those torsos with different legs, the contiguity was no warrant for continuity. Although the thin border between live immediacy and mediatized unreality might have seemed blurred, the collage was exhibiting its own impossibility in the realm of representation. Such impossibility became even more obvious later, with an image of Willem Dafoe's face prolonging his body as he reclined in profile like a Renaissance painting of Deposition. But the projected face was clearly not as clean-shaven as Dafoe actually was in the show: it belonged to another time and place and belied the idea of prolongation in favor of fragmentation. The assemblage did not quite fit. Still later, Dafoe's bare torso transformed into iconic representations of antique male statues as if by a morphing operation, and the referee ironically called for the projection of different slides showing those statues after Theseus' invocation to Neptune (IV.3).

Thus, visual technology added another level of commentary on the play. Not only could the stage action seem superimposed on the reading of a "revisited" version of Phèdre, but it also juxtaposed the physicality of the performers and images – their own and others. The text and the body were equally submitted to a method of fetishization, and this method further extended to the aural layer of the performance as individual sounds were singled out and blown up. During the badminton matches, every hit of a racket, every hiss of the birdie, every wipe of a towel was amplified, as were the steps of Theseus when he came on stage like a marching colossus or the suction operation when Phaedra defecated. Technology was an integral part of Elizabeth LeCompte's take on the play, rather than a gratuitous apparatus which self-consciously exhibited the postmodernity of her directorial perspective.

What the triple bill also emphasized was the variety of architectural devices and spatial configurations, each echoing the others and yet standing on its own terms. *North Atlantic* was played on a ramp standing on top of the stage floor's metal scaffolding and sharply tilted toward the audience at a forty-five-degree angle. As the performers shuffled and skittered on the platform, sliding down, climbing up or trying to maintain their balance, the view afforded the audience was often a view from below. Along with the performers, it was America that could be seen falling down, plunging into the Atlantic. In *The Hairy Ape*, the set relied on the stage floor's complex support of metallic poles, being more vertically oriented and split between two levels linked by a staircase. Hung with video monitors, it made room for two main playing areas: the lower level represented the stokehole or the sailors' headquarters, complete with hammocks, and later the prison on Blackwell's Island, while the upper level stood for the ship deck, and later Fifth Avenue and the zoo where Yank met with the gorilla. Furthermore, the verticality of the set spread to the verticality of the performing style in that the performers were equipped with a one-legged seat affixed to their buttocks: they could stop and sit in an almost upright position as they bent their knees ever so slightly. In *To You, The Birdie!*, on the contrary, the space was organized horizontally and divided into cross-sections or corridors from downstage to upstage: in the foreground were the sliding Plexiglas panels with the screens; behind was the badminton court, and at the rear the table at which Scott Shepherd sat on one side and Suzzy Roche (Venus) on the other. Stair railings protruding from the stage floor suggested a pool, representing the ocean or Hades. But never was its depth to be seen. And just as verticality was the global concept of *The Hairy Ape*, a good part of the action in *To You, The Birdie!* took place with the performers sitting or lying on the floor, which added to the horizontality of the view. Aside from being attracted upward toward the screen hanging overhead, the spectator's eye moved from front to back, as well as from side to side: Phaedra urinated, defecated or was douched on a commode stage left, and Œnone hung herself with a tube of the suction instruments attached to another commode stage right, amidst a flushing reminiscent of her original drowning.

Those different spaces (tilted, vertical, horizontal) and the different kinds of gaze they called for make it possible to think of Elizabeth LeCompte's work in terms of construction as much as deconstruction, according to the term that is generally, perhaps too systematically, applied to her work. She uses the stage as a workbench to assemble her productions and she controls it like a machine in which all components (actors, gestures, images, words, sounds) function together as cogs or dysfunction as counterweights. In that sense, her work may recall the constructivist movement of the 1920s, with its tendency to rear up the stage and uplift the eye. Just as props were then turned into playing partners, the technological devices here become genuine performers, and not simply elements of the set design. Accordingly, it may be more than a coincidence if LeCompte once claimed that "the most radical theatre work being done today belongs to a tradition that Meyerhold created for us" (Schmidt, 1996: back cover). Running counter to a naturalistic style of acting, she seems to follow in the footsteps of the pioneering director-auteur from a distance. She confers on her shows a similar sense of heightened theatricality and dense musical choreography, and proceeds to reinvent American theatre in her own experimental laboratory; a laboratory resembling an anti-Actors Studio just as Meyerhold's theatre stood in contrast with Stanislavsky's Moscow Art Theatre.

The Americanness of the Wooster Group

Undoubtedly, the Wooster Group speaks the language of America in the late twentieth century and turns that language against itself. It plays with the idiom of today's culture in order to target the militaristic ideology and the role of technology in shaping American culture (*North Atlantic*), the degrading image of hyperfemininity (*The Hairy Ape*), male narcissism and fetishistic body worship (*To You, The Birdie!*). In Paris, it came to be seen as an American company on tour, as opposed to artists used to criss-crossing all over the world to the point of losing track of their cultural roots. "They are American, that is to say madly in love with the real, its drunken chaos and racket," wrote a critic at the beginning of his review of *To You, The Birdie!*, which he called "a lethal cabaret" (Ferney, 2001). As Americans, he continued, "they do not experience blood, firearms, microphones, violence, and speed, the way we do." It was as if the experience could not be apprehended in terms other than American: the productions were foreign by French standards, perhaps even alien – whether alienated from the audience or alienating them to a degree that the same elements in a film would not.

But the Wooster Group's triptych was not simply linked to a particular culture, whose poignant details and more subtle references may or may not have escaped the audience's attention. More importantly, it gave an extraordinary lesson on the use of technological devices as contemporary tools for a new theatrical language, rather than instruments of a technical achievement for its own sake, and it manifested the benefits of a tight group working together over a long period of time. The clarity and intelligence of Elizabeth LeCompte's understanding of the stage became as prominent as the versatility of the performers – not only as actors of different roles and in different styles, but also as singers, dancers, and to some extent athletes. Moreover, the triple bill showed that the idea of a repertoire is not necessarily a dusty notion serving the conservative preservation of the classics, but a moving concept aiming to keep the most radical expressions of the past alive.

Within the dialectical tension between otherness and assimilation, the Wooster Group looked exemplary in its foreignness. Even the older pieces seemed new, although nearly twenty years separated the premiere of *North Atlantic* and the Paris performances, and the French spectators are regularly exposed to the most recent experimental work. Perhaps *North Atlantic* was less startling than it would have been two decades earlier; perhaps the quality it brought along was not quite "the shock of the new," to borrow Richard Hughes's phrase, but it appeared neither comfortable nor familiar. It belonged to the present as much as to history.

More generally, the Wooster Group breathed fresh air into the possibly "museumized" image of American theatre, as guarded by the secure values that Robert Wilson or Peter Sellars have come to stand for year after year (Carmody). No doubt there have been other American artists in Paris aside from those two leading directors in today's international circuit: ironically enough, between the "marginal" performances of *Fish Story* in 1994 and the highly mediatized performances of *House/Lights* in 1999, the Exit Festival invited two Wooster Group offshoots in 1998 – Marianne Weems with the Builders Association and Roy Faudree with *No Theater*; and in the course of the years, several other alternative artists like Paul Lazar, Jennifer Lacey, Bill Shannon, and Richard Maxwell have been given a degree of cultural visibility perhaps higher in France than in the United States. But willy-nilly, as one of the most "established" companies within the alternative New York scene, as an heir to the avant-garde of the 1970s (Foreman's Ontological-Hysteric Theater would be a survivor), the Wooster Group's presence in Paris at the start of the twenty-first century was essential in filling a gap: the gap between the golden age of the American avant-garde and today's perhaps less flamboyant relief troops, the gap in an unsuspected tradition of radical innovation still on the march.

Appendix: The Wooster Group in France

Route 1 & 9: Le Printemps du théâtre, Théâtre de la Bastille, Paris, 25-30 June 1985.

Brace Up!: Sigma Festival, Hangar 5-2, Bordeaux, 10-14 November 1992.

Fish Story : Exit Festival, Maison des Arts, Créteil, 13-17 May 1994.

House/Lights: Festival d'Automne à Paris, Théâtre de la Bastille, 8-18 December 1999.

North Atlantic: Festival d'Automne à Paris, Centre Pompidou, 14-17 November 2001.

The Hairy Ape: Festival d'Automne à Paris, Centre Pompidou, 22-26 November 2001.

À vous, volant! ou Phèdre *revisitée* (*To You, The Birdie!*): Festival d'Automne à Paris, Centre Pompidou, 3-7 December 2001.

Framing the Fragments

The Wooster Group's Use of Technology

Jennifer PARKER-STARBUCK

Scarborough School of Arts, Hull University

Placing a specimen on the instrument's stage and closing one eye to peer through the viewfinder, the microscopist sees the body in a manner that effectively distances the observer from the subjective experience of the body imaged. Excised from the body, stained, blown up, resolved, pierced by a penetrating light, and perceived by a single squinting eye, the microscopic specimen is apparently stripped of its corporeality, its function, and its history even as it serves as a final proof of the health, pathology, or sexuality of the subject whose body it represents. (Cartwright: 83)

The arts of presentation and, particularly, video installation, are the privileged art forms for setting this mediated, built environment into play for purposes of reflection. Indeed, the underlying premise of the [video art] installation appears to be that the audiovisual experience supplemented kinesthetically can be a kind of learning not with the mind alone, but with the body itself. (Morse: 161)

"The Wooster Group is about an art of the body itself, as well as the mind," concludes one of the many favorable reviews for *House/Lights*, the Group's 1999 presentation (Zimmerman: 40-41). While the mind may seem an obvious choice, describing a Wooster Group piece as "an art of the body" is a more curious phrase to describe a company that is often thought of for its postmodern deconstruction of texts, a reliance on the technological, and a "dissociated" (Brantley, 2002), "Wooster aesthetic." (McNulty, 2002) The quotation reflects the contemporary critical thought that the "human subject" is no longer a unified whole, but a fragmented complex of systems: body, mind, constructed identities, multiple, cyberized, cyborg – and the Wooster Group's technological tendencies reinforce this mode of thought. Using examples from *To You, The Birdie!* (seen at St. Ann's Warehouse, Brooklyn, NY.

9 February and 2 March 2002), I will explore how the Group's use of technology ultimately returns to the "art of the body," rethinking the idea of subjectivity through a metaphoric film loop between the bodies and technologies on stage generating a cyborg performance model.

A foundational assumption of this essay is that the condition of Western society in the early twenty-first century is now what theorist Katherine Hayles calls the "posthuman," signifying it is no longer possible to imagine daily operations that are not surrounded by, immersed in, and/or intersecting with technology. Just as the idea of the body has evolved from the "natural" to the "constructed," so too has technology evolved from "tool" to "systems," including artificial intelligence. The body as cultural construct is no longer a mere biological given, but a site for inscribed meanings and readings of identity, class, gender, race, and state control. The sophistication with which technologies have extended beyond the idea of "tool" has led to machines that think, create, and function as replicas of the human system. The posthuman is, to Hayles, a "point of view" that "configures human being so that it can be seamlessly articulated with intelligent machines." (22-3)

An ironic tone resonates in the prefix "post," for despite many literal examples of prosthetic devices augmenting the human body, most of us are still committed to our "human-ness." In their edition called *Posthuman Bodies*, Judith Halberstam and Ira Livingston distinguish the term: "The posthuman does not necessitate the obsolescence of the human; it does not represent an evolution or devolution of the human. Rather it participates in re-distributions of difference and identity [...] the posthuman does not reduce difference-from-others to difference-from-self, but rather emerges in the pattern of resonance and interference between the two." (10) I am not disputing the validity of each of our individual bodily identities, but only suggesting that the currents of theory around this term cannot be overlooked and that the word posthuman is written as an ethical question in order to retain the sense of what has been called "human." My larger concerns and argument are in part an attempt to re-think certain "screened" modes of representation in live performance acting as sites of resistance against mythologized notions of able-bodied norms, technologies of global capital, and bodies as commodified objects. I would like to follow Matthew Causey's call when he writes, "ethically and politically, that the object of posthuman performance should be to configure a map of the terrain of identity in digital culture while challenging failed models of human subjectivity that threaten to return continually if different systems of subjectivity are not engaged."

I use the term posthuman as a condition in which to locate the cyborg as a site for the re-imagination of performance that relies on both live bodies and varying forms of technology. Building on Donna Haraway's cyborg, which she calls a myth "about transgressed boundaries, potent fusions, and dangerous possibilities which progressive people might explore as one part of needed political work" (1991: 154), I call this form of performance "Cyborg Theatre," and of my examples, the Wooster Group's use of technology on stage marks a de-stabilization of presence and subjectivity through the use of video, framing, and aural manipulation that can ultimately be read as a reconstituted alternative presence for a media driven age (see also Parker-Starbuck, 1999). Unlike more advanced forms of computer technology that actually attempt to merge with the live body on stage (such as George Coates in San Francisco, or virtual reality experiments like the Institute for the Exploration of Virtual Realities at the University of Kansas), the Wooster Group explores the potential of technology to disrupt, frame, and multiply the body, exposing the gaps between the two that produce a multiplicity of meanings for a new cyber-subject.

In discussing video installation art, Margaret Morse asks:

Who is the subject of the experience? Performance, even where it has installation-like sets, differs from installation, because the artist occupies the position of the subject within the installation world. Interactive work differs in yet another way. Room is made for the visitor to play with the parameters of a posited world, thus taking on a virtual role of 'artist/installer' if not the role of artist as declarer and inventor of that world. (163)

While it is so that the "viewer/audience" attending the Wooster Group's performances is not interactive in the sense of installation art, I find Morse's ideas relevant in that the Wooster Group is clearly asking many of the same questions of subjectivity as installations do, only on the stage. The play of subject/object crucial in Morse's analysis of video art installation is taken up in the performance structure of the Wooster Group as well.

I will take as a premise what I term the "object body" of the Wooster Group aesthetic. I do not see them originating ideas from a central subject on stage, but rather, from bodies onto which ideas are inscribed. This body is a filter for certain historically mediated constructions of the body. It is objectified, a *tabula rasa* for the meaning imposed upon it. Like Foucault's disciplined body, the body objectified by the gaze, or the racialized body,[1] the Wooster Group body begins as an object on stage, equal to and balanced by the objects of technology. By objects of technology I mean a variety of screens and the use of aural manipulation that co-exist in the stage picture. Sue Ellen Case, drawing on Elizabeth

---

[1]   While for Foucault, the disciplined body is a "subject," in the sense of a subject of the state, I consider this body as being subject-ed, thereby turning object, rather than a possessor of agency, which distinguishes my subject body categorization.

Grosz's work, describes the basic idea of the socialized, disciplined body and writes, "Moreover, the body loses its fleshly integrity as it intertwines with other 'surfaces and planes.' The term 'body' thus ascends into a trope for the matrix of social forces." (107) I argue that instead of losing agency through its entwinement with the surfaces of technology, the Wooster Group's objects, body and technology, both become subjectified as cyborg through their association with each other – creating a resistant site for re-placing object bodies.

Much has been written about the loss of embodiment through computer interface and the need to put the body back into the "real" mix. I shall hold this anxiety in abeyance, and simply state that I am willing to believe that society is "mediatized" (Auslander, 1999: 4-6) and that this mediatization frames our understanding of the world, whether one has access to technology or is withheld from it. I would like to return now to the two opening epigraphs. These epigraphs are taken from theorists who question the role of subjectivity in a mediatized age. Lisa Cartwright's *Screening the Body* exemplifies ways in which screened, specifically medical cinema technologies have affected and controlled the way life is thought of culturally, and Margaret Morse's *Virtualities* offers intermedial spaces of cyberculture as means of understanding communities in a techno-driven world.

Cartwright looks at uses of cinema in medical science to "analyze, regulate, and reconfigure the transient, uncontrollable field of the body." (xiii) She says that the purpose of her study is to "demonstrate how the cinema, an instrument of popular entertainment, functioned as a part of a social apparatus through which the cultures of Western science and medicine shaped and built the life they studied, and how individual subjects and cultures aided, confounded, or resisted Western medical science's normative life-building projects in the first half of this century." (xvii) Specifically, her discussion of the microscopic motion picture, or cine-microscope, depicts a cultural shift through microscopy that begins with seeing the body as unified which shifts to a systematized view of isolated parts and fragments that set up "microcosms of cultural norms about the body and subjectivity," not of a "seeing subject" but of a "social subject." (105)

Morse, on the other hand, begins with the idea that cultural exchanges are "automated" and that machines now function within a cyberculture to facilitate these exchanges. For Morse, the accretion of technology has created a dizzying world of postmodernism and fragmentation and types of virtualities – in the case of this epigraph, video art installation – allow the "visitors" of the installation to reflect on their worlds by immersing themselves in the technology where an "experience" can occur, implying a reconnected "wholeness" through the immersion.

The Wooster Group's use of technology exemplifies a shift from a conception of "whole" to the fragmented and back again but in a recon-figured form.[2] The Wooster Group's space of performance – i.e. the world of their stage – is like that of the "experience" Morse refers to. The Wooster Group illustrates Lisa Cartwright's notion that "the body is rendered part of a living system that incorporates the technologies of its representations." (xiv)[3] Through the meticulous balance of techniques and ideas of framing, gaps, presence, and layering, the "Wooster Group body" resituates Cartwright's "social" subject and the authority of a "speaking subject" described by Morse, as a way to see a radically reconfigured, potentially even feminist, model of cyber-subjectivity, a model developed by Donna Haraway's *The Cyborg Manifesto*. Haraway writes:

> Communications technologies and biotechnologies are the crucial tools re-crafting our bodies. These tools embody and enforce new social relations for women world-wide. Technologies and scientific discourses can be partially understood as formalizations, i.e. as frozen moments, of the fluid social in-teractions constituting them, but they should also be viewed as instruments for enforcing meanings. The boundary is permeable between tool and myth, instrument and concept, historical systems of social relations and historical anatomies of possible bodies, including objects of knowledge. Indeed, myth and tool mutually constitute each other. (164)

The cyborg theatre as constructed by the Wooster Group is developed through a series of explorations into the mutual constitution between myth and tool.

To You, The Birdie!, a loose adaptation of Racine's *Phèdre*, is instal-lation-like as performance. The Wooster Group's deconstruction and blending of "texts" brings together: the story of Phèdre, the tormented queen who struggles over the lust for her stepson Hippolytos; the game of badminton; gliding three-foot screens and television-like monitors; Greek "ghosts in the machine"; a sophisticated vocal score of human narration and syncopated sound effects – as screens slide into place or birdies fly through the air; and scatological explorations of the body.

---

[2]   I use quotation marks around the term whole, because I agree with Case's notion that fragmentation presumes a whole from which to fragment – she instead prefers the term "net of notions." (7)

[3]   I am also indebted to Vanden Heuvel (1991), which opened up an investigation of the lenses of seeing I use in this essay. Although Vanden Heuvel focuses on the use of alternative texts to analyze the Group's contribution to a form of theatre that inter-faces what he defines as "drama" and "performance," he does not specifically ana-lyze the texts of technology in their work.

The piece opens to expose the Wooster Group world – in the large hangar-like St. Ann's Warehouse, (a move to a larger space for this production) Hippolytos and Theramenes, his friend, enter the typical grid-like frame and sit downstage center, behind a large screen on which a pre-recorded projection of their lower halves merges with the action of their upper bodies, creating a cyborgean illusion. The men chat, eyes following a match (a ball? a birdie?) as they fidget, reaching down with their live arms which then simultaneously appear on the screen below as they adjust their exposed genitals beneath their kilts. The screen image, shot slightly larger-than-life, creates a microscopic view that moves slightly faster and often out of synch with the live bodies. Upstage, live, and on a TV monitor overhead, Venus, the referee watches over the whole scene, perhaps controlling or foretelling the events that are about to unfold. The voices are amplified and precise pops and whirrs fill the space, indicating how far from the neoclassical world Racine inhabited the Wooster Group has come.

Or, perhaps it is not as far as it looks. I will agree with Morse's description that within the "automated cultural exchange" of today's (at least Western) society, "there is a basic human need for reciprocity and the reversibility of 'I' and 'you' in discourse – seeing and being seen, recognizing others and being recognized, speaking, listening and being listened to." (10-11) In choosing the text of *Phèdre*, the Wooster Group emphasizes the isolation that today's technology can offer, an isolation not without fear and confinement. Morse goes on to explain that "Social institutions of family, education, politics, religion, and the economy [...] have converged to some degree or other with the media. The television is virtual babysitter, matchmaker, educator, (non)site of electoral, legislative, and executive political events, a judicial body, a church, and a mall." (9) With society's convergence with the media, a sense of community is lost. Theatre is under-attended, but chat rooms are over-flowing.

The *mise en scène* of *Birdie!* could be Phèdre's personal chat room. A world of isolation has paradoxically rendered Kate Valk's Phèdre incapable of relating as individual to the world. She rarely speaks un-mediated for herself, cannot use the bathroom without attendants, and is lost behind screens in a false world of desire. In her downtime, she demands that an array of shoes be brought to her. As she tries on several pairs on the screen that connects imaged legs and live upper torso, she could as easily be doing some internet shopping as being attended to by servants. Director Liz LeCompte may not have intended so clearly to find parallels between Racine's world and today's but in this production LeCompte and her company comment on and question the social subject of both worlds through ideas of isolation, surveillance, and desire that are expressed here through a convergence with technology, yet one that takes place in a theatre space, retaining the sense of community so often thought lost through mediatization. In the same fashion as microscopy, LeCompte isolates moments and frames parts of the body with a series of screens that give the viewer the feeling of looking through a lens, giving an illusion of control to the viewer/audience, but ultimately creating an environment for reflecting that gaze.

The use of fragmentation and dislocation is a trademark of LeCompte's stage view. Video screens often isolate the live actors from their mediatized selves, either creating split personalities that obliquely question essentialist identity formation, or acting as literal representations of the multiple texts and characters within those texts (as in *House/Lights*, which spliced the 1964 soft-core sex film *Olga's House of Shame*, and Gertrude Stein's 1938 *Dr. Faustus Lights the Lights*, a text in which the "protagonist" is the doubly-named Marguerite Ida and Helena Annabel.) In *Phèdre*, the fragmentation begins with the example discussed earlier, the slight close-up of the lower halves of the two men. This initial split sets up a viewing process whereby we the viewers, like Cartwright's microscopists, are given an "insider" view, a sectioned-off fragment of bodies to analyze differently from the whole, which was historically "a mode geared to the temporal and spatial decomposition and reconfiguration of bodies as dynamic fields of action in need of regulation and control." (xi) LeCompte's beginning with images of male genitalia may need more time to deconstruct than space will allow, but I will speculate that by allowing us to enter the world of the isolated, fragmented image with this one in particular, instead of leading us directly to the protagonist Phèdre, LeCompte immediately parallels and then reconfigures the traditional mode of viewing Cartwright describes, commenting ironically on the tiresome types of representations of the same toned, thin, and exposed female "screened" bodies in the public media (billboards, magazines, films, television in the U.S.) by opening with an image that is never seen. The screen is itself exposed as a method of surveillance, control, and isolation, and like Cartwright's assertion that cinema was used in medical science to "analyze, regulate, and reconfigure the transient, uncontrollable field of the body" (xiii), *Birdie!*'s opening suggests this regulation, but this screen's eye view of itchy, sweaty, exposed male bodies, begins to reconfigure stereotypical media representations as a form of surveillance shrouded in voyeuristic desire. By "embodying" the technology, that is, by situating it in a cyborgean relation to the two live actors interacting with it, LeCompte lets the composite images gaze back, empowering a dialogue, or a give and take with the bodies imaged that resists screens of regulation and fragmentation that impose the "impossibly perfect" mediatized bodies upon passive viewers.

Evolving out of techniques in previous works, the use of fragmentation in *To You, The Birdie! (Phèdre)* layers isolation and desire upon
ideas of multiple imaging. Unlike Racine's Phèdre, Valk's is not only
trapped in an unrequited and forbidden love, but in a disjointed world of
technological anxiety. LeCompte deftly uses techniques that can either
comment on the stage world, or the "real" world outside the theatre.
Whereas the technique of exposure I mentioned above served to convey
an outside reflection of society's use of mediatized bodies, the same
technique is expanded to create an interior world of the play, a world
where the surveillance is imposed from within, and desire emanates
through the screen. In the following examples, the gaps between the
bodies and the screens serve as a space of dislocation and desire that
require a reconsideration of the location of subjecthood.

Within the world of the play, Phèdre searches for a way out of her
struggle with lust, her anxiety, her desire. At one point Valk stands
alone behind a head-height screen that holds a projected image of her
head. Merging her live lower body and recorded, emotionally imploring
face, the composite Phèdre performs a gesture of intense longing and
sadness. Valk's live arms rise up and in synch with the recording,
become enscreened as her hands press the recorded surface in what
might be an attempt to get out. After a moment, she steps out from
behind the screen, leaving the now larger than life head still in motion
beside her. The recorded moving image lingers beside the live Valk,
leaving a dislocated space of identity, of subjecthood. Can Racine's
queen live split between desire and reality? Does the body embody
technology or technology embody the body? What is in the space
between ourselves and our relationship to technology? Later, these
questions are taken up again when Dafoe's Theseus has returned from
war and is being massaged by his attendants. He rests his body on the
floor, half immersed in a screen onto which his head is projected. The
projected head is slightly out of focus at first, and with the beginnings of
a moustache not found on the live Dafoe, indicating a disjointed time
and place between the live and the tech. The head stares out at the
audience and "talks" flirtatiously while being massaged by attendants.
After a while the image adjusts in focus, and Dafoe rises from the floor,
leaving the head to linger, perhaps longing for the massage to continue,
perhaps showing his level of comfort, as compared to Valk's uneasy
immersion in the technology. After all, Theseus is a warlord, comfortable with the "tools" of the time, whether they are for pleasure or
destruction. As Sue-Ellen Case has written, "critical models [of technol-
ogy] derive from chaos theory, semiotics, postMarxist studies of value,
and theories from men whose work by and large ignores issues of
gender and sexuality, such as Martin Heidegger, Walter Benjamin, Paul
Virilio, Gregory Ulmer, Mark Poster, and Deleuze and Guattari." (72)

Leaving gaps and spaces that reverberate between the live and the technologized on stage, LeCompte creates her own space in which to pose questions, if not answers, of gender and sexuality in relation to the controlling and regulating forces of these mergings. Additionally, that the techniques of screening in *Birdie!* are used only for the characters of higher status, rather than those of the nurse and attendants bears further consideration about representations of class within technological structures.

In this section I would like to take the idea of re-constructing subjectivity through a cyborgean model a bit further. Already building on what Marvin Carlson has referred to as "body ghosting [is] made possible by a combination of the group's general recycling of material and its duplication of bodies within a single production by the use of video" (169), LeCompte and the Group in *Birdie!* continue the layering process: from the earlier use of small video monitors to larger-screened surveillant and regulatory double imaging systems. Upon that, gaps between the live and the screened are exposed to create an experiential and resounding space for questions of subjectivity. Onto this deeply layered terrain, the technique of mediatized narration is applied, decentralizing ideas of subjectivity emanating from a "speaking subject" and allowing mediatized voices to have an equivalent authority in the character's subjectivity. This layering reinforces Morse, who, relying on semiotic analyses of Derrida, Austin, and Greimas, says, "to call oneself 'I', for instance, has to begin from the basis of a not-I and its negation. Thus, a rupture or break is and remains at the heart of subjectivity." (12) In the Wooster Group's work I argue for the reconfiguration of object body and object technology through the relationship with each other as a cyborg model of performance. Both body and technology thus attempt to speak as "I" for the other but the failure to do so completely strips either of the authority of the "I" subject. Morse explains that while we understand the slippage in digital representations such as photography, the fallacy of electronic media, specifically news television, is that "the subject or 'I' in the utterance or image is the one who actually enunciates it, here and now." The fallacy here is that the body we see actually "belongs to another order of reality than the subject 'I' in the linguistic utterance," (12) and that once the utterance is disengaged from the speaker "I," it may be interpreted endlessly, questioning the authority of the speaker.

In *Birdie!*, the utterance is doubly disconnected. The actors playing Phèdre, Theseus, and Hippolytos rarely use their own voices and the bulk of the text is read through a microphone by Scott Shepherd, in the disassociated and deadpan Wooster Group fashion. The bodies become objectified as visual commodities, destabilized through a separation

between the speaker, the spoken, and the body ascribed to these utterances. Concerning cyberculture, Margaret Morse writes:

> The argument to be made here, is not that once there was something sincere
> and unmediated called face to face conversation of which exchanges medi-
> ated by television and the computer are inherently inauthentic or debased
> simulations. If anything, machine subjects are made possible by the
> fundamental gap that has always existed between language and the world
> and between utterances – be they subjective or impersonal – and the act of
> enunciation – whether it is produced by a human subject or has been
> delegated to machines. (14)

In *Birdie!*, narration, then, becomes another form of "subject technology," like moving screened body parts interacting with live bodies in a
dialogue about representation, the narration technique separates the
utterance from the body and filters it through a microphone – the voice
is live but it is not the voice of the "speaker-actor." This and the embodied screen techniques give technology a "voice" on the Wooster Group's
stage. Morse writes that, "such language-using, or more precisely,
language-simulating machine subjects, insofar as they are embodied,
belong to a category of 'intelligent' robots." (14) While this concept is
not literalized on the stage of *Birdie!*, the idea carries over as the Wooster Group develops a new form of subjectivity on stage. Like the seg-
menting of body parts, the emphasis upon the gaps between the speaker
and the spoken are at first disorienting – who is speaking, whose words
are these, are they thoughts in the character's head? But like a "chat" on
the computer, the spaces between utterances allow room for interpretation, for reflection – who are we speaking to? Who are we as speaker?
These gaps destabilize a traditional speaking subject while constructing
an embodied machine subject with an alternate subjectivity.

As Kate Valk's Phèdre confesses her illicit love for her stepson to
her nurse Œnone, played by Frances McDormand, the narrator, Scott
Shepherd, hides behind a screen placed upstage center, again forming a
cyborg relationship between live lower body and projected head. As the
women whisper, Shepherd turns his on-screen, disproportionately large
head to eavesdrop and his on screen ear begins to grow larger, creating a
humorous moment that both makes visible the regulatory control technology often invisibly carries, while also itself mimicking the kind of
fantastical techniques frequently employed by television shows such as
Ally McBeal. Technological surveillance is also made plain through the
character Venus, who sits upstage throughout the show, and frequently
appears on the small video monitors overhead, controlling the badminton game that is a play on rules – of the game, the neoclassical rules of
Racine's time, of love and desire, and rules each character must uphold
within the overall social world of the play. However, the Wooster

Group's layering makes any one reading impossible, and through the specific examples of framing and fragmentation, manipulating vocal subjectivity, and juxtaposing the live with the screened partial perspective, a cyborg model emerges to alter essentialist thinking and binary constructions of the natural and the constructed, or the subject and the object.

Donna Haraway writes that "the cyborg is a kind of disassembled and reassembled, postmodern collective and personal self. This is the self feminists must code." (163) To be at once a collective and a self is a monumental task. Isolated within a technological age, typing alone at a screen populated by millions of other presences, the idea of the contemporary subject is an amalgam of its parts. But without a critical understanding of the ways in which that screen functions the subject will be misunderstood, unable to assume any (one) political code. The physically isolated cyber-subject of the chat room desires a community to interact with. Sharing secrets, transferring erotic tales of lust and longing, gathering information, instant messaging and carrying on conversation with other users (including mechanized "chatterbots" [Auslander 2002]), the cyber-subject exposes fragments of the whole, creating a composite on-line "persona." However, to retain any sense of political agency within the dizzying world on-line, the cyber subject must question how all its components have been constructed: in what ways is it shaped by the ways its parts – identifying, physical, or electronic – have been shaped? How have its desires been shaped because of these constructs? The self Haraway seeks is cyborg. But to step beyond the many uncritical, masculinist and militaristic formations of cyborg subjectivity, is to recognize that the "I" is formed by the "not-I" and that the spaces between the live and the technological are as important to examine as the seamless mergings of the two. Morse writes, "In an era when cameras can travel under the surface of the skin, the desire to experience, interact, and even touch the image in an apparently unmediated way refuses to stop at the screen itself." (177)

Although I have not focused on a specifically feminist critique nor read any indication that LeCompte and the Group consider themselves political or feminist, as Cartwright has pointed out, technologies shape our lives and "Women must actively reconfigure technologies of representation – precisely because these technologies have been invested with the power to transform the body physically [...] Although medical technologies may not be a cure, they are a critical – and heavily funded – area of visual culture. Thus this field is in need of active feminist technological refunctioning and counter surveillance." (170) As I continue to watch the Wooster Group layer ideas of technology's isolating forces, of surveillance, and regulatory image-making, I consider their work political because it inspires me to see between the images, to hear

the resonating sounds that are so often missed as television and even
film hold our attention so passively, to enter an environment where I can
see and be seen, and where the live interrelationship with technology on
stage is palpable, visceral. LeCompte and the Wooster Group place both
the live and the technological on stage but neither for their own sake.
The bits and pieces, the fragments and frames on the Wooster Group
stage do not stand as isolated moments of the whole – we, the viewers,
set in the position of the microscopist, watch the feedback from live to
screen, from speaker to spoken, from the world of the stage to the world
of today. I began by hoping to develop the idea of a feedback loop –
Morse describes one way in which this can take place: "Once the simultaneity of liveness becomes instant feedback between images and the
world, an inversion takes place in what was once called representation:
neither image nor the world is 'first,' and each is likely to shape the
other." (21) The Wooster Group achieves just such an exchange.

PART III

SPIN-OFF

Double Take

Elevator Repair Service's
Highway to Tomorrow and Euripides' *Bacchae*

Julie BLEHA & Ehren FORDYCE

Columbia University & Stanford University

Elevator Repair Service and Performance Theatre (Bleha)

In May 2002, Mark Russell, former artistic director of New York City's acclaimed performance venue P.S. 122, surveyed in the *Village Voice* the growth and maturation of a generation of artists making theatre that "[moves] under the radar of our American culture," theatre that is "influenced by hip-hop, burlesque, dance, and the experiments of longtime renegades like the Wooster Group, Mabou Mines and Richard Foreman." He termed the work by artists such as Richard Maxwell and Elevator Repair Service "performance theatre" because in the spirit of those "longtime renegades," it "[focuses] on the joy and power of presence, the act of performing and witnessing the act."

Elevator Repair Service (henceforth ERS), like the Wooster Group, claims "hi-fi sound" as a production hallmark, but the flip side of that is ERS's dedication to "low-tech design" (a marked contrast to the Wooster Group's technically elaborate stage constructions). However, what again links both companies is their focus on presence – which necessarily relies on intimacy with an audience. By shining the spotlight on "the ambiguity that exists between the actor and the character and the setting and the theater," ERS explores the tension between "the real and the pretend" (ERS Artists' Statement). Much like the Wooster Group in their Performing Garage, ERS works with the exigencies of the rehearsal and performance space, and will design a show predicated on the physical reality of their workspace. There is no call to imagine anything outside "the girdle of these walls," as we hear in *Henry V*; in an ERS play, what you see is what you get, and what you see is in and of itself noteworthy. ERS falls under Russell's rubric because they "reduce the theatrical experience to the basics," and through their "fascination with the presence of the performer and the act of acting," acknowledge artifice – the basis of their work and the key to their success.

By now, ERS has become a stalwart of New York's experimental theatre scene. Like the Wooster Group, ERS is a collective of artists who make devised theatre, developing their work over lengthy periods of time (even continuing to shape the material throughout the course of a run). Also like the Wooster Group, the membership of the collective has changed over time (causing cast changes within a run), yet the company continues to project a strong aesthetic profile through its artistic directorship. Since ERS's founding in 1991, executive director John Collins has helmed each project, with company member Steve Bodow joining him as co-director in 1997. Collins, a sound designer as well as a director, has worked with Foreman and the Wooster Group. Sound cues function as lines in the script or gestures in the choreography, and the sound operators work in total parity with the actors. As with a Wooster Group show, sound design is built into the very fabric of an ERS show – there are no cue sheets. It is not difficult to detect the influence of this earlier generation of artists in ERS's work: in a review of their 1996 show *Shut Up I Tell You (I Said Shut Up I Tell You)*, *Artforum*'s Steven Drukman hailed the commingling of "the mind-bending perception play of [Foreman] with the hi-tech [sound] hijinks of the [Wooster Group]."

Since its debut with *Mr. Antipyrene, Fire Extinguisher*, ERS has produced eight shows, and at the time of writing were working on their tenth, *Room Tone*. Earlier productions focused on topics as far-ranging as Salvador Dalí's mythical lost screenplay for the Marx Brothers (who have been a constant source of inspiration for Elizabeth LeCompte), an infamous bar (McGurk's Suicide Hall) in late nineteenth century New York, to the peculiar life and mindset of Andy Kaufman. These shows theatricalized abstract ideas through found objects (i.e. carpet remnants with tape markings) and found texts (i.e. physics lectures). In 1996, ERS for the first time embraced a text written specifically for the theatre, using Tennessee Williams's *Summer and Smoke* as the basis for *Cab Legs*. They "translated" Williams's play into a loosely contemporary text by paraphrasing his words (leaving room for moments of improvised dialogue), around which they performed dances inspired by Bollywood musicals and Betty Boop cartoons (which also feature in the Wooster Group's *House/Lights*). In their next show, *Total Fictional Lie*, ERS returned to found text by mining a number of documentaries on vaudeville, serial killer Aileen Wuornos, Paul Anka, turkey hunters, and traveling Bible salesmen. *Total Fictional Lie* is concerned with how people present themselves in seemingly non-fictive moments; ideas of presence and presentation are turned inside out (and literally upside down) in this show. Prefiguring their transformation of the *Bacchae*, the company plumbed the differences in varying versions of truth: In a documentary, can we believe the omniscient narrator? Can we believe seemingly objective witnesses? Or are they, as much as anyone, subject to a misrecognition of their own subjectivity and impulses? Questions like these highlighted the relative conjunction and disparity between performers and the personae they present to their audience. *Total Fictional Lie* caromed back and forth from dance to appropriated documentary dialogue, eschewing text-driven narrative logic and relying primarily on the show's singular choreography for structural cohesion.

Perhaps in reaction to the lack of conventional theatrical components in *Total Fictional Lie*, namely a narrative structure built on plot and character, ERS's next project, which would become known as *Highway to Tomorrow*, showed a renewed interest in tackling dense text. In fact, ERS increased the stakes of the challenge, selecting F. Scott Fitzgerald's novel *The Great Gatsby* as their source text. Both Bodow and Collins felt that the best way for the company to engage with text was to attack an abundance of words, hence the choice of a novel. (In 2004, ERS started work on their next multi-year project, a revisiting of Fitzgerald's work; they called it, simply, *Gatsby*.)

This first version of *HTT* (*HTT1*) was performed in an August 1999 workshop. Actors sat at a table and manipulated a motley assortment of hand-made puppets (a shoe and a mallet both with sunglasses taped to them, a thermos with a pair of self-adhesive googly eyeballs) while they read aloud from segments of the novel. When *HTT* was next mounted in November 1999 (*HTT2*), the company had switched its source text to Fitzgerald's *The Last Tycoon*. Two of the five actors from *HTT1* were replaced; likewise, only some of the puppets from *HTT1* remained in use, most notably the thermos.

Rehearsals for *HTT3* resumed in the spring of 2000 with the intention of revising and expanding the piece. Steve Bodow suggested yet another shift in text, to Euripides' *Bacchae*, and the company agreed that it was a challenging idea for them to tackle a Greek play. Their encounter with the novels had shown that the most fecund texts were those replete with material resistant to dramatization. Greek drama, wherein large-scale action is often heard about but neither physicalized nor seen, met the working parameters established in *HTT1* and *HTT2*. Moreover, the *Bacchae*'s inherent examination of theatricality itself was in perfect consonance with one of ERS's long-standing concerns, the presence of the performer. The play offers, in the character who plays Dionysus to the audience, but who "acts" the "role" of the stranger from Lydia to the other characters, a deliberate confusion between actor and character. This work continued in the fall of 2000.

Double Take (Fordyce)

In its final guise *Highway to Tomorrow* is a representation based on the *Bacchae*, but it does not try to be an exact reproduction of Euripides' play. ERS recognizes the necessary disparity between source and copy, and rather than try to diminish that difference, the company expands upon the possibilities offered by such doubling. *HTT* is a "double take" on Euripides' *Bacchae* in both a metaphorical and literal sense. Metaphorically, *HTT* uncannily doubles the *Bacchae* by offering a seemingly familiar classical text at some points, a strangely contemporary adaptation at others. Literally, ERS often stages *HTT* in such a way as to tell and then retell Euripides' *Bacchae* in two versions of the same story from slightly different perspectives. Moreover, when these narrative doublings occur, characters often perform the literal gesture of a comic "double-take," looking at another character or the audience twice, playing up the humorous failure or shock of not being able to see a thing clearly the first time round.

HTT had two directors, John Collins and Steve Bodow, and this double direction, along with the basic multiplicity of perspectives offered by working with a company, may be one basis for the interesting tensions in interpretation created in *HTT*. On the one hand, Collins has professed some skepticism about language's ability to be transparent. His early work with ERS was often distinguished by finely executed physical comedy that played with the border between the intelligible and the absurd. On the other hand, Bodow has expressed more of an interest in texts, yet, as mentioned, it was Bodow who suggested Euripides' drama in part because the text resists easy theatricalization.

In regard to the *Bacchae*, this dual attitude of resisting and engaging with text yields an interpretation in *HTT* that often seems most authentic to Euripides when it is most skeptical about the production's ability to cut through the centuries and see its classical, tragic source in a transparent way. Indeed, one of the most rewarding aspects of *HTT* is its humor, a skeptical humor that forthrightly acknowledges the strangeness of Euripides' ancient world, but that also curiously succeeds in revealing a strangeness already imminent in the *Bacchae*'s relationship to the tragic genre. Is the *Bacchae* after all, ERS seems to ask in *HTT*, a tragedy? Or is it more like what T.S. Eliot called "savage farce"? Or is the play a comedy of mistaken identity where the audience laughs at Pentheus because he confuses the god with a charlatan? Additionally, if Dionysus is the god of both tragedy and comedy, then how does that affect our reading of this self-referential Greek tragedy about Dionysus? Is this tragedy also, at times, a travesty of tragedy?

Elevator Repair Service and Devised Theater (Bleha)

Of the many thematic and performative through-lines in ERS's aesthetic that have developed over the past decade, an emphasis has emerged on the company members' shared sense of humor and on a literal conception of "play" – in their view, both fundamentals of theatre. Bradley Glenn, a veteran of many ERS shows, has joked about the company's "love-hate" relationship with theatre.

> In rehearsal we have always joked about something Richard Foreman said, to the effect that "A jar rolling across the stage [...] could qualify as theater." Although we joke about that, since the beginning the group has always asked time again "What is Theater?" and I think the most successful shows offer several options and answers.[1]

In conversation with LeCompte, Foreman once said that what made theatre interesting for him was "only the distractions [...] only the suggestion that life goes off in a million different directions at all moments [...] provide[s...] an interesting subject for art" (139). Proving themselves true disciples of Foreman's and LeCompte's theatre, ERS thrives on distractions as it seeks to answer its own question: What is theatre?

Once rehearsals for a new show commence, all available company members and occasional guest artists assemble, and from this conjunction of minds and bodies are planted the seeds of a play. Projects proceed from a kind of *tabula rasa*, as if the artists have to review and relearn how to build a show. Taking seriously mundane questions – "What do you want to see?" "What takes up an hour?" – someone starts "playing" with an object, a text or a sound source. Here is where the fun begins, as the ludic tone that pervades every ERS piece is teased to the fore during the rehearsal process. Because of this commitment to the possibility of chance and change, it is difficult to predict from an ERS play's inception what it might be "about" in more than a general sense or indeed how it might ultimately look and sound.

ERS answers its fundamental question – "What is theater?" – by privileging experience over narrative. Perhaps this is why they emphasize humor; laughter is a physical response and experience, an embodied experience. Laughter is an immediate, palpable response that reminds us

---

[1] Interestingly, Glenn then says that he thinks *Language Instruction* (1994 & 1999) was not wholly successful "because of the lack of a cohesive story line that [the] audience could hang their sensibility hat on while indulging the group in its pursuit of that question 'What is theater?'" To a lesser degree, the same could be said for *Total Fictional Lie*; while it was a crowd-pleaser, one could appreciate the individual vignettes and dances more readily than any inherent dramaturgical logic which tied the scenes together.

of our own corporeality even as it reflects the theatre's corporeality. Such performance work elicits from its audience a reaction in the present tense: an instinctual response, a response unmediated by familiarity and expectation. Although not explicitly cited by ERS as an influence, Brecht's dictum that theatre should "be turned from a home of illusion to a home of experience" certainly anticipates their theatrical philosophy.

Thermos or *Thyrsis*? (Fordyce)

"A jar rolling across the stage […] could qualify as theater." Foreman's image suggests how simple, even poor the means of theatre can be. It also implies how the notion of an "actor" need not always be human. To test this credo, ERS used a jar as a central character in *McGurk: A Cautionary Tale*. In a further example of thrifty, downtown theatricalism, the opening scene of *HTT4* presents a similarly simple, yet elegant meditation on the nature of theatre, in this case through the figure of an animated thermos. The scene serves as a useful emblem for ERS's serio-ludic practices generally and for its reinterpretation of the *Bacchae* specifically.

When the lights rise at the beginning of *HTT*, they reveal a bare, monochrome brown, chest-high flat in the upstage right corner of the stage. From behind this flat a silver thermos floats up, on which two large googly eyes are attached. Although it may not be apparent to the entire audience, the thermos is an intentional mistranslation, a visual and aural pun based on one of the *Bacchae*'s major textual symbols. It also echoes the Wooster Group's doubling of a microphone stand as sceptre and viper in *House/Lights* (1998), a magic feat in which John Collins participated (Callens, 2001: 395). In place of the ritual appearance of a *thyrsis*, the emblematic fennel-stalk staff of Dionysus and his Bacchantes, ERS presents a *thermos*. The phallic *thyrsis* entwined with fertile vines is replaced by a phallic *thermos*, later shown to be full of an intoxicating potion. While the audience may not register the linguistic game at work, the thermos's anthropomorphic, googly eyes hint at its divinatory associations with the figure of Dionysus: thermos as ecstatic seer. More pronouncedly, the thermos begins to reveal its Dionysian, as well as theatricalist, agenda when from behind the flat it draws up and reads from a book entitled *Hypnotism for Everybody*.

Foreshadowing the moment when Dionysus hypnotizes Pentheus into cross-dressing, a moment represented in *HTT* by his donning a pair of googly eyes, the thermos reads from its book and then tries to hypnotize the audience. However, the audience laughs at the thermos. This is a skeptical, savvy, resistant audience of interpreters, not yet willing to lose their "I"s as Pentheus ultimately will. The thermos goes back to reading its book and then redoubles its efforts at hypnosis by shaking its eyes and straining out towards the house. This time, after several seconds of intense staring, the thermos falls over in a daze. Apparently the thermos has succumbed to its own auto-suggestion and hypnotized itself. The audience laughs again; the thermos awakes and exits in seeming embarrassment; the show goes on.

ERS seems to be telling the audience to be skeptical of its own performance's ability to hypnotize them. At the same time, the audience's very laughter at the thermos suggests a vestigial form of theatrical seduction and suspension of disbelief. Although the audience may laugh at the anthropomorphism of the thermos and the hubris of its attempts to hypnotize them, they *get the joke*. The audience may be wryly skeptical of a stage world in which a thermos stands in for the god Dionysus, but underlying their skepticism is a basic faith in the doubling stage of representation itself, where signifiers come to stand in for signifieds and other signifiers. The thermos may fail to hypnotize the audience, but it succeeds in *signifying* its failure.

The point may seem slightly sophistic, but it is an important one. Skepticism about particular representations still relies on a faith in the feasibility of representation in general, so that the efficacy of the splittings and substitutions accomplished by representation requires a provisional acceptance of the holism of representation as a system. At the same time, a sense of identity within representation requires a certain suspension of disbelief in the splittings and substitutions of representation. Without identification across the splits of representation, the self would become inert. Excessive and ecstatic over-identification with an endless, substituting stream of representations becomes hysteria.

In his essay on "The Mirror Stage," Lacan suggests that the child's illusory recognition of its wholeness, its *Gestalt*, in the differently-sized and reversed image of the mirror is basic to the formation of the phantasmatic, symbolic unity of the ego. Lacan rests the development of the ego on a premise of "*méconnaissance*," on the premise that the symbolic recognition of truths is ineluctably predicated on misrecognizing one's self as whole in the substituted and split-off form of one's mirror image. Lacan's model is pertinent to understanding the *Bacchae* and particularly the character of Pentheus since we can understand Pentheus' hubristic fall as emerging, to some degree, from his initial, excessive faith in and misrecognition of his ego's wholeness. He believes himself master of Thebes, and more importantly master of himself. Faced with Dionysus whose provenance is the world split and substituted – the god of wine, theatre, madness, ecstasy, and even of death, in some of his figurations – Pentheus can only distance himself from Semele's son. He cannot recognize his cousin as anything but alien to himself.

Unlike Pentheus, who cannot recognize his own capacity for mis-recognition, ERS's interpretative strategy self-consciously plays with misrecognition. The substitution of a thermos for a *thyrsis* is a "mis-translation" with intent. *HTT4*'s opening scene with the thermos comically sends up for the audience the way in which both religious and theatrical belief are kinds of signifying hypnosis. Moreover, the scene establishes one of the basic interpretive techniques – comic and intentional misrecognition – underlying ERS's approach to Euripides throughout *Highway to Tomorrow*.

Elevator Repair Service's Past *Tomorrows* (Bleha)

One of the first things the company did was to rename the people and places of Euripides' play to something contemporary and geographically recognizable. In doing so, they welcomed an absurd dissonance between matter and nomenclature. Thebes became St. Louis, the "stream of Dirce/ and the waters of Ismenus" (ll.5-6) became Susquehanna. Teiresias morphed into Teri the Seer, Cadmus into Carl, Pentheus became Paul (the name of the actor), and his mother, Agave (played by Rinne Groff), was re-named Holly. Interestingly, Dionysus, the focal point of the play, remained Dionysus. During the runs of *HTT3* and *HTT4*, the audience found this playful "misnaming" quite humorous, but their laughter masked how the new nomenclature underscores the textual distinction between the god and the other characters, while highlighting a consonance between the actor Paul and the character Paul. Just as the *Bacchae* subverts and simultaneously reinforces the paradoxical theatrical conventions of disjunction and communion, so do ERS's tactics in *Highway to Tomorrow*.

Some of the most interesting examples of the slippage in identification and meaning come from the group's effort to work the pre-*Bacchae* elements into the new framework (thereby following an incremental method recognizable from the Wooster Group). In *HTT2*, the company had transcribed actions from a scene in the film version of *The Last Tycoon* (1976, dir. Elia Kazan) where Tony Curtis's character is trying to explain his impotence to Robert de Niro. Movements culled from this scene congealed into the dance named, appropriately, "Impotence." Selected gestures of de Niro and Curtis were copied by the group in real time as best they could. The video monitor was in a corner of the room, forcing the performers to refer to it while executing the moves and circulating in the space according to Collins and Bodow's direction. As they did this, Collins videotaped them. The performers' being caught between monitor and camera again recalls the Wooster Group practice. "Impotence" opened *HTT3* but moves taken from taped earlier rehearsals had been copied, expanded, and subsequently "translated" by the company into a new dance sequence. Like images from an infinite mirror, second- and third-generation moves filtered through the performer's body exponentially expanded the roster of gestures.

A repeated action in this version of "Impotence" was to look at the position where the video monitor had been in the room for *HTT2*; onstage, this translated to the down right corner. This move became a foundational step in the dance, with the performers all trying to retain a sense of fidelity to the experience of their (or their earlier counterpart's) looking to the monitor for guidance. Of course, the audience had no knowledge of the monitor's ever existing, but in performance, the dance's potency stemmed from a sense of latent anxiety as the actors craned their necks towards downstage right. The dance thus became a celebration of high-energy that was also fraught with tension, a perfect opening gambit for the *Bacchae*. As in the Wooster Group's work, ERS's strategic uses of video as a layering device deepened the dramatic resonance.

Also in the manner of the Wooster Group, the play had not been cast, at least not in the traditional sense, at the time work began on "Impotence" in *HTT3*'s rehearsals. Actors had merely been trading reading assignments. Character relationships were grounded only in the contingencies of a particular rehearsal. Once the show was cast, the choreography reflected these relationships. Paul/Pentheus and Randall Curtis Rand/Dionysus faced off at one point in the dance, as Paul and Dionysus did later in the play. Even the title "Impotence" prefigured the dissipation of Paul's power throughout the course of the play, his failure to thwart Dionysus, his inability to effectively rule his city, and ultimately his disgrace as a fallen son, murdered by a mad mother.

A similar example of what the company terms "dance translation" can be found in the choreography for "Butt Dance." Also created without an idea of where and how it would fit into the play, it was inspired by a 1960s text brought in by Bodow, which showed exercises prescribed for facial muscles. Company members then transferred the facial moves south to the *gluteus maximus* (and its surrounding muscles), basing the dance on the spontaneous flexing of these muscles in isolation from the rest of the body. Notwithstanding its name, the dance also retained (exaggerated) versions of the source book's facial poses. Used to set the tone for the maenads' mountainside activities, it was termed an "ecstatic ritual" in the scene breakdown of *HTT4*'s program.

Comic Misrecognition and Substitution (Fordyce)

In *HTT4*, the "Butt Dance" follows Dionysus' prologue to the audience in which he summarizes his life-story and foreshadows his coming maneuvers in Thebes. As Dionysus, Rand enters wearing a tan, vaguely country-and-western-style shirt, a pair of metallic silver-blue disco pants, and shit-kicker leather boots. He is the image of a rurally-styled urban dancer who is ready for a fight. He walks to a small table mid-stage left, sits, and proceeds, with a childlike smile on his face, to scatter a pile of books neatly stacked on the table. Then he introduces himself into an amplified microphone on the table as "Dionysus, son of Zeus."

Like the opening scene with the thermos, the physical action of scattering the books is an elegant and deceptively simple piece of action. It suggests Dionysus' unruly, disorganizing character. At the same time, the action neatly points to the metalevel of interpretative strategy that ERS is pursuing in relationship to the *Bacchae*. Like Dionysus, ERS eschews a neatly ordered image of literary history. Indeed such an image would seem to be merely a misrecognition of a more basic complexity. Instead, through selective uses of disorder and misrecognition (similar to the Wooster Group's deconstructions), ERS self-consciously embraces the potential for comedy in acts of (mis)representation.

While critics have frequently debated the merits of seeing comic elements in the *Bacchae* (Seidensticker), *HTT* is the rare performance that embraces the generic fluidity of Euripides' play and does so convincingly. One of the more widely acknowledged comic episodes in the *Bacchae* occurs between Teiresias and Cadmus, where the two old men debate with Pentheus the use-value of pledging their faith to the new god Dionysus. ERS retains the humor of sophistic argumentation contained in the episode, but they subtly shift its source in several ways. First, the text of Cadmus' character is basically cut, although his presence is represented in other ways, as will become clear later. Second, Teiresias' long rationalizing argument in favor of respecting Dionysus is replaced by the story of how Teiresias was turned into a woman, then back into a man. And third, perhaps most importantly, the scene is no longer played to Pentheus, but to the audience. Although ERS may appear to be playing fast and loose with their literary history here, the company's substitution of Teiresias' story of gender change neatly fits the thematic patterning of Euripides' original, since the story succeeds in foreshadowing Pentheus' own ultimate gender travesty. Even better, the way in which ERS performs the scene develops a pattern of character-audience relationship which is vital to their reinterpretation of the *Bacchae*.

As Teri the Seer (Teiresias), Susie Sokol delivers her monologue directly to the audience, frequently pausing with just the right sense of comic delay so that the audience can savor the outrageousness of her story of not one, but two magical sex changes. S/he seems to understand how skeptical the audience is about the truth of her story, yet earnestly perseveres in trying to communicate the mythic truth of the gender play.

In a sense, Teri is setting up the audience in the role of Pentheus, the cult's uninitiated who requires patient explanation and persuasion. So while Dionysus' disposition towards disturbance and play sometimes seems to align with that of ERS (albeit not exclusively), on other occasions *HTT* appears to imply how the audience's point of view may align with Pentheus'. The audience is forewarned: do not be too skeptical about Teri's stories of sex and gender fluidity; do not, like Pentheus, misrecognize ego or gender as stable and whole.

Tragedy, Comedy, and Catharsis (Bleha)

The *Bacchae* negotiates several boundaries: the divide between male and female, divine and human, sacred and profane, character and actor, insider and outsider, and the generic modes of comedy and tragedy. Highlighting the comedy, perhaps in a way that is long overdue, *Highway to Tomorrow* is a funny, raucous, silly yet serious, energetic play about Dionysus – and the scheming for and wreaking of revenge on his inattentive family and native city. Yet, it is through the *Bacchae*'s comedy, rather than despite it, that *HTT* achieves tragedy. The story's basic elements – the disastrous competition between god and mortal, the breakdown of a family, the loss of a child – are very much part of the production. The tragic mood caused by the unclean conclusion of these crises is palpable for the audience. The laughter is uneasy: finding humor in the absurd, we also find ourselves laughing at calamities – destruction, exile and death wrought by an almighty temper.

Helene Foley has noted that Euripides transposed many Old Comedy formulae to the *Bacchae*, to stunning effect. Rarely in Greek tragedy "does the meaning of a scene depend primarily on role-playing and on the costume changes that a character makes onstage [but the] reverse is true for Old Comedy." Here, "the change of costume" works toward "rejuvenation or restoration to heroic status," goals which are "arguably [...] essentially more characteristic of comedy than of tragedy." Thus, in the *Bacchae*, "costume change serves as a sign of conversion to Dionysiac worship, and what are largely comic techniques [...] are used for the first time in a play that has a disastrous outcome." This "unsettles the audience": when the two old men, the ex-king Cadmus and the seer Teiresias, "gracelessly but strategically accept the worship of the god by donning his fawnskin and *thursos* [*sic*] and adopt a hobbling dance," the audience laughs at this moment, one which in fact anticipates the impending tragedy (225). Foley cites Pentheus' "ludicrous fussing" (226) with his costume as another instance of Euripides' "striking merging of comic and tragic stage business" (225), a concept effectively rendered in *HTT4* as Paul wheels himself around on a stool with a puffy pink prom dress awkwardly draped over his lanky frame.

Perhaps most shocking, both to an Athenian audience and to us if we consider its import, is our awareness of Dionysus' comic mask. According to one of Pentheus' men, Dionysus "stood there smiling" (l. 439) and the Chorus can invoke the god with "O Bacchus, come! Come with your smile!" (l. 1018) The implications are moving: essentially, Dionysus is directing a scenario, a play if you will, that is simultaneously a comedy for him and a tragedy for Pentheus, whose very name means "man of sorrow." Pentheus is the hapless, and ultimately useless, *pharmakos*, or scapegoat. There is no comforting promise of knowledge-through-redemption allowed the tragic hero, much less the players, or even the audience, at the end.

The *Bacchae* paves a rough road to catharsis, if there is one to be found at all. In fact, there is no "recovery of tragic vision," as Foley terms it (234) – an ambiguous ending which may have made the play all the more attractive to ERS. Like the Wooster Group in *Nayatt School*, its take on T.S. Eliot's *The Cocktail Party*, ERS is not concerned with providing a pure catharsis in its theatrical output. Rather, their work demands of each audience member its own unique act of interpretation, its own working-out of the problem.

Dionysus' Double Story/Double Laugh (Fordyce)

Throughout *HTT*, Dionysus' monologues to the audience, like that of Teri, subtly suggest that he is interpellating them in the position of the uninitiated. Moreover, Dionysus frequently tells a story not once, but twice, in the process calling into question the tragic import of his monologue even as he seeks to reinforce it. Finally, Dionysus' narrative doublings often conclude with a piece of comic business, a physical double-take.

After Dionysus' prologue and the "Butt Dance," Pentheus/Paul gives a speech to the audience that serves as his own competing prologue, a speech that alerts the audience to his fears about the "girl-man" Dionysus and about the "woman-on-woman action" he suspects is transpiring in the hills outside St. Louis. Following Paul's speech, Dionysus resumes material from Euripides' original prologue with the story of his mother's impregnation by Zeus. He dwells on how Holly (Agave), repudiated her sister Semele's story of a divine coupling. Then he concludes with the legend of St. Louis's founding when King Carl (Cadmus) planted his dragon-seed men.

At first, Dionysus tells these stories in a formal, narrative manner, sticking closely to Euripides' original text, whereupon he encounters a series of laughs from the audience at the apparent ridiculousness of such mythic stories. At that point, Dionysus leans forward and repeats the story of Susan/Semele's impregnation by Zeus, but now in an informal, conversational tone, using everyday, rather than heightened word choice. ("See, in other words, once Zeus hooked up with my mother Susan...") Here the comedy of the physical double-take turns into a linguistic double-take, which accentuates the fact that the Greek of Athenian tragedy was never in the first place everyday Athenian speech. Euripides' language demanded that its original audience interpret and translate. More importantly this double translation into two speech registers recognizes, rather than avoids, the basic difficulty of translation posed by performing the *Bacchae* today. And it does so by playing on the way translations *must* misrecognize their originals in order to speak to new audiences with different cultural, historical, and linguistic frames of reference. Finally, Dionysus performs this double translation with the utter seriousness upon which the humor of ERS's presentation depends. When the second retelling also provokes laughter and fails to arouse the audience's respect and awe for Dionysus, the character glances once, then twice over the audience, as though to remind them that the joke may ultimately be on them as much as on the unbelieving Pentheus/Paul.

This serio-comic double-take by Dionysus receives its most elaborate performance in his last speech before he takes Paul up the mountain to meet his fate. In this speech, Dionysus anticipates Paul's coming sacrifice, as well as the exiles and transformations in store for Holly and Carl. Unlike in Euripides' drama, however, in *HTT* Dionysus keeps spinning his tale, suggesting that Thebes' travails will not end once his rites have been instituted. He recounts how one of Carl's dragon-teeth men, Laius, will come to rule and have "a son named Oedipus who..." In one of those virtuoso pauses difficult to convey on the page, Rand here holds back until he receives a laugh of recognition from the audience. Perhaps its reaction derives from the recognition of the overdetermined quality of suffering in Thebes, its banality as it strikes not only Cadmus' family, but also Laius'. Perhaps the audience is laughing at the stubbornness of storytellers in promulgating such tales of grotesque misery. In any case, Dionysus waits out this first laugh by the audience, scans the audience left to right, very slowly, and then he himself laughs.

In an embodiment of the cunning infelicity of the gods, which Nietzsche saw as prompting a cheerfully haughty pessimism in sixth and early fifth-century Greeks and which he suspected was lacking in the so-called Socratic rationalist Euripides, Dionysus seems to laugh at the audience's laughter, neither joyfully nor wryly nor caustically, but with a laugh that is long, belly-deep, and uncannily silent. This Dionysus seems deeply comfortable with whatever drives him to assert the "I" of being Dionysus. He is not the vaguely sinister or vaguely feminine or vaguely atavistic mystery which so many productions of the *Bacchae* resort to; nor is he the rationalizing, sophistically rational, Apollonian degeneration of Dionysus that Nietzsche projects onto the poet Euripides. Instead, Rand and ERS present a Dionysus as *raisonneur*, yet one who also appears skeptical about reason; a very New York Dionysus who is also, perhaps, not totally alien to the skeptical culture of urban Athens.

Objets Trouvés, or Teri Meets Carl (Bleha)

Aside from the replacement of the thermos for the *thyrsis*, another substitution took place in *Highway to Tomorrow*'s rendition of the *Bacchae*. Like the Wooster Group, ERS allows aspects of the rehearsal space to resonate in the performance space. This means that even its limitations can serve as fodder for invention. HERE, the downtown arts center where all versions of *HTT* were presented, has a big pole upstage center of the playing area. One early casting decision in *HTT3* (that remained for *HTT4*) was to cut the character of Cadmus – or at least, to "deanimate" him. Instead, some of his lines were given to other charac-ters, and more interestingly, a static persona, christened Carl, was born out of the pole in HERE's space. During the performance, two plastic googly eyeballs were affixed to it by James Hannaham, and the pole, like the thermos, was thus quickened into theatrical life. Bodow and Collins struggled with staging the scene in which Cadmus and Teiresias dress up to join the maenads, given the obvious problem that a pole cannot converse, let alone dress itself. In the show's bittersweet comedic highlight, Susie Sokol (playing eccentric) as Teri the Seer comes to meet Carl. She calls out Carl's name from offstage, then enters, calling his name again. She looks around, finds him, walks up to him, and greets him. Expecting an answer, she is treated to silence. Sokol then goes through a routine where she taps Carl, pokes him, waits for long moments, and even pulls out her script to show him where they are in the play, hoping he will be prompted to say "his" lines. She finally surrenders, commencing her monologue to the audience described above. In this moment, the actress is as prominent as the character, and in fact it is hard to tell who is in possession of the limelight. Sokol was present as both herself and as a character, and it was difficult to say who was standing in for whom. When the line between performer and char-acter elides, the presence of the performer (and the tension between performer and character) must be acknowledged.

Tragic Finale (Fordyce)

While ERS persuasively developed the comic elements of the *Bacchae* in *HTT*, they needed to return their presentation and their audience to a tragic frame of mind at the production's conclusion. To avoid falling into a reductive parody of the play, they needed to represent as tragic the doubled *anagnoreses* in which Holly (Agave) recognizes first that her son is dead and second that she was his murderer. As usual, the company's staging and acting of this scene was thrifty, elegant, and sure-footed. Since the audience had been so thoroughly convinced of the comic potential of the *Bacchae*, however, it is open to question whether they entirely joined the company in this sharp turn at the end of *HTT*.

Before Holly's customary final entrance with the head of her son, ERS has her make a number of fleeting entrances and exits in which she pursues and finally drinks from the thermos/*thyrsis*. In one of the show's most literal representations of Dionysus' ecstatic powers, the scene evokes the money shots of porno films as Holly shakes and strokes the thermos until it explodes on her, whereupon she laps up the dregs of its liquor. Whether the scene is to all audiences' tastes seems less important than the question of whether it is useful to show Holly before her usual final – and only – entrance. (A similar distinction between taste and dramaturgical use has been made with regard to the hard core porn in *Route 1 & 9 (The Last Act)*, through which the Wooster Group foregrounded Wilder's repression of sexuality in *Our Town*.) While it can be argued that having Holly enter previously detracts from the power of her final entrance, making her visible throughout *HTT* usefully deflates the hyperbolic fantasies that Paul/Pentheus has about the Bacchic rites. In contrast to his commingled desire and fear about "woman-on-woman" action going on in the hills above St. Louis, the audience sees Holly's actions. Her relationship with the thermos, whether it represents getting drunk, or having sex, or both, may be ecstatic, but it is visibly ecstatic for all to see, thereby removing some of the sense of danger attached to representations which remain bottled away in the imagination. As a result, ERS avoids the problem of treating what Dionysus represents as merely exotic or mysterious. They retain a sense of his possible threat, but as a threat within this world, not outside it.

In the presentation of the *anagnoreses* surrounding Paul's death, ERS continued to pursue this strategy of making things visible that would customarily be unwritten or offstage in Euripides. Most obviously, the murder of Paul occurs onstage. As Holly, Rinne Groff wears a pair of googly eyes, like those of the thermos, to show that she is outside herself, that she has succumbed to the ecstatic embrace of Dionysus. She takes a red picnic cooler and twists it around her son's head. Once it has twisted enough to hide Paul's face, we hear the sound effect of a painful cracking, and we infer that the warrior maenad has snapped the neck of her prey. Whereas Greek tragedies assiduously stage violence offstage, ERS moves Pentheus' death onstage, obscured only by a blood-colored cooler.

However, as part of ERS's partly comic, partly serious deflation of Holly, she is treated less as a warrior than as a mad society woman. She has returned from the hills in a rain slicker over her brown velvet evening dress. So while Paul is feminized in a pink prom dress, Holly is not equally masculinized. She does not wield her thermos as a mace, for example; nor does Holly perform her lines in a particularly bellicose manner. The interpretation is convincing given the production's pattern of quasi-mythical Americanizations and modernizations of names, place-names, and costumes. It is, however, one instance where ERS does not play Euripides' gender inversions to the hilt.

After starting to talk Holly down from her high, Teri then persuades her to look at the supposed lion cub in her cooler. Tentatively she sticks her head into the cooler. Although Paul's murder is revealed in *HTT*, the moment of Holly's first *anagnorisis*, the recognition that the captured head belongs to her child, not to an animal, is hidden. Quietly and modestly, the production makes a tragic gesture towards representation's failure in the face of terror. When Holly rises from the cooler again, her intoxication has dissipated, her googly eyes have disappeared and her sight has cleared, but her understanding of the situation remains obscured. When she asks Teri how her son has died, she experiences the second *anagnorisis*, the revelation that she herself has killed her son. At that point, still confused, she asks Teri, "But where is his body?" In a comic deflation that stops shy of cruel irony, Teri points down at the body of Paul and says in shock, "It's right there." The audience laughs.

Throughout the *Bacchae*, Pentheus misrecognizes his identity as cohesive and authoritative, so when the Bacchantes finally tear him apart, there is an awful sense in which they have held up a radically dissolving mirror to him, as though to teach him just how split apart his self has always been. By maintaining the wholeness of Paul's body at the end, ERS forgoes, to some degree, their customary comic splintering of the *Bacchae*. Since that splintering has worked to such comic effect previously, it may be necessary at this point to turn away from that mode in order to move towards the play's tragic denouement of Holly's and Carl's exile from St. Louis. And those final moments of leave-taking, quiet and unforced, do succeed in conveying the unredeeming and utterly unheroic loss that Dionysus has inflicted on Holly, Carl, and the community of St. Louis. Yet it is hard to say what lies behind the audience's final laughs. Perhaps some of the audience still reads the work as comic hyperbole. Perhaps others are laughing at a kind of truth, a laugh at that which is unhappy. Perhaps still others are laughing in a kind of grim and defensive baring of the teeth against an aggressive world. And perhaps some of the laughs turn and double back on themselves in the recognition, at such a uselessly cruel moment, that it is impossible to laugh and impossible to do anything but laugh.

The Builders Association
S/he Do the Police in Different Voices

Johan CALLENS

Vrije Universiteit Brussel

The Builders Association, directed by Marianne Weems, was officially founded in 1993 by a group of like-minded artists including
Weems, Jeff Webster, David Pence, Jennifer Tipton, Coco Mcpherson,
and John Cleater. Several of these had lengthy associations with the
Wooster Group. Weems was its assistant director and dramaturg from
1988-94, apart from performing in *Brace Up!* and assisting Richard
Foreman, who directed LeCompte's company in *Miss Universal Happiness* (1985) and *Symphony of Rats* (1988). Weems also co-directed
Wooster Group member Ron Vawter's solo performance *Roy Cohn/Jack
Smith*, and co-produced the film version with Good Machine, executive
produced by Jonathan Demme. In the meantime she also performed for
The V-Girls (1986-1995) and became board president of the private
foundation, Art Matters. The link with the Wooster Group extends to
other Builders Association members – like Webster, who performed
extensively in LeCompte's stage and video work (1983-94); video
designer Christopher Kondek (1987-95); lighting designer Jennifer
Tipton (who lighted *House/Lights* and *To You, The Birdie!*); and
costume designer Ellen McCartney (*Fish Story* and *The Hairy Ape*) – as
well as to members of the Advisory Committee (Norman Frisch, Peyton
Smith and Kate Valk). These names notwithstanding, the Builders Association's production and performing teams keep changing with each new
project, according to artistic needs, financial resources, and people's
availability. Such flexibility in the assembly of the cast is typical of the
more informal theatre ensembles that emerged in the 1980s, as opposed
to those rooted in the countercultural 1960s.[1] The work of both the

---

[1]   According to Soloski, LeCompte has always encouraged the creative work of "staff"
       members (designers, technicians, administrators, etc.), listing John Collins (Elevator
       Repair Service), Jim Findlay (Collapsable Giraffe), Richard Kimmel (Cannon
       Company) and Marianne Weems (the Builders Association) as cases in point. This
       support was formalized in July 1999 by the first three-week-long Emerging Artist

Builders Association and the Wooster Group is bound by a recognizable intermedial vocabulary, in addition to a degree of professionalism unknown to earlier alternative companies and a refusal to distinguish between high art and popular culture or to leave the classics to mainstream theatre (Shewey: 280-1).

The purported affinity between the aesthetics of the Builders Association and those of the Wooster Group may, however, obfuscate rather than elucidate their specificity. At times it indeed becomes symptomatic of the levelling imprecision of certain critics' lingering impatience when dealing with intermedial theatre, reduced as it is to any production featuring video monitors. In a supportive letter to Marianne Weems, dated 14 October 1994, Susan Sontag stressed the originality of the Builders Association's second show, *Master Builder*, and of the way in which it departed from the Wooster Group's scenic language. "You have used," she said, "this scenic language to take it one step further – toward a greater intimacy of effect." No matter how truthful and well-meant, the letter, which is included in press files, functions both as a tribute to the influence of Elizabeth LeCompte on the contemporary avant-garde scene and as a way of removing, right away, the prickly issue of indebtedness for artists staking out their own terrain. Successfully so, as I hope to demonstrate in the following discussion.

Actually, the specificity of the Builders Association's approach is already encapsulated in its name, which becomes self-evident in the light of the company's self-expressed intention (on their website) to set up "performances exploring the languages of theater, media, and architecture," by "re-animat[ing] classic theatrical texts," often "outside of conventional theatrical sites." The interest in architecture gets reflected not just in site-specific productions, but also in their sources of inspiration and collaborators. Among the former rank the American artist Gordon Matta-Clark, with his "rough cuts" or interventions on buildings scheduled for demolition[2] (e.g. in *The Master Builder*), among

---

Series, which grew out of the annual Visiting Artist Series, begun as early as 1978, with the assistance of outside curators. The new series "grants three individuals or groups a week of rehearsal time[, facilities] in the Performing Garage and a weekend of performances."

[2] The unsuccessful attempt to save *Office Baroque* (1977-1980), Matta-Clark's last European site project in Antwerp, Belgium, by Flor Bex, then director of the International Cultural Center (ICC), led to the founding of the city's museum of contemporary arts (MUHKA), two years after Matta-Clark's death on 27 August 1978. For a discussion of the project and its intertwining of real estate and art, see Lee 220-233. The set of *Visitors Only* (2003), which Anna Viebrock made for Meg Stuart's Brussels-based dance company, Damaged Goods, was a pseudo-"rough cut," an eerily lit-up, squatted building, ghost house on memory lane, or subconscious realm "beyond the looking glass," with some of the effects provided, courtesy of Chris Kondek, the Wooster Group's video designer.

the latter John Cleater (e.g. in *Imperial Motel* (*Faust)*) and the architectural team Diller + Scofidio (in *Jet Lag*). Despite Weems's claims of indepen-dence, however, Matta-Clark (1943-78) is crucial, too, for the Wooster Group, whose activities began three years prior to his premature death. LeCompte's subversions of domestic realism call for a gutting, splitting, fracturing, layering, or shifting of the con-ventional box set, interventions similar to Matta-Clark's "rough cuts," besides building on Richard Schechner's environmentalism. Elizabeth Diller and Ricardo Scofidio are both professors of architecture, the first at Princeton University, the second at The Cooper Union. Their joint, interdisciplinary projects, like those with the Builders Association, combine architecture, the visual and the performing arts. Their own *Jump Cuts*, not to be confused with *Jump Cut (Faust)*, consisted of a video marquis for the United Artists Cineplex Theater in San Jose, CA.

Added to the Builders Association's architectural sources of inspira-tion and collaborators should be the choice of the company's first two productions, Ibsen's *Hedda Gabler* (1993, No Theater, Northampton, MA)[3] and *The Master Builder* (1994, Industrial Space, NYC). In the context of a discussion of Faust's techno-offspring it may be worth recalling that the hero of *The Master Builder* (which premiered in 1893) has been interpreted as "Man rebelling against God." Halvard Solness is an arrogant and ambitious architect of churches and houses with spires, fearing as well as "yearning for youth," hubristically venturing every-thing, children born and unborn (symbolized by Mrs. Solness's nine dolls), to the point of self-destruction, that fall from great heights. In short, he is a man cast (or cast down) in the mould of Faust, and Lucifer for that matter (Michael Meyer: 726, 729, 732).[4]

The Builders Assocation's name also bespeaks a witting or unwitting feminist agenda. Susan Harris Smith (103-108) has thoroughly docu-mented how the history of American drama has been shadowed by explicit fears of being feminized. Such fears were harbored by the likes of George Pierce Baker and Brander Matthews. They can be explained (though hardly condoned) by their one-time need to establish the disci-plinary field and the canon as a "masculine" science, in the face of the allegedly feminine sentimentality and moralizing of the late eighteenth

---

[3] No Theater is an initiative of associate Wooster Group member Roy Faudree. For a brief introduction to his work, see my review of *Dupe* (1995).

[4] Meyer sums up the theme of *The Master Builder* in the playwright's own words: "Our whole being is nothing but a fight against the dark forces within ourselves" (660), which the Builders Association rendered as Faust "wrestling with his de-mons." In *The Quintessence of Ibsenism* Shaw already established the lineage bet-ween Ibsen and Goethe, adding that Solness is "really daimonic, with luck, a star, and mystic 'helpers and servers', who find the way through the maze of life for him." (116)

and early nineteenth century novel, in the face, too, it needs to be said, of a British monopoly on art. When it came to writing drama, women, Matthews claimed, could not handle "largeness in topic," nor were they capable of

> strictness in treatment [...] And here we come close to the most obvious ex-
> planation for the dearth of female dramatists in the relative incapacity of
> women to build a plan, to make a single whole compounded of many parts,
> and yet dominated in every detail by but one purpose. (120, qtd. in Smith:
> 105)

Insofar as he agreed with Ibsen that drama is like architecture,[5] Matthews added that it requires a scientific and allegedly male sense of "plan and proportion" and the equally male "faculty of construction," whereas women were said to have gained fame only in the "subordinate art" of "decoration" and the narrowly domestic field (120, 124, qtd. by Smith: 105-6). By co-founding and heading the Builders Association, Marianne Weems, like Liz LeCompte before her, has begged to differ of opinion.

Imperial Lab

The company's capable and innovative perspective was well demonstrated by their idiosyncratic confrontation with the Faust tradition. It was a confrontation taking several years (1995-1998) and resulting in intermittent embodiments in different cities, each one newly enriched by earlier experiences. Their first stab at the tradition occurred in *Faust Lab*, a residency at the Clocktower Gallery, NYC (under the aegis of P.S.1), in October 1995. Its generic title designated your common enough theatrical workshop as well as Faust's traditional laboratory-and-library-in-one. In a set-up with several television monitors a variety of Faust texts were explored and cross-cut with conversations picked up on an illegal scanner, making for Cagean disruptions of the fourth wall.

Faust Lab fed into *Imperial Motel (Faust)*, a co-production with the Zürich Neumarkt Theater. It was developed in New York (at the Broad Street Space, then an abandoned office building on Wall Street) and in Zürich, from the spring of 1996 onwards, premiering later that year on 17 October. Zürich incidentally is also where Thomas Mann (1875-1955), author of a famous Faust novel, settled upon returning from his exile in the U.S., an exile not so incidentally speeded up by his altercation with the Nazis over the nationalist significance of Wagner and Goethe's lyrical drama (Schröter: 108-9). At this point during the

---

5   Meyer has noted that from Ibsen's youthful poem, "Building Plans," onwards, the
     dramatist had "regarded himself as a builder and his plays as works of architecture."
     (730)

Builders Association's drawn-out wrangling with the material, Weems commissioned a new version of the story from John Jesurun, which took full advantage of her extensive dramaturgical research.

Jesurun's own stage productions, experimenting with technological mediation and shifting perspectives, compounded by his sculptural and spatial imagination, made him a more than suitable collaborator. The script he furnished[6] – by itself an exciting collage where Camelot, Kennedy, Tiepolo, Cartland and Polanski rub shoulders with the Beatles – reflected and added to the welter of sources already delved into: Marlowe's *Doctor Faustus* (1588-1589), William Mountfort's English farce (1688), eighteenth century German and English puppet shows, Goethe's *Faust*, especially Part I (1773-1832), transcripts of the trial of childmurderer Susanna Margaretha Brandt (1774) (which inspired Goethe's play and Heinrich Leopold Wagner's *Die Kindermörderin*, 1776), Gounod's romantic opera (1859), and film versions by Georges Méliès (1898, 1903, 1905) – after Berlioz's 1845-6 *La damnation de Faust (légende dramatique)* – F.W.Murnau (1926), Gustaf Gründgens, and Peter Gorski (1960). Such is the abundance of adaptations one cannot help but speculate how the story's obsession with transformation (Faust's learning, dabbling in alchemy, worldly rise, travels, and rejuvenation; Mephisto's disguises and conjurings, etc.) keeps affecting the shape it assumes, ever forcing it to morph from one genre, nation, and era into another, forcing the Builders Association, too, into reconceiving and renaming their production over a three-year period.

In my subsequent comments I will by force be selective and limit myself in the first part to Weems's ideological inscription of her *Faust* cycle by way of Gründgens, Murnau, Reinhardt, and Brandt – paying attention to their recuperations and resistances regarding gender, nation, religion, and ethnicity. In the second part I move on to more technical aspects, such as the Builders Association's use of filmic techniques (match cuts, jump cuts, suturing) and the architectural conception of their art, as part of the productions' overall dynamic between embodiment and disembodiment.

Imperial Motel (Faust) was set in an anonymous transitional realm along Route 66, invoking right away the road novel and movie. Spatial and developmental simultaneity was aimed for by having video cameras reveal what was happening "off stage," in the hall behind the Venetian blinds of the reception desk, in addition to the directly visible action in

---

[6] References to the script version dated April 1998 are provided parenthetically. I hereby thank John Jesurun, Marianne Weems, and Crescentia Dünsser of the Neumarkt Theater for their assistance in providing material. That year Jesurun himself produced the play to much acclaim in Mexico City. More recently, he presented *Faust/How I Rose*, at the Faustival, 1-5 April 2003, University of Calgary.

the two scenically conveyed onstage rooms. In this composite setting a contemporary American Faust was paired off anachronistically with a German one, bent on recovering older personifications of the tale, partly real, partly the psychotic results of some drug taken by the road-weary traveller. The cast included Kyle DeCamp (as a leather-clad, female Mephisto) and Jeff Webster (as Faust), both from the Builders Association, as well as Susanne-Marie Wrage (a young stage Gretchen, in charge of room service) and Michael Neuenschwander (the motel manager, doubling as Faust, his assistant Wagner, and a male devil), from the Zürich Neumarkt Theater. Far from a mere practical matter, these doublings and mirrorings helped to convey the devilish visions, deceptions, and transformations at the heart of the Faust myth. That these were no male prerogative followed from DeCamp's cross-gender devil and the seduction of Marthe, who suddenly appropriated Mephisto's speeches and gestures, being equal to her opponent in terms of manipulative match-making. More worrying is of course that this kind of female empowerment easily shades off into sexist calumniation, a point made in the show through the fiendish accusations of female provocation in rape cases and of Gretchen's female mendacity in court to safeguard her acquittal, giving rise to Faust's misogynist outbursts. After all, everyone in this show is enthralled by the devil and the distinction between true and false has become hard to make. All the same, Weems questioned the patriarchal bent of the Faust tradition, already evident in Marlowe and hardly weakened by Goethe's Part I, whose female protagonist remains very much a passive victim.

Given the bicultural cast, German words were sprinkled across the English dialogue, as in "I never invited you into my Traumkopf" or "I take whatever Gestalt wants me." The international cast and bilingual dialogue of *Imperial Motel* (*Faust*) enhanced the hybrid nature of the production and the material – partly historical, partly legendary – which different cultures have submitted to different treatments, ever since Johannes Spies's 1587 *Faustbuch*. The most eminent cast member in the Swiss run was Ella Büchi. She played Martha but was magically transformed into an older Gretchen, when brought face to face with a rerun of Gründgens's Hamburger *Faust* on television – the scene in which Gretchen finds the jewel case, argues with her suitor, and finally undresses, singing the love song about the King of Thule.[7] While mimicking the gestures of her movie image Büchi abandoned herself to the youthful desire of the part she enacted decades earlier (a mirror to

---

[7]   Inter Nationes (Bonn) released the Hamburg *Faust* on videotape, as produced by Divina Film (Munich) and also featuring Willi Quadflieg as Faust and Gustaf Gründgens as Mephisto, a part he had been performing on stage since 1932 (Michalzik, 1999).

Faust's desire for youth). By contrast, the production's opening shots reversed the direction of the media-crossing, tracking Jeff Webster on screen before he arrived, in the flesh, on the stage set.

The reliance on Gründgens's *Faust* (as filmed by Peter Gorski) was not just a thematically relevant means of paying tribute to a great actress. Nor was it a case of site-specificity dwindled to a touch of local color. The Zürich premiere for that matter took place, quite symbolically, in a plant midway between the railway station and the airport. The incorporation of Gründgens's *Faust* actually short-circuited public history (next to Büchi's private one), as a foil to the spatial simultaneity achieved by the video cameras and the collapsing of theatre history through the doubled Faust (one contemporary, one traditional). In this manner Weems forcefully opened up a controversial metatheatrical and political realm, dominated by Germany's traumatic past. The early career of Gründgens (1899-1963) was indeed inextricably entwined with the rise of Fascism and its ideological appropriation of *Faust*. Despite Goethe's possibly "impure" racial origins, the play's hybrid source history, and its ultimate condonement of a birth out of wedlock, its aspiring character was opportunistically promoted into the exclusive "essence" of the Germanic soul. Accordingly, Faust's lethal transgressions were presented as necessary and natural acts of spiritual and artistic, military and technological creation or progress. Such appropriation for propagandistic purposes was also the fate of Gründgens's 1941-1942 *Faust*, whether he had intended it to or not (Mahl: 124-130).

Actually, the one-time communist sympathizer had already compromised his reputation as an innovating theatre director and as a former in-law of the Mann family (married to Thomas's daughter Erika from 1926-29) through his personal friendship with Reichsmarschall Goering and his function as Chief Intendant of Berlin's State Theatre during the Third Reich (1933-45). To all appearances Gründgens's subsequent sparse, metatheatrical Hamburger staging of *Faust* (1957-59) was marked by a formalism possibly reflecting a desire to steer clear of politics. It retained Goethe's double prologue (in the theatre and in heaven) and relegated the play proper to the bare platform of an inner stage, visibly surrounded by the performers when not on. Yet, by presenting Faust as an overreaching modern physicist (through reference to the Brussels Atomium and film projections of nuclear explosions during the Walpurgis night), Gründgens offered an ironic reflection on his personal past. This reflection nevertheless remained far more reserved than that constituted by *Mephisto: Roman einer Karriere* (1936), the novel which Klaus Mann (Erika's brother) based on Gründgens and whose publication the actor/director opposed until his very death by suicide, driven by lingering guilt.

254 The Wooster Group and Its Traditions

Gründgens's entanglement in the vicissitudes of Goethe's *Faust* is far from unique. The equation of this play with the essence of German nationhood during the Weimar Republic (1918-33) already emanated into a clarion call for territorial expansion (Eisner, 1973b: 12-5), intimated by the tell-tale adjective, "imperial," in the title of the Builders Association's production and by its travel metaphor. A similar attempt at ideological appropriation therefore underlay the cultural and economic exploitation of Murnau's movies, including his *Faust* (1926, after Hans Kyser's script), which the American performance company relied on.

Following the box-office success of Robert Wiene's horror movie *The Cabinet of Dr. Caligari* (1919) it was believed that Germany's expressionist movie makers (including Fritz Lang and Georg Pabst), could re-establish, in a move parallelling the attempts at territorial expansion, the country's international artistic prestige. This, ironically, was to be achieved with a genre whose excessive (originally anti-bourgeois) style partook of popular melodrama and the gothic, but which the intellectual elite quickly enough relegated to the sphere of high-brow art, even if directors like Lang and Murnau went to work in Hollywood during the late 1920s and early 1930s, thereby contributing to its commercial success and growing monopoly (Hayward: 166-168). Another irony is that Lang and Murnau's move to America – coinciding as it did with the advent of sound – also signalled the end of the heyday of Germany's silent cinema (Eisner, 1973b: 7). Finally, the limited financial and artistic success of his *Faust* had convinced Murnau to accept an offer by Fox Film Corporation. But unlike Lang (1890-1976), who reached the venerable age of 86, Murnau died of a car crash on the Pacific Coast highway in the vicinity of Santa Barbara, on 11 March 1931, five years after his arrival in the U.S. and a week before the premiere of *Tabu*, his last international success. The contrast between the exotic *Tabu*, set and shot outdoors among the sun-drenched Pacific Isles, and the gothic *Nosferatu, A Symphony of Terror* (1922), which signalled Murnau's breakthrough, could not be greater. The expressionist style (never that excessive in Murnau because of his lingering post-Romanticism) is still prominent in his 1926 chiaroscuro *Faust*, particularly in Emil Jannings's performance of the devil, less so in the semi-abstract architecture of the lavish studio sets (created by Herlth and Röhrig), and even less in Gösta Ekman's rather bland demeanor as the scholar (Eisner, 1973b: 285, 292; 1973a: 165).

While no screen adaptation of an earlier stage performance, as was the case with Gründgens and Gorski's 1960 film, the aesthetics of Murnau's *Faust* (its architectural conception, ingenious lighting, and visual imagination) were informed by his (and Jannings's) training as an actor under Max Reinhardt (1873-1943) and by his subsequent assistantship to the Austrian in the very period that he first embarked on Goethe's *Faust* (1909-11). Insofar as Reinhardt's revival of *Faust* Part I during the 1933 Salzburger Festspiele met with a racist-inspired critique from the Nazis, the Jewish director (born Goldmann) left for the U.S. by way of London, thus making room for Gründgens's rise at the Deutsches Theater, Berlin. In a similar way, Murnau's earlier emigration in 1926, following his own *Faust*, had been partly motivated by his homosexuality, as it made him an outcast in Germany. The resistance of these two artists to Germany's nationalist ideological interpellation is all the more remarkable, in the light of Reinhardt's autocratic deployment of theatrical masses (providing a rather unsettling parallel with the Nazis' megalomania) and the inauspicious beginnings of Murnau's film career during World War I. While his involvement as a pilot was terminated by his internment in Switzerland, following a forced landing amidst a fog, he soon afterwards won the first prize in a contest by staging the Swiss nationalist play *Marignano*, as well as embarked on propaganda films for the German embassy, before cofounding in 1919 with some former Reinhardt students the Murnau-Veidt Film Society. From this early stage onwards, then, Murnau's life and art (much like that of Gründgens and Reinhardt) were suffused with ideology. Here again lay one of the Builders Association's primary interests, besides the ground for biographical allusions to Murnau's double crash – in Switzerland and California – encapsulating the moviemaker's stylistic evolution from a nightmarishly dark to a sun-lit palette.

Given the course history would take, Weems's concluding film footage from the intro to Leni Riefenstahl's *Triumph of the Will* (1935) acquired ominous overtones, collapsing as it were the light-infested heavenly opening and closing of Murnau's *Faust* with the end of his career. By offering a perfect counterpart to Murnau's often praised subjective camera in Hitler's grandiose aerial approach, through a ballet of clouds, of Nüremberg for the 1934 Nazi Party Convention, Weems to all appearances simply matched the blissful prospect of redemption terminating Murnau's movie (Eisner, 1973a: 165). Yet with the inevitability of hindsight, the Builders Association's "Damnation" scene (the thirteenth and last), which textually recalls the 1945 burning of Dresden, also harked back to the death foretold of Murnau's opening sequence, in which the immense shadow of Mephisto's "wing" or cape darkens the medieval town upon which he is to inflict the plague. Conversely, Faust's burning of his books and subsequent pact with the devil – film sequences retained by Weems – prefigured the Nazis' book burnings and own blood-drenched devilish pact, events barely fictionalized in Mann's encyclopedic *Doctor Faust*, begun in his Californian exile to the rhythm of the collapsing German Empire. In her study of expressionist cinema Lotte Eisner has left no doubt as to how its "flight" into the fantastic and supernatural (what the early, *Sturm und Drang* Goethe called the "daemonic" [Eisner 1973b: 8, 15]) was rooted in the everyday reality of the poverty-stricken, war-defeated Weimar republic (a name indissolubly attached to Goethe), and how, by feeding on the romantic nostalgia for a sense of greatness lost, the expressionists' transcendence of their extreme subjectivism in a (male) power-driven unanism (as in Reinhardt's crowd scenes), would lead to another European disaster (Eisner, 1973b: 9-15).

Jump Cut

Spelling out Europe's crash course even more explicitly, the penultimate stage of the Builders Association's work-in-progress opened in October 1997 at Munich's Spiel.Art Festival under the title, *Jump Cut (The Last Hour)*, before losing some of its explosive site-specificity during its December run at the Thread Waxing Space in New York as *Jump Cut (Faust)*. By the time it reached Brussels, where it was shown at the Lunatheater on 16-17 March 1998, the production had a newly constituted, mono-lingual cast and further adapted script. Webster remained present as Faust, but absent was DeCamp, whose female Mephistopheles had reverted to Moira Driscoll (with horn-like braids), further doubling as Martha, Gretchen's neighbor, and the Judge at the trial. David Pence was the male devil, while Heaven Phillips replaced Wrange as Gretchen and Rhonda Kindermoerd. In the absence of Büchi (formerly playing Martha), the scene in which she confronted her younger self (as Gretchen) in Gründgens's movie had to be adapted, too. As a result, the production now lay a more exclusive emphasis on Murnau, sequences from which, with or without intertitles, "jump-cut" to Jesurun's script. Occasionally these intertitles were accompanied by an ominously whispered, readerly voice-over ("A knave like all others! He preaches good and does evil! He seeks to turn base metal into gold!"). Adding to the ironic distance thus achieved were the section titles and synoptic catchphrases derived from Jesurun's text, highlighting ideas and themes ("God was jealous," "A frozen beauty," "Baby you can drive my car,"etc.).

The earlier scenes of *Jump Cut (Faust)* leaned heavily towards Murnau's film classic, whose excerpts were projected onto a large-size, rectangular screen, covering the upper half of the backstage wall. In the later scenes the live performance dominated, notably the court scenes with Gretchen or Rhonda Kindermoerd as she was now called. Susanne Brandt's inquisition was indeed updated into a publicly "broadcast," melodramatic rape trial, pitting the abortionist against the pro-lifer viewpoints. Both the movie images and stage action were in turn framed by Faust's opening and closing letters, resp. to his "Dear One" and to

"Gretchen" (Jesurun's alternative to Murnau's and Goethe's heavenly frame). "Dear One," Faust's punning salutation to his "Letter #1," exposed the perfunctory nature of his love, whether the "first" in a series or an "impersonal" one. Such perfunctoriness adds to the parallels with Mephisto, who forgot the name of the angel he fell in love with (his capital sin), and towards the end is accused by Faust of not knowing how to kiss. Both men, therefore, represent the lackluster reality behind Gretchen's romantic song about the king who remained faithful, even to his departed beloved. The epistolary frame was returned to only once in an intermediate letter to "Phaedra," in which the devil's biting comment keeps interrupting Faust's unctuous self-exculpation. Still, together with the already mentioned intertitles and the occasional readerly voice-over, this frame sufficed to ground the entire intermedial performance in writing and retrospective story-telling, i.e. language or Mephisto's perfectly honed tool of seduction. Whether deliberately or not (given Weems's parenthetic title for the show's Munich run) the retrospection recalled the albeit more physical and ritualistic montage by Grotowski's Laboratory Theatre of Marlowe's *Doctor Faustus* (79-96). That "biographical travelogue" supposedly also took place in "the last hour" before Faust's martyr-like death, in that Grotowski presented him very much like Goethe did, as a saintly rebel against heavenly intrigues, incapable of saving god's offspring through his magic (Bevington and Rasmussen: 55-6).

The differences with Grotowski notwithstanding, *Jump Cut (Faust)* was a similar dream or hallucinatory ride down memory lane. Triggered by a photograph of his love(s), Faust's mental trip takes place while his plane is "flying on empty" above an apocalyptic, post-United Nations landscape, plagued by computer and communication breakdowns amidst a post-holocaust, post-nuclear conflagration. The whole resonates with David Bowie and Stanley Kubrick's space odysseys, spiced by the popular metaphysics of Bob Dylan ("knocking on heaven's door") and Robert Plant ("highway to hell" instead of "stairway to heaven"). Jesurun's lyrically dense intertext is set among the ruins of Western humanist culture, like an offshoot of T.S. Eliot's "Wasteland" or Heiner Müller's *Hamletmachine*, though it is Stoppard's adaptation, *Rosencrantz and Guildenstern Are Dead* (1966), which is quoted, and Shakespeare's original, too, notably Claudius' inability to pray as long as he enjoys the crown. The cumulative effect of this rich allusiveness is another short-circuiting of time and place. Just so, the murder trial, whose sharp-tongued altercations were stalled by Gretchen's mesmerizing evocations of her laboring body, turned into a gothic séance as the ghost of her dead foetus testified to the court in an advanced case of video conferencing, across temporal and spatial divides. Ultimately the perspectival dislocations erupted into the fleeting eternity of an ethereal no man's land, which an exhilarated Faust contemplates before his fall. Until then the referential overkill and saturation deliberately threaten this bursting "omniverse" (ts. 5) with fragmentation and dissolution. Each new reference – jumping wildly from high to low culture, across national heritages and literary periods, mixing up archaisms, Latin, techno-talk, foul-mouthed street slang, and legalese – requires a constant recontextualization, at the risk of exploding the text, the world, the self. Dismemberment is way too slow an end for this postmodern Faust, whose delirious psychodrama already split him up into a full-fledged cast after his own image. Here speed is all, the painful enough modern mobility accelerated in Faust's intergalactic travels through a "haunted history house" (ts. 12), that psychedelic "rush through an amnesiac, bulimic billenia in 2 seconds flat" (ts. 15). Supported by The Beatles' "L.S.D.," a.k.a. "Lucy in the Sky with Diamonds" (ts. 12), it ends abruptly with a bathetic crash into the House of Pancakes, whose deflated flapjacks and ruined sweets nauseatingly anticipate Gretchen's lost child.

Keeping the verbal excesses and sledgehammer assaults on Romanticism within bounds, however, was the restrained acting and delivery, the rhythmic apportioning of Jesurun's witty and richly allusive speech among silent scenes from Murnau. The relationship between the screen images and stage action deserves special attention, linked as they were by having the live performers carefully adopt the very postures of the movie actors (much as Büchi had done with Gründgens's film track) and by matching their real-time images with Murnau's prerecorded ones. Often it was difficult to ascertain which was which, whether filmic action was mimicked or stage action filmed, because of the smoke effects, style-copying, and technological processing – a collaborative feat of the performers and designers, among whom featured Christopher Kondek (video), Dan Dobson (sound), Jennifer Tipton (light), and Ellen McCartney (costumes). The perceptual manipulations of their artful game recall Murnau's "trick photography," itself an attempt to emulate the "magical" effects of the earlier vaudeville stage tradition, performed with a view to solliciting the spectator's appreciation, much as in what Tom Gunning has called the cinema of attraction (Elsaesser and Barker: 56-62, 95-103). Technically speaking, Murnau combined the best of both worlds, contrasting to great dramatic, psychological and emotional effect, the flat, fore-shortened spaces or frontal compositions reminiscent of the (melo-)dramatic stage tableau, with the deep-focus sets and depth-of-frame from outdoor photography and natural locations, which he introduced in his movies (Elsaesser: 250). Added to this should be his personal transformation of painterly pictorialism from Romanticism (David Friedrich Caspar) and the Renaissance (Christ in Mantegna's *The Lamentation over the Dead*, a Flemish Madonna, etc.), leading to

Rohmer's conclusion that Murnau in his *Faust* combined pictorial with architectural and filmic space (Eisner, 1973b: 98; Vacche: 161-196; Rohmer).

So did Weems, with the match cuts functioning either independently or enhancing the jolting effect of the jump cuts and textual dislocations (regarding space, time, register, tone, and cultural source), whether to debunk Murnau's and Goethe's romantic elevation by exposing the artifice, or simply to enjoy that artifice. Thus the sentimental incitement to compassion for Gretchen's unwanted motherhood, in perfect painterly Madonna poses, was undercut by the Builders Association's reliance on a rather low-tech sugar dispenser to create a snow effect. The express staging, marked by positioning, makeup, and costuming (Martha's headdress, Gretchen's monk cape), followed by an equally explicit filming and projection of the images (delineated by a sonar-like beep), problematized the audience's immersion in the melodramatic narrative. This freed the critical space to invoke the spec(tac)ularization and commodification of women in cinema, especially Hollywood mainstream films, operating according to Murnau's melodramatic principles, yet fostering the audience's secretly enjoyed voyeurism rather than the stage's explicit exhibitionism. So much greater then was the audience's consternation when Weems's performers suddenly appeared *within* rather than *next to* Murnau's film footage, as if they were latter-day Alices stepping through the screen rather than the looking glass. After all, Jesurun possibly alludes to the mad tea party from *Alice in Wonderland* (ts. 23). The derisively cool mimicry therefore did not exclude illusory effects in the manner of the cinema of attraction (say of Méliès's *Faust* fantasies), and this despite the blatant intertextual layering of the Faust material. Much of the audience's pleasure derived precisely from the fluctuations between the illusion and its disruption, the embodiments and disembodiments of the fiction.

The use of a cinemascopic screen as opposed to individual monitors here proved crucial. To begin, it allowed for the double vision or simultaneity of screen close-ups (hard to achieve on stage) and panoramic or wide angle "stage" shots (what is commonly offered the average theatre spectator beyond the first rows). Next, the large-scale screen facilitated a theatrical play with filmic suture (Hayward: 81, 371-379), the stitching of the spectators into the narrative only to rip them out of it all the more violently. Most common among the means to achieve suture are subjective angle shots and reverse-angle shots, as well as ocular contact between the performer and spectator, e.g. when Pence's Mephisto exculpated himself, in contrast to Camilla Horn's demure looks, recovered by Phillips. Effective, too, are reflections of all kinds. Thus, Phillips displayed the devil's gift directly to the spectators through a translucent vanity mirror, though Murnau's necklace with a heart-shaped pendant had been replaced by a literal chain. A voice-over topped the effect – Mephisto's exclamation, "Look what she found in her dresser drawer" – words whose unidentified source was assigned to the spectators until the devil's distorted face materialized in a lateral section of the mirror, which earlier had displayed only Pence's magnified eye like an evil charm. In "The Fall or How I Fell" (scene 5) the exchange between Faust (Q: "They say you can take any form you want.") and Mephisto (A: "You create me in your own image.") resulted in the tell-tale title "What do I look like?", addressed straight to the camera and audience, as if both were indeed mirrors of sorts.

How well-considered the interactions between stage and screen could become, emerged when at the trial Phillips as Rhonda Kindermoerd suddenly broke the silence to take the initiative. Without qualms she assumed the subject position by peremptorily insisting that the question of whether she did or did not kill her baby be dealt with right away. So far the defendant had only been talked about, objectified and marginalized. The paradox of her position was conveyed by her sitting in semi-profile to the side of the stage, eyes cast down, while being granted centrality on the screen as the bone of contention between the (female) Judge and Faust. Consequently, her looking up and speaking into the microphone registered all the more forcefully on the already blown-up image (taken frontally and cropped at the waist). Rhonda's sudden, real-time call for attention further clashed with the delayed images of the Judge and Faust, which could be interpreted as an effect of her initial dreamy absent-mindedness. Alternatively the desynchronization of their speech and images conveyed the characters' lagging behind the fast-talking, devilish public prosecutor (representing the Symbolic Order or Patriarchal Law), and the speaking subject's secondariness (Lacan's *futur antérieur*) when it comes to expressing repressed desire (signified by Faust and Gretchen's illegitimate child). If Weems here came up with an extension of Murnau's subjective camera, the Prologue, during which Pence was seen driving along a nightly, wind-blown highway (Route 66 from Jesurun's "Letter #1"), stuck to the (by now) more traditional method. By filming the sequence across the performer's shoulder (as when Murnau shows Faust's pursuit of Gretchen through Mephisto's eyes) (Eisner, 1973b: 291; 1973a: 65), the character's point of view is made to coincide with the movie viewer's. During Faust's intergalactic travels, though, the method used was the old-fashioned one of filming stable figures against a moving background, which Murnau precisely made redundant.

All in all, the Builders Association's combination of different cinematographic techniques (suture, subjective camera, match cuts, jump cuts, close-ups) abolished their transparency or invisibility, as was the case with the discrepancy between words (e.g. Faust's talk of a plane ride) and images (the highway), the dephasing of stage and screen action, or the stage action's implausible "incorporation" into Murnau's images. As with Goethe's Prologue in the theatre, Weems's formal manipulations re-embody the audience's perceptual activity and the performance company's technical mediations. The inset of Faust's rearview mirror in the windshield of his car e.g., by reflecting the driver's eyes, invoked the formerly invisible frame, i.e. the off-screen space occupied by the camera and the spectators identified with it. While screening the stage activity, the Builders Association thus simultaneously countered film's ideological screening as well as the fictionalization and virtualization of our media-dominated age, a disembodiment of sorts (whether merely ascertained or castigated as evil) prolonging the dissolution of physical reality through the extensive verbal intertextuality and the possibility that the play is Faust's recollection or psychotic daydream. In this regard Peter von Becker's review of *Imperial Motel (Faust)* touched upon the production's ironical crux in the contrast he set up between the (regrettably) superficial and exchangeable glossy images of a video culture (allegedly including the kind of theatre produced by the Builders Association) and the physical fascination, the virtuosity rather than virtuality, exerted by Ella Büchi and Susanne-Marie Wrage, two "unique" actresses, no matter that they were playing alter-egos in the part of two namesakes, that of Maggie (Margarethe, Gretchen) and Susanna Margaretha Brandt. These two actresses, von Becker argued, allowed for the two-fold wonder of *Imperial Motel (Faust)*, despite the profusion of American-made technology. What comes across as an outburst of nationalist fervor hence touches upon the problematical but ever more precious status of the physical body in an intermedial age. So, too, does his comment that Webster possesses the typical movie actor's gift of doing little and being "present" all the same. Far from having pinpointed a weakness of the Builders Association's *Faust* adaptation(s), von Becker identified the intentional terms of their intermedial exploration, by situating Büchi and Wrage's performance in-between Webster's allegedly "empty" movie "presence" and Murnau's expressionist or Gründgens's more rhetorical style.

The Burden of Irony, the Onus of Cool

The Wooster Group's Influence
on Cannon Company and Richard Maxwell

Daniel MUFSON

Brooklyn College

Dominating the downtown theatre scene in New York, the Wooster Group has become a magnet for artists making their way on the New York scene. Numerous younger experimental theatre artists have passed through the Performing Garage practically as a rite of passage to their own self-fruition; people who have worked at the Garage have gone on to collaborate with or form most of the major young ensembles working in New York's downtown scene: Collapsable [*sic*] Giraffe, Radiohole, and the Builders Association, to name just a few.[1] Both Richard Kimmel, director of the Cannon Company, and Richard Maxwell have worked with the Wooster Group: Maxwell interned at the Garage for six months in 1994, just after moving to New York from Chicago[2]; Kimmel began interning at the Garage before he received his MFA in directing from Columbia University in 1998, and he continues to work with the Group today, recently serving as Assistant Director on the Group's *To You, The Birdie!* But even before Richard Kimmel or Richard Maxwell actually set foot in the Performing Garage, they had both studied the Wooster Group as part of their university coursework in the performing arts.

Although other young groups are doing worthwhile work and will hopefully continue to do so, I want to focus on the work of Richard

---

[1] Two examples, beyond those listed elsewhere in this volume: Michelle Stern, co-founder and producer of GAle GAtes, performed in the revival of *North Atlantic* and Collapsable Giraffe founder Jim Findlay has designed and built sets for the Wooster Group.

[2] To illustrate the continuing connection, it is perhaps worth mentioning that Liz LeCompte's sister, Ellen, acted in Maxwell's production, *Drummer Wanted*, which moved to the Performing Garage in the spring after having opened at P.S. 122 at the end of 2001.

Kimmel and Richard Maxwell primarily because the two of them have taken a more critical and revisionary stance *vis-à-vis* the Wooster Group than most of the others. Taking a concept from Harold Bloom, I am thinking here about "influence" not necessarily in terms of source-hunting or allusion-counting but rather in terms of relations between works and the way one production implies a critique of another by any variety of tactics – a "corrective swerve," an effort at taking a gesture one or more steps further, or an attempt at negation. In the present discussion, questions of influence come into play when considering fascination with multimedia technology, the use of irony, and the attitude a work seems to have to the possibility or legitimacy of genuine and visceral emotional responses in the context of formally challenging work.

The events of September 11, 2001 precipitated a flood of self-questioning, not least within the artistic community, and one of the consistent refrains came in the form of the questions, "Is this the end of irony? Will we now see a reawakening of political commitment that the formalist experimenters of the downtown scene have – with the note-worthy exception of queer and feminist artists – largely avoided?" And yet in looking at *Puss*, the Cannon Company's adaptation of Ludwig Tieck's *Der gestiefelte Kater*, or any number of Richard Maxwell's plays, one realizes that the air of irony and intellectual detachment that has lain at the heart of the Wooster Group's work for many years now was already being challenged long before the myth of America's isolation was so forcefully punctured.

Before discussing the work of Kimmel and Maxwell, it might be worthwhile to review briefly notions of irony and detachment in the context of the Wooster Group's work. The Wooster Group began making theatre in the highly charged political environment of the mid-1970s. At the time, its partial move towards apolitical postmodern performance was in itself tantamount to a gesture of dissent from the politicization of countercultural artists and ensembles. Influenced in part by the politically engaged work of Richard Schechner yet admiring the more insular worlds of Richard Foreman and Robert Wilson, LeCompte staged a retreat of sorts from commitment to themes such as the Vietnam War, racial prejudice, and sexual oppression, a commitment that had pervaded the work of so many other artists and ensembles at the time. For example, the Group's first productions, the first parts of *Three Places in Rhode Island*, used the personal life of Spalding Gray as a starting point.

But, as mentioned, the retreat from political and social issues proved itself to be partial rather than full. The Wooster Group toyed with issues of militarism in *North Atlantic* (1984) and race in *Route 1 & 9* (1981), but its treatment of such issues was allergic to the slightest tendentiousness, reveling in the coy and ambiguous. Indeed, the opacity of their "position" vis-à-vis their themes precipitated on occasion considerable controversy, as in their use of minstrelsy in *Route 1 & 9*. In that instance, without the security provided by an explicit critique of blackface, the Wooster Group left itself open to accusations of racism to the point of jeopardizing their funding from state arts organizations.

The Wooster Group has become known for a number of practices that can more or less be codified: the exposed rows of harsh fluorescent lighting; the metal, skeletal grid that either frames or in fact constitutes the set; dance as an interruption device; the use of audio samples to caricature certain movements in the manner of certain children's cartoons or kung fu movies; actors, either sitting at tables or standing, speaking into microphones, while facing out towards the audience; an ironic mode of acting, in which the actor often seems to smirk at or undercut the emotion suggested by the words of a line of dialogue; and of course the use of video and sound technology to alter the visual and auditory landscapes of performance.

All of these devices constitute *Verfremdungseffekte*, distancing the audience from the traditions of empathy so ingrained in psychological realism. As a result, Wooster Group performances often provoke laughter or surprise; an admiration for their precision and ingenuity; and perhaps occasionally a feeling of shock or anger – although I think even that is less and less the case. Seldom, if ever, do the performances evoke fear or pity or sorrow, all of which usually require a degree of identification with the stage characters. Indeed, in reviewing the Wooster Group's *To You, The Birdie! (Phèdre)*, critic and Brooklyn College professor Charles McNulty aptly compared the layers of traditional avant-garde technique to the emotionally cincturing effects of Racine's alexandrine lines, the formal rigor sharply restricting – if not completely stifling – any visceral sense of the pathos of the tragedy.

Much of the distancing employed by the Wooster Group stems from its use of irony, which manifests itself in at least three ways: first, there is a discrepancy between the literal meaning of the lines of dialogue and the meaning conveyed by the actors' delivery; the second type of irony is derived from the first, namely, the irony that Schlegel spoke of as a "permanent parabasis," or turning out to the audience; third, the productions take place in Northrop Frye's sense of the Ironic Mode, that is, the manner of depiction suggests characters who are "inferior in power or intelligence to ourselves, so that we have the sense of looking down on a scene of bondage, frustration, or absurdity" (34). For example, in *To You, The Birdie! (Phèdre)*, the Group presents a scatological Phèdre paralyzed by her neuroses and a Theseus reduced to a caricature of a flexing bodybuilder. Finally, as D.C. Muecke points out in *Irony and the*

Ironic, in the twentieth century the traditional definition of irony – saying one thing and suggesting the contrary – has given way to a notion of irony as "saying something in a way that activates not one but an endless series of subversive interpretations," "a perpetual deferment of significance" (31).

The type of irony referred to by Muecke has manifested itself consistently throughout the Wooster Group's work. As members of the ensemble have themselves conceded, it contributes to a sense of emotional coolness (Savran, 1988: 53). Though it would be an exaggeration to say that the triggering of a visceral emotional response is unknown in Wooster Group productions, the Group has also clearly been aware for some time that the "perpetual deferment of significance" and the constant layering of *Verfremdungseffekte* reduce the pointedness and frequency of emotional connections with an audience.

Kimmel and Maxwell have explored different ways of responding to these practices, but their impulses share some common roots. Each one has acknowledged that a certain level of irony is essential in creating artistic work of integrity today; at the same time, each has expressed frustration with an irony that suffocates emotion or undermines ideas of emotional genuineness or authenticity. Both are musicians who have played in and continue to play in rock bands and who speak admiringly of the energy and emotion generated by rock concerts. One of Richard Kimmel's more recent projects was a piece of paratheatre called *Pleasuredome*, a weekend-long experience in which the audience's dancing and revelry would be interrupted by choreography and scenes by his performers. Richard Maxwell, for his part, recently performed with his rock trio, the New York City Players, as part of the Phat Tuesdays series at the Galapagos venue in Brooklyn. But after one acknowledges those interests and concerns, any similarities become much more difficult to find. Their answers to the Wooster Group model pivot on the question of irony, but at angles virtually opposite to one another.

Kimmel immediately signals his preoccupation with irony by directing an adaptation of Johann Ludwig Tieck's *Der gestiefelte Kater* (1796), which in its own time was a radical challenge to contemporary bourgeois tastes as well as to techniques of undermining illusion, incorporating self-referential commentary into the action of the play. Aside from featuring actors falling out of character, the play itself appears to slip out of its position as a play. As Nicholas Saul has pointed out, *Der gestiefelte Kater* was an attempt at conducting a dialogue with the public in which the poet "must plead grovelingly for understanding" (236); Tieck, critiquing his contemporaries, was also grappling with what many of the Romantics perceived as an overwhelming literary tradition, a problem which Kimmel himself perceives as confronting theatre artists today. Tieck's play ends with the character of the Author asking the audience to "forget [its] knowledge," and longing for "a new kind of poetry which can be better felt than described." Upon having these sentiments scorned, with the audience throwing rotten fruit and crumpled paper at him, the Author realizes the futility of his proposition, saying, "No, the gentlemen out there [in the audience] are better than I am at this new kind of poetry. I withdraw."[3]

In *Puss* (1999), Kimmel re-stages techniques of the Wooster Group as well as those of Foreman and a handful of other representatives of what might be considered the contemporary canonical avant-garde. He indulges, self-consciously, in flagrant imitation and quotation. Exploring the depths of the derivative gesture, Kimmel draws attention to the familiarity of Wooster Group staging techniques within the downtown New York theatre community. By staging Tieck's *Der gestiefelte Kater*, Kimmel in essence traces a lineage of parodic self-referentiality in modern performance.

Kimmel's version of *Puss* does not limit its theft to the Wooster Group but steals from all of the icons of New York's experimental scene. Plexiglas and strings colored white and black cut through the stage à la Foreman; a dance scene is performed to music from Robert Wilson's *Einstein on the Beach*; movements are copied from Anne Bogart productions. Clearly though, the overwhelming stylistic presence is that of the Wooster Group. Aside from the fact that the production itself takes place in the Performing Garage, two of the most salient characters are shaped by Wooster Group productions. The character of Hanswurst, the court fool who in Tieck's hands represented a type of Commedia-influenced character whose presence on German stages was at that time being actively discouraged by critics, becomes a blackface figure from *Route 1 & 9*. Tieck's Leander, the wise man, plays his role in Kimmel's production over a video screen, the actor's image supposedly conveyed from his apartment via internet under the (false) pretext of his having sustained an injury in rehearsal; the reference, however, is to Wooster Group productions such as *L.S.D.*, *Brace Up!*, and *Fish Story*, where actors who had to leave the show were replaced by videos – sometimes of themselves, sometimes of other actors. In the

---

[3] Gerald Gillespie's widely used English translation presents the last line as, "No, the gentlemen out there are better than I am at farce. I withdraw," but the German text refers not to farce but "dieser Dichtungsart," which the poet has just described as something "die sich besser fühlen als beschreiben lässt." These last lines, and the throwing of fruit and paper, are omitted from Kimmel's version, although the production fizzles out in a comparably deflated fashion.

famous case of *Brace Up!*, the missing actor who had played Solyony was replaced in Act One by blasts of a Godzilla video.[4]

Kimmel makes important alterations in the play. Aside from changing Tieck's writer-author into a twentieth-century director-auteur, the self-referential, self-destructing fiasco of the play results not from the excessive education and aesthetic preconceptions of the critics in the audience but rather from the excessive education and aesthetic preconceptions of the artist. It is Kimmel's directorial character – or Kimmel himself? – who burdens the stage with too much knowledge, a knowledge that stifles creativity. In the Tieck text, the performance is consistently interrupted by critics chattering in the gallery, until one of the more negative of the lot, Bötticher, is urged by his peers to leave the theatre instead of burdening them with his opinion. In Kimmel's version, the critics' banter is kept quiet for most of the production and is generally limited to barely audible muttering until quite late in the play, at which point a critic and her companion get up and leave, loudly condemning the production's lack of originality. The remarks that the critic yells are by this time usually shared by a noteworthy portion of the audience, many of whom were not aware that the critics were plants. On any given night, audience members applauded the critic's comments in apparent sympathy.

The New York press either ignored or rejected the production. In the *Village Voice*, Charles McNulty confirms the impression that audience members shared the opinions anticipated by the critic of Kimmel's own creation: "[T]here are times," McNulty writes,

> when one can't help but rue the legacy of Richard Foreman and the Wooster Group. This is not to undervalue the way these contemporary legends have invigorated our alternative theater; it's just not always easy to sit through the work of their disciples. Of course, for every bona fide genius, there's an army of admirers trying to duplicate the magic. But couldn't the new crop of downtown directors evince just a little more anxiety of influence? (84)

According to Kimmel, many members of the artistic community were enraged by the production. Some were angry that they had been fooled by the critics planted in the audience; other artists, apparently sensitive to the charge of derivativeness, viewed the production as a critique by Kimmel of their own work. Kimmel has said that he welcomed the negative reactions because one of his chief aims was to provoke a genuine emotional response of the sort that, in his view, is not a typical facet of downtown productions today (Mufson, 2002b). In a sense, he is returning from a twentieth-century breed of irony to a Romantic one in

---

[4]   Via live video Production Manager Clay Shirky gradually replaced Godzilla over the course of the evening.

that he deploys irony not to eliminate emotion but to balance it. He highlights the avant-gardist's dilemma today: as he puts it, "How do we keep making it strange when it's already been made so strange?"

One could beneficially compare *Puss* to a somewhat similar project, namely, the 1997 production of *Three Sisters* by Richard Schechner and East Coast Artists, in which Act I was played à la Stanislavsky, Act II using Meyerhold's biomechanics, Act III set in a Stalinist gulag, and Act IV in a Wooster Group-influenced style of postmodernism. What sets *Puss* apart is its attempt to use self-referentiality and ironic devices in order to decrease the audience's critical distance rather than to increase it; it is a parody of the culture of sampling and undermines the postmodern assumption that originality is a fiction. It accomplishes its ends by wallowing in creative bankruptcy to the point of provoking fury. Originality may or may not be a fiction, but derivativeness definitely becomes intolerable. In *Puss*, it is no longer only the characters on stage who are the victims of dramatic irony, unaware of the reality of the performance, but the audience as well. Finally, Kimmel reconstructs rather than deconstructs *Puss*, in that he revives Tieck's initial use of the play as a weapon of critique against the stage practices of his contemporaries.

Richard Maxwell pursues another path. Where Kimmel indulges in *Verfremdungseffekte* and the fetishization of technology in order to question them, Richard Maxwell rejects the outer trappings of technological finesse perfected by the Wooster Group and revels in the absence of sophisticated stage machinery. Where the Wooster Group has used advanced sound technology such as digital vocal harmony processing, Maxwell's actors in *House* and *Drummer Wanted* use a cheap, handheld tape player to provide the musical accompaniment for their songs. The sets are deceptively plain; for example, as the set for *House*, Maxwell replicates the plain white wall with a pay phone that existed in the space where the production was rehearsed.

Rhetorically, Maxwell bases his style on the idea of a rejection of style; in interview after interview, he talks about his aim of "eradicate[ing] any evidence of a style" even though he says he "understand[s] the ridiculousness of the statement" (Mufson, 2002a). In contrast to the line delivery of Wooster Group actors who seem to comment on their dialogue even as they recite it, Maxwell has his actors recite their lines under the pretense of removing any type of attitude whatsoever towards what is being said; delivery is almost completely stripped of tonality. The actors make faint vocal gestures at emotions that seldom achieve anything even close to full expression. This eliminates the brand of irony associated with Wooster Group actors but in fact creates another kind of irony insofar as there remains a disjunction between the words themselves and the way in which they are spoken. On the one hand, draining a passionate dialogue or monologue of its emotion provokes laughter from the audience; on the other hand, this tonal stepping-out-of-the-way exercised by the actors allows the audience greater liberty to consider the emotional possibilities of the line, almost as if reading the text on the page. Meanings may be variable, but not infinite. Emotions, muffled as if being suffocated under a pillow, feel all the more vigorous in their imagined struggle to break free. We are no longer in Frye's Ironic Mode, looking down on the people on stage; the characters are similar to those found in the audience, and the portrayals, directorially speaking, show more compassionate humor than snide mockery.

Maxwell takes a path away from the Wooster Group markedly different from Kimmel's, but both recognize the unavoidability of self-referentiality, irony, and the tradition of the avant-garde while expressing frustration with what they perceive as the eradication of vulnerable sentiment. Maxwell is acutely aware of the difficulty involved in balancing the two concerns. With his band at Galapagos in February 2002, Maxwell played a song by a honky-tonk singer named Lefty Frizzell called "The Mom and Dad Waltz," with the following lyrics:

And in my heart, joy tears start, 'cause I'm happy

And I pray every day for Ma and Pappy

And each night I'd walk for miles, cry and smile

For my Mama and Daddy

I want them to know I love them so.

Maxwell prefaced the song by telling the audience, "You can laugh at this, but it's not supposed to be funny."

Although this was not theatrical performance *per se*, I think it reveals a great deal about Maxwell's approach to his drama. His band, consisting of a six-string guitar, a bass guitar, and drums, was a stark contrast to the trio in which Kate Valk played at a fundraiser at New York's downtown presenting theatre, HERE, in 1998, in which her trio of musicians filtered their voices through vocoders and the music was not played on musical instruments but rather programmed on computers and synthesizers. Maxwell's approach to theatrical staging is more sophisticated than his straightforward – but enjoyable – performance of honky-tonk music, yet there is still this idea that, "You can laugh at this, but it's not supposed to be funny." In *Showy Lady Slipper*, for example, a moment comes at the end of the play where the three young women learn from a phone call that the love interest, John, has just died in a car accident. On stage, the revelation provokes laughter because of the accelerated and deceptively blasé presentation of events, but the moment was inspired by the actual death of Maxwell's brother-in-law. I would argue that the serious roots of the incident penetrate the staging. After the news of John's death has come, the three women hurriedly and unconvincingly sing the final song, "O how I loved you / I can't live without your love," after which they exit stoically and the play comes to an abrupt finish. The saccharine, trite harmonies contradict the weight of the moment as well as their stony facial expressions, yielding an effect more hollow than humorous. The absence of dialogue after the event suggests a milieu which, because it is incapable of expressing thought about events of such magnitude, makes a gesture at expression through the contemporary layman's poetry of a pop song, realizes the inadequacy of that gesture, and then shuts down into silence.

Although his work has been described as depicting awkwardness – a statement which must mainly be based on the young women portrayed in *Showy Lady Slipper* – most of the plays possess strong narratives with characters not afraid to make important – albeit sometimes circuitous – statements and to take decisive actions. *House* is a classic revenge narrative; *Cowboys and Indians* tells a story based on a true account of an 1846 journey across America's Oregon Trail; *Boxing 2000* also bears the marks of a classic tale of an underdog stepping into the ring. Whereas physical awkwardness almost always entails a restless shifting to and fro, Maxwell's actors remain still as statues for most of the dialogue, and when they move, they move with precision and economy.

In two of Maxwell's more recent works, one senses the director starting to wrestle with his own legacy. As Philippa Wehle has pointed out, the intonation used by several actors in *Boxing 2000* started to veer surprisingly close to what one might encounter in conventional psychological realism (78). The movement in that piece was also less restricted, as actors seemed less conscious of every move and in some cases twitched their arms and hands as they spoke – minimally compared to the work of most other artists, but for Maxwell there was an uncharacteristic amount of stage business. At about the time *Boxing 2000* was being developed in a workshop with NYU students, Maxwell wondered aloud if "maybe the way to go is the realism route. Maybe you almost have to play a trick on the audience [...] to convince them that there is no style. [...] The most common reaction I get from the audience is that it's about the formalistic nature of it, the stylization of it [...] Even though I understand it's probably unavoidable, it's something that gets under my skin" (Mufson, 2002a).

But in Maxwell's more recent work, *Drummer Wanted*, he has shied away from realism. The actors' movement – or lack thereof – regains its rigid artificiality. The line readings are again done with a feeling of highly attenuated but not completely deadened emotion. Here, however, in a story about a young man trying unsuccessfully to get his life in order, so that he can move out of his mother's house after having injured his leg in an accident, the two actors punctuate the dialogue and movement with jarring outbursts. Suddenly, an actor will break his or her quasi-monotone with a shouted phrase; a still pose will rupture into a paroxysm of movement.

The writing itself begins to deploy playful repetitions as well as an almost desultory logic, a sometimes almost surreal quality of incongruous juxtapositions, all of which serve as a type of *Verfremdungseffekt*. Towards the end of the play, the son, Frank, learns that he has won a $150,000 insurance settlement, but at about the same time, his relationship with his mother breaks down and she throws him out of the house. (The father, by the way, died long ago.) The last lines of the play are as follows:

MOM: Get out fucker.

(*pause*)

FRANK: What? What the hell was that? What are you talking about? Are you talking about breaking a vicious circle? I mean, I guess you are, because there's no other way out. Are you willing to take it to the next level? Willing to take the consequences of breaking a vicious circle? Because you don't know what that means. We don't know what that means. That's okay. I got balls, see? You saw 'em. I don't apologize for the money. I get the money. I get the money. The money is MINE. Don't look back like that. I can do it myself. Just got to break through it, I want to get at it. This is it Rey. I'm coming for ya. I'm outta here. I'm flyin' I see my opening. This is not a conflict with any of you this is a conflict with me. This is the easiest thing and I never saw it. All that agonizing over nothing. All the songs and pieces of songs. They're all on tape. 15 fucking years, dude. 5,000 miles of tape. But there's a lot of music left. It's all written down. I still have 'em all, and I can play them any time. That's the record. Right there. There's no other record than that. Tapes and tapes of it. That's the record. That's the circle. What do you know? It's about time. It's about time. It IS about time. Can you let go of the idea. Can I let go of the idea. Can I let go. Go with the flow. The idea makes me sick. But what would happen if I let go? Who knows. Might be nice! You never know. I want to let go. I want to let go so bad. I see the other side. It's a beautiful thing. But it takes balls, right? That's what you're saying? Well, I see your point. I know you. You're from my dream. And I never took you seriously. All those nights added up to something. They did didn't they. Here I am. Oh no. Oh no! There's the threshold, dude. Dad, I'm beginning to feel a little cheated. You were right... No need to worry.

Throughout that entire closing monologue, Frank and Mom stay motionless, and yet the language seems to imply several perceptive shifts and there are several points where one is no longer sure that Frank is addressing his mother. What Maxwell is proving himself expert at doing is exploring the means of balancing the emotional and intellectual engagement of the audience, communicating a point of view as a writer and director without pinning things down so narrowly as to remove all flexibility of interpretation.

In essence, Kimmel's and Maxwell's works signal that reports of the death of irony were, to say the least, premature, as both have taken different, provocative tacks in questioning the inherited techniques of the avant-garde without totally abandoning them, heating up the cooling effect of irony and making audiences wonder about the nature of "making it strange." Richard Kimmel's production of *Puss* seems as though it might have been a dead-end experiment that cannot be taken further; on the other hand, several critics, including myself, underestimated the potential variety of Maxwell's work when it first started to win widespread notice in 1998. Nevertheless, it is hard not to imagine *Puss* as a question about the benefits and burdens of the Wooster Group's legacies while Maxwell's work constitutes at least one possible answer – paradoxical and straightforward, self-conscious and sincere.

Works Cited

Ades, Richard. "Stimulating." *The Other Paper* (Columbus, OH) 16-22 Oct. 1997.

Adorno, Theodor W. "The Actuality of Philosophy." *Telos* 31 (1977): 120-33.

_____. *Negative Dialectics*. Trans. E.B. Ashton. New York: Seabury, 1973.

Agate, Nicky. "Stage proves a Valk in the park." *Sunday Herald* 11 June 2000.

Amin, Samir. *Spectres of Capitalism: A Critique of Current Intellectual Fashions*. New York: Monthly Review Press, 1998.

Arratia, Euridice. "Island Hopping: Rehearsing the Wooster Group's *Brace Up!*" *The Drama Review* 36.4 (T136) (Winter 1992): 121-142.

Aronson, Arnold. *American Avant-Garde Theatre: A History*. London: Routledge, 2000.

_____. "The Wooster Group's *L.S.D. (...Just the High Points...)*." *The Drama Review* 29.2 (T106) (Summer 1985): 65-77.

_____. *The History and Theory of Environmental Scenography*. Ann Arbor: UMI Research Press, 1981.

_____. "Sakonnet Point." *The Drama Review* 19.4 (1975): 27-35.

Atlan, Henri. *Entre le cristal et la fumée: Essai sur l'organisation du vivant.* Paris: Seuil, 1979.

Auslander, Philip. "Live From Cyberspace or, I was sitting at my computer this guy appeared he thought I was a bot." *Performing Arts Journal* 70 (2002): 16-21.

_____. *Liveness: Performance in a Mediatized Culture*. London: Routledge, 1999.

_____. *From Acting to Performance: Essays in Modernism and Postmodernism.* London: Routledge, 1997.

_____. *Presence and Resistance: Postmodernism and Cultural Politics in Contemporary American Performance*. Ann Arbor: Michigan UP, 1992.

_____. "Toward a Concept of the Political in Postmodern Theatre." *Theatre Journal* 39.1 (March 1987): 20-34. Rpt. in *From Acting to Performance* 58-72.

_____. "Task and Vision: Willem Dafoe in *L.S.D.*" *The Drama Review* 29.2 (T106) (Summer 1985): 94-98. Rpt. and extended in *From Acting to Performance* 39-45 and *Acting (Re)Considered*. Ed. Phillip Zarrilli. London: Routledge, 1995.

_____. "Staying Alive: The Living Theater in the '80s." *American Theatre* 1.4 (1984): 10-14.

Barthes, Roland. *Empire of Signs*. Trans. Richard Howard. New York: Farrar, Straus and Giroux, 1982.

_____. *Image – Music – Text*. Trans. Stephen Heath. New York: Noonday Press, 1977.

_____. *The Pleasure of the Text*. Trans. Richard Miller. London: Jonathan Cape, 1976; New York: Hill and Wang, 1987.

Benjamin, Walter. *Selected Writings*. Vol. 2, 1927-1934. Cambridge: Harvard UP, 1999.

_____. *The Origin of German Tragic Drama*. Trans. John Osborne. London and New York: Verso, 1998.

_____. *Understanding Brecht*. London: Verso, 1973.

Bennett, Susan. *Performing Nostalgia: Shifting Shakespeare and the Contemporary Past*. London: Routledge, 1996.

Bergson, Henri. *Matter and Memory*. Trans. N.M. Paul and W.S. Palmer. New York: Zone Books, 1991.

Bevington, David, and Eric Rasmussen, intro. and ed. *Doctor Faustus*. By Christopher Marlowe. Manchester UP, 1993.

Bierman, James. "*Three Places in Rhode Island*." *The Drama Review* 23.1 (1979): 13-29.

Birringer, Johannes. *Theatre, Theory, Postmodernism*. Bloomington: Indiana UP, 1991.

_____. "Debating 'Ways of Speaking, Loci of Cognition'." *The Drama Review* 32.2 (T118) (Summer 1988): 4-13.

Blau, Herbert. *Blooded Thought: Occasions of Theatre*. New York: Performing Arts Journal Publications, 1982.

_____. *Take Up the Bodies: Theatre at the Vanishing Point*. Urbana: Illinois UP, 1982.

Bloom, Harold. *The Anxiety of Influence: A Theory of Poetry*. Oxford: Oxford UP, 1997.

Bogard, Travis. *Contour in Time: The Plays of Eugene O'Neill*. New York: Oxford UP, 1988.

Bourcier, Jean-Pierre. "La folie Wooster au Centre Pompidou." *La Tribune* 19 Nov. 2001.

_____. "Docteur Faust, vidéos et petites pépées." *La Tribune* 13 Dec. 1999.

Bourdieu, Pierre. "The Production of Belief: Contribution to an Economy of Symbolic Goods." *The Field of Cultural Production: Essays on Art and Literature*. Ed. Randal Johnson. New York: Columbia UP, 1993. 74-111.

Bowers, Jane Palatini. *"They Watch Me as They Watch This": Gertrude Stein's Metadrama*. Philadelphia: Pennsylvania UP, 1991.

Bradby, David, and Maria M. Delgado, eds. *The Paris Jigsaw: Internationalism and the City's Stages*. Manchester: Manchester UP, 2002.

Bragg, Melvyn, ed. *South Bank Show:The Wooster Group*. London: Weekend Television, 1987.

Brantley, Ben. "Racine's Pale Queen, Struggling With Racket Sports." *New York Times* 19 Febr. 2002: E1+.

_____. "Watch It, Nellie Forbush, They're Rockin' the Boat." *New York Times* 18 Febr. 2000.

_____. "A Case for Cubism and Deals with Devils." *New York Times*, late ed., 3 Febr. 1999.

_____. "Chekhov Through a New Dimension." *New York Times* 22 Nov. 1994: C20.

Brecht, Bertolt. *Brecht on Theatre: The Development of an Aesthetic*. Ed. and trans. John Willett. London: Methuen, 1964.

Brietzke, Zander. Rev. of *The Emperor Jones*. By the Wooster Group. *Theatre Journal* 50.3 (Oct. 1998): 382-385.

Brown, Mark. "Theatre: House/Lights." *Scotland on Sunday* 18 June 2000.

Builders Association, The. 1997 <http://www.thebuildersassociation.org/_about_the_company>.

Bürger, Peter. *Theory of the Avant-Garde*. Trans. Michael Shaw. Minneapolis: Minnesota UP, 1984.

Butler, Judith. *The Psychic Life of Power: Theories in Subjection*. Stanford: Stanford UP, 1997.

Callens, Johan. "'Black is white, I yells it out louder 'n deir loudest': Unraveling the Wooster Group's *The Emperor Jones*." *The Eugene O'Neill Review* 26 (Spring 2004): 43-69.

_____. "From Dismemberment to Prosthetics: The Wooster Group's *House/Lights*." *Homo Orthopedicus: Le corps et ses prothèses à l'époque (post)moderniste*. Ed. Nathalie Roelens and Wanda Strauven. Paris: L'Harmattan, 2001. 393-415. Rpt. as "Going Public, Performing Stein." *Staging a Cultural Paradigm: The Political and the Personal in American Theatre and Drama*. Ed. Barbara Ozieblo and Miriam López-Rodriguez. Brussels: P.I.E.-Peter Lang, 2002. 113-130.

_____. "Negotiating Class and Gender Differences in the Wooster Group's Production of *The Hairy Ape*." *Culture and Power IV: Cultural Confrontations*. Ed. Chantal Cornut-Gentille D'Arcy. Zaragoza: Departamento de Filología Inglesa, 1999. 149-163.

_____. "*FinISHed Story*: Elizabeth LeCompte's Intercultural Take on Time and Work." *Anthropological Perspectives. Contemporary Drama in English* vol. 5. Ed. Werner Huber and Martin Middeke. Trier: Wissenschaftlicher Verlag, 1998. 143-158.

_____. "Sex, Lies, and Videotapes." *Andere Sinema* 127 (May-June 1995): 51-55.

Cameron, Neil. "Design: Tramway." *The Scotsman* 12 June 2000.

Carlson, Marvin. *The Haunted Stage: The Theatre as Memory Machine*. Ann Arbor: Michigan UP, 2001.

Carmody, Jim. "Creating the Theatrical Museum: Theatrical Visions of an Alternative America. Cultural Politics and the Festival d'Automne." Bradby and Delgado 248-266.

Cartwright, Lisa. *Screening the Body: Tracing Medicine's Visual Culture.* Minneapolis: Minnesota UP, 1995.

Case, Sue-Ellen. *The Domain-Matrix: Performing Lesbian at the End of Print Culture.* Bloomington: Indiana UP, 1996.

Causey, Matthew. "Posthuman Performance." *Crossings: eJournal of Art and Technology* 1.2. May 2002 <http://crossings.tcd.ie/issues/1.2/Causey>.

Chekhov, Anton. *Plays.* Trans. Elisaveta Fen. Harmondsworth: Penguin, 1959.

Cilliers, Paul. *Complexity and Postmodernism: Understanding Complex Systems.* New York: Routledge, 1998.

Clayburgh, Jim. "Letters." *Theatre Crafts* 18.4 (April 1984): 6.

Coe, Robert. "Making Two Lives and a Trilogy." *Village Voice* 11 Dec. 1978.

Cole, Susan Letzler. *Directors in Rehearsal.* London: Routledge, 1992.

Conti, Chris. "Double Talk: The Wooster Group's Kate Valk." *Columbus Alive* (Columbus, OH) 8-14 Oct. 1997: 12.

Cooley, John R. *Savages and Naturals.* Newark: Delaware UP., 1982.

Cooper, Neil. "Scottish Theatre: 'House/Lights'." *London Times* 16 June 2000.

Davis, Fred. *Yearning for Yesterday: A Sociology of Nostalgia.* New York: The Free Press, 1979.

de Baecque, Antoine, and René Solis. "Star superscénique." *Libération* 6 Dec. 2001.

Deleuze, Gilles. *Bergsonism.* Trans. Hugh Tomlinson and Barbara Habberjam. New York: Zone Books, 1990.

Deleuze, Gilles, and Felix Guattari. *Nomadology: The War Machine.* Trans. Brian Massumi. New York: Semiotext(e), 1986.

de Man, Paul. "Autobiography as De-Facement." *Rhetoric of Romanticism.* New York: Columbia UP, 1984. 67-81.

_____. *Allegories of Reading.* New Haven and London: Yale UP, 1979.

Demastes, William C. *Theatre of Chaos: Beyond Absurdism into Orderly Disorder.* Cambridge: Cambridge UP, 1998.

Derrida, Jacques. "La parole soufflée." *Writing and Difference.* Trans. Alan Bass. Chicago: Chicago UP, 1978. 169-95.

Dort, Bernard. "The Liberated Performance." Trans. Barbara Kerslake. *Modern Drama* 5.1 (1982): 60-67.

Drukman, Steven. Rev. of *Shut Up I Tell You (I Said Shut Up I Tell You).* By Elevator Repair Service. *Artforum* March 1996: 104.

Ehrenreich, Barbara and John. "The Professional-Managerial Class." *Between Labour and Capital.* Ed. Pat Walker. Montreal: Black Rose Books, 1979. 5-45.

Eisner, Lotte H. *Murnau*. Trans. Gertrud Mander. London: Secker and Warburg, 1973a [1964].

_____. *The Haunted Screen: Expressionism in the German Cinema and the Influence of Max Reinhardt*. Trans. Robert Greaves. Berkeley: California UP, 1973b [1965, 1952].

Eliot, T.S. "Tradition and the Individual Talent." *The Sacred Wood: Essays on Poetry and Criticism*. London: Faber and Faber, 1997.

Elsaesser, Thomas. *Weimar Cinema and After: Germany's Historical Imaginary*. London: Routledge, 2000.

Elsaesser, Thomas, and Adam Barker, eds. *Early Cinema: Space, Frame, Narrative*. London: British Film Institute, 1990.

Etchells, Tim. "Replaying the Tapes of the Twentieth Century: An Interview with Ron Vawter." *Certain Fragments: Contemporary Performance and Forced Entertainment*. Foreword Peggy Phelan. London: Routledge, 1999. 84-93.

Euripides. *The Bacchae*. Trans. William Arrowsmith. *The Complete Greek Tragedies: Euripides V*. Chicago: Chicago UP, 1959.

_____. *Bakkhai*. Trans. Reginald Gibbons. Oxford: Oxford UP, 2001.

Feingold, Michael. "North Pedantic." *Village Voice* 7 Febr. 1984.

Féral, Josette. "Performance: The Subject Demystified." *Modern Drama* 25.1 (1985): 170-80.

Ferney, Frédéric. "Un cabaret électrique. " *Le Figaro* 6 Dec. 2001.

Finter, Helga. "Die Theatralisierung der Stimme im Experimentaltheater." *Zeichen und Realität*. Ed. Klaus Oehler. Tübingen: Stauffenberg Verlag, 1984. 1007-1021.

_____. "Experimental Theatre and Semiology of Theatre: The Theatricalization of Voice." *Modern Drama* 26 (1983): 501-517.

Fischer-Lichte, Erika. "The Avant-Garde and the Semiotics of the Antitextual Gesture." *Contours of the Theatrical Avant-Garde: Performance and Textuality*. Harding 79-95.

Fisher, Mark. "Funny Peculiar." *The List* (Glasgow and Edinburgh) 25 May-8 June 1999.

Flaubert, Gustave. *The Temptation of Saint Antony*. Trans. Kitty Mrosovsky. Ithaca: Cornell UP, 1981.

_____. *Selected Letters*. Trans. Geoffrey Wall. Harmondsworth: Penguin, 1997.

Foley, Helene. *Ritual Irony: Poetry and Sacrifice in Euripides*. Ithaca: Cornell UP, 1985.

Foreman, Richard and Elizabeth LeCompte. "Off-Broadway's Most Inventive Directors Talk About Their Art [1994]." *Richard Foreman*. Ed. Gerarld Rabkin. Baltimore: Johns Hopkins UP, 1999. 133-142.

Foucault, Michel. *Language, Counter-Memory, Practice: Selected Essays and Interviews*. Ed. Donald F. Bouchard. Trans. Donald F. Bouchard and Sherry Simon. Ithaca: Cornell UP, 1977.

Frank, Tom. "Hip is Dead." *The Nation* 1 April 1996: 18.

Freud, Sigmund. "Das Ich und das Es." *Psychologie des Unbewußten.* Studie-nausgabe Band III. Frankfurt: Fischer, 1982. 273-330.

Frye, Northrop. *Anatomy of Criticism.* Princeton: Princeton UP, 1957.

Fuchs, Elinor. *The Death of Character: Perspectives on Theater After Modernism.* Bloomington: Indiana UP, 1996.

_____. "Presence and the Revenge of Writing: Re-Thinking Theatre after Derrida." *Performing Arts Journal* 26/27 (1984): 51-54.

Fusillier, Didier. "Destruction, Decomposition, Reconstruction." Statement of purpose for the 1994 Exit Festival.

Garner, Stanton B. *Bodied Spaces: Phenomenology and Performance in Contemporary Drama.* Ithaca: Cornell UP, 1994.

Gibb, Eddie. "Power Struggle." *Sunday Herald* 4 June 2000.

Giesekam, Greg. "The Wooster Group." *Postmodernism: The Key Figures.* Ed. Hans Bertens and Joseph Natoli. Oxford: Blackwell, 2002. 327-333.

_____. *Luvvies and Rude Mechanicals? Amateur and Community Theatre in Scotland.* Edinburgh: Scottish Arts Council, 2000.

Glenn, Bradley. "Re: ERS." E-mail to Julie Bleha. 12 Nov. 2000.

Godard, Colette. "Les États-Unis en images éclatées. " *Le Monde* 17 Nov. 1992.

Goldman, Albert, and Lawrence Schiller. *Ladies and Gentlemen, Lenny Bruce!!!* New York: Random House, 1974.

Gray, Spalding. "About *Three Places in Rhode Island.*" *The Drama Review* 23.1 (T81) (March 1979): 31-42.

Grogan, Molly. "'House/Lights' A postmodern dance with technology." *Paris Free Voice* Dec. 1999-Jan. 2000.

Grotowski, Jerzy. *Towards a Poor Theatre.* Ed. Eugenio Barba, intro. Peter Brook. New York: Touchstone, 1968.

Grünberg, Roland, and Monique Demerson, eds. *Nancy sur scène: au carrefour des théâtres du monde.* Nancy: Festival mondial du théâtre de Nancy, 1984.

Guay, Hervé. "Les plaisirs des choses complexes." *Le Devoir* (Montréal) 29-30 May 1999.

Gussow, Mel. "Stage: Wooster Group." *New York Times* 31 Oct. 1984: C28.

_____. "The Stage: 'Route 1 & 9'." *New York Times* 29 Oct. 1981: C15.

Halberstam, Judith, and Ira Livingston, eds. "Introduction." *Posthuman Bodies.* Bloomington: Indiana UP, 1995.

Hamacher, Werner. "(Das Ende der Kunst mit der Maske)." *Sprachen der Ironie-Sprachen des Ernstes.* Ed. Karl Heinz Bohrer. Frankfurt: Suhrkamp, 2000. 212-55.

Haraway, Donna. "A Cyborg Manifesto: Science, Technology, and Socialist Feminism in the Late Twentieth Century [1985]." *Simians, Cyborgs, and Women: The Reinvention of Nature.* New York: Routledge, 1991.

Harding, James, ed. *Contours of the Theatrical Avant-Garde: Performance and Textuality*. Ann Arbor: Michigan UP, 2000.

Hayles, N. Katherine. *How We Became Posthuman: Virtual Bodies in Cybernetics, Literature, and Informatics*. Chicago: Chicago UP, 1999.

Hayward, Susan. *Key Concepts in Cinema Studies*. London: Routledge, 1996.

Hegel, G.W.F. *Phänomenologie des Geistes*. *Werke* vol. 3. Frankfurt: Suhrkamp, 1986.

Highway to Tomorrow. Dir. John Collins and Steve Bodow. Perf. Paul Boocock, Rinne Groff, James Hannaham, Randall Curtis Rand, and Susie Sokol. Elevator Repair Service: video, 2000.

Holden, Stephen. "Critics' Choices: Theater." *New York Times* 1 Nov. 1987: 2A 2.

Iampolski, Mikhail. *Memory of Tiresias: Intertextuality and Cinema*. Berkeley: California UP, 1998.

Jameson, Fredric. "Pleasure : A Political Issue." *Formations of Pleasure*. Ed. Tony Bennett. London: Routledge & Kegan Paul, 1992. 1-14.

Jesurun, John. *Jump Cut (Faust)*. Ts. April 1998.

Jonas, Susan, Geoffrey Proehl, and Michael Lupu, eds. *Dramaturgy in American Theater: A Sourcebook*. Fort Worth: Harcourt Brace College Publishers, 1997.

Kalb, Jonathan. Rev. of *House/Lights*. *New York Press* 10-16 Febr. 1999.

Kaufman, David. "'House/Lights' not a shining hour: Meanings are dim in Wooster Group's offbeat Faust tale." *Daily News* (New York) 3 Febr. 1999.

Kershaw, Baz. "The Politics of Performance in a Postmodern Age." *Analysing Performance: A Critical Reader*. Ed. Patrick Campbell. Manchester: Manchester UP, 1996. 133-52.

Kittler, Friedrich. *Gramophone, Film, Typewriter*. Trans. Geoffrey Winthrop-Young and Michael Wutz. Stanford: Stanford UP, 1999.

Koschorke, Albrecht. "Platon/Schrift/Derrida." Neumann 40-51.

Kostelanetz, Richard, ed. *Gertrude Stein Advanced: An Anthology of Criticism*. Jefferson, NC: McFarland, 1990.

Lacan, Jacques. *Écrits: A Selection*. Trans. Alan Sheridan. New York: W.W. Norton & Co, 1977.

Lawliss, Chuck. *New York's Other Theatre Guide*. New York: Rutledge [*sic*], 1991.

LeCompte, Elizabeth. *A Video Interview with Lin Hixson*. Video Data Bank, 1990.

Lee, Pamela M. *Object to Be Destroyed: The Work of Gordon Matta-Clark*. Cambridge, MA: MIT Press, 2000.

Leich-Galland, Claire. "Un théâtre high-tech: le Wooster Group." *Du théâtre (la revue)* 16 (1997): 32-37.

Leon, Ruth. *Applause: New York's Guide to the Performing Arts*. New York: Applause, 1991.

Levine, Mindy. *New York's Other Theatre: A Guide to Off Off Broadway.* New York: Avon, 1981.

Lowenthall, David. "Nostalgia Tells It Like It Wasn't." *The Imagined Past: History and Nostalgia.* Ed. Malcolm Chase and Christopher Shaw. Manchester: Manchester UP, 1989.

Lyotard, Jean-François. "Acinema [1973]." *The Lyotard Reader.* Ed. Andrew Benjamin. Oxford: Basil Blackwell, 1989. 169-180.

Mahl, Bernd. *Goethes "Faust" auf der Bühne 1806-1997.* Stuttgart: Metzler Verlag, 1999.

Mahoney, Elisabeth. "Devil and the Detail." *The Guardian* 10 June 2000a.

_____. "A World Apart." *The Guardian* 5 June 2000b.

Matthews, Brander. *A Book About the Theatre.* New York: Charles Scribner's, 1916.

Maurin, Frédéric. "Did Paris Steal the Show for American Postmodern Directors?" Bradby and Delgado 232-247.

Maxwell, Richard. *Drummer Wanted.* Ts., 2001.

McGlone, Jackie. "Back on track." *Scotland on Sunday* 28 May 2000.

McGrath, John. *A Good Night Out.* London: Eyre Methuen, 1981.

McKenzie, Jon. *Perform or Else: From Discipline to Performance.* London: Routledge, 2001.

McMillan, Joyce. "Lights, Camera, Interaction." *The Scotsman* 12 June 2000.

McNulty, Charles. "Shuttlecock Tragedy in Brooklyn." *Village Voice* 5 March 2002.

_____. "Sons of Frankenstein." *Village Voice* 20 June 2000: 84.

Muecke, D.C. *Irony and the Ironic.* London: Methuen, 1982.

Menke, Bettine. "De Mans Prosopopöie der Lektüre. Die Entleerung des Monuments." *Ästhetik und Rhetorik. Lektüren zu Paul de Man.* Ed. Karl Heinz Bohrer. Frankfurt: Suhrkamp, 1993. 34-78.

_____. "Prosopopoiia. Die Stimme des Textes – die Figur des 'sprechenden' Gesichts." Neumann 1997: 226-251.

Mennessier, Florence. "Dafoe sur les planches." *Le Figaro* 23 Nov. 2001.

Merleau-Ponty, Maurice. *The Phenomenology of Perception.* Trans. Colin Smith. London: Routledge and Kegan Paul, 1962.

Meyer, Michael. *Ibsen.* Harmondsworth: Penguin Literary Biographies, 1985 [1974].

Meyer, Petra Maria. "Ästhetik des Gegenwartstheaters im technischen Zeitalter." *Theater der Region-Theater Europas.* Ed. Andreas Kotte. Bern: Theaterkultur Verlag, 1995. 369-384.

Michalzik, Peter. *Gustaf Gründgens: Der Schauspieler und die Macht.* Berlin: Quadriga Verlag, 1999.

Minwalla, Framji. "Postmodernism, or, the revenge of the onanists." *Theater* 23.1 (1992): 6-14.

Morse, Margaret. *Virtualities: Television, Media Art, and Cyberculture.* Bloomington: Indiana UP, 1998.

Mufson, Daniel. "The Hydras of Irony and Style." 15 April 2002a <http://www.alternativetheater.com/CommentaryMaxwellInterview.html>.

_____. "How Do You Make Strange What's Already Strange." 15 April 2002b <htttp://www.alternativetheater.com/CommentaryKimmelInterview.html>.

Neumann, Gerhard, ed. *Poststrukturalismus. Herausforderung an die Literaturwissenschaft.* Stuttgart: Metzler, 1997.

Nietzsche, Friedrich. *The Birth of Tragedy and Other Writings.* Ed. Raymond Geuss and Ronald Speirs. Trans. Ronald Speirs. Cambridge: Cambridge UP, 1999.

_____. *The Geneaology of Morals.* Trans. Francis Golffing. New York: Doubleday, 1956.

Obejas, Achy. "Wooster Group stuns the crowd with 'HOUSE/LIGHTS'." *Chicago Tribune* 14 Nov., 1997.

O'Neill, Eugene. *The Hairy Ape. The Collected Plays of Eugene O'Neill.* Intro. John Lahr. London: Jonathan Cape, 1988. 428-449.

_____. *The Emperor Jones.* New York: Vintage, 1972.

Owens, Craig. "The Allegorical Impulse: Toward a Theory of Postmodernism." *Beyond Recognition: Representation, Power, and Culture.* Ed. Scott Bryson et al. Berkeley: California UP, 1992. 52-87.

Parker-Starbuck, Jennifer. Rev. of *Triangulated Nation* by George Coates and *Lizard Monitors* by Cathy Weis. *Theatre Journal* 51.4 (1999): 445-450.

Pavis, Patrice. *Analyzing Performance: Theater, Dance and Film.* Trans. David Williamson. Ann Arbor: Michigan UP, 2003.

Peitz, Christiane. "Der Leibhaftige [The Devil]." *Die Zeit Magazin* 13 June 1997: 12.

Perrier, Jean-Louis. "De New York à la Bastille, les feux de la rampe enflamment le théâtre." *Le Monde* 14 Dec. 1999.

Pontbriand, Chantal. "The eye finds no fixed point on which to rest..." Trans. C.R. Parsons. *Modern Drama* 25.1 (1985): 154-58.

Poole, Gabriele. "'Blarsted Niggers!': *The Emperor Jones* and Modernism's Encounter with Africa." *Eugene O'Neill Review* 18.1 (1994): 21-37.

Prigogine, Ilya, and Isabelle Stengers. *Order out of Chaos: Man's New Dialogue with Nature.* New York: Bantam, 1984.

Rabkin, Gerald. "The Play of Misreading: Text/Theater/Deconstruction." *Performing Arts Journal* 19 (1983): 42-47.

Rich, Frank. "Theater: 'Atlantic,' Mixed-Media Work." *New York Times* 1 Febr. 1984: C16.

Rohmer, Eric. *L'organisation de l'espace dans le "Faust" de Murnau.* Paris: Union Générale d'Editions, 1977.

Rosten, Bevya. "The Gesture of Illogic." Interview with Kate Valk. *American Theatre* Febr. 1998: 16-19.

R.S.. "Culture et la lumière Faust: La pièce du Wooster Group de New York jette sur le mythe un éclairage désaxé." *Libération* 10 Dec.1999.

Russell, Mark. "The Happy Awkward Moment: Performance Theater's Intimate Surprise." *Village Voice* 28 May 2002.

Ryan, Betsy Alayne. *Gertrude Stein's Theatre of the Absolute.* Ann Arbor: UMI Research, 1984.

Saul, Nicholas. "Aesthetic Humanism." *The Cambridge History of German Literature.* Ed. Helen Watanabe-O'Kelly. Cambridge: Cambridge UP, 1997.

Savran, David. "Revolution... History... Theatre: The Politics of the Wooster Group's Second Trilogy." *The Performance of Power: Theatrical Discourses and Politics.* Ed. Sue-Ellen Case and Janelle Reinelt. Iowa City: Iowa UP, 1991. 41-55.

_____. "Adaptation as Clairvoyance: The Wooster Group's *Saint Antony.*" *Theater* 18.1 (Winter 1986-87): 36-41.

_____. *Breaking the Rules: The Wooster Group, 1975-1985.* Foreword Peter Sellars. Ann Arbor: UMI Research Press, 1986; New York: Theatre Communications Group, 1988.

Schechner, Richard. "Ron Vawter: For the Record." *The Drama Review* 37.3 (Fall 1993).

_____. "Ways of Speaking, Loci of Cognition." *The Drama Review* 31.3 (T115) (Fall 1987): 4-7.

_____. "The Decline and Fall of the (American) Avant-Garde: Why It Happened and What We Can Do About It." *Performing Arts Journal* 5.2 (1981): 48-63 (Part One); 5.3 (1981): 9-19 (Part Two).

_____. *Environmental Theater.* New York: Hawthorn Books, 1973.

Schlegel, Friedrich. "Zur Philosophie [1797]." *Philosophische Lehrjahre 1796-1806, Erster Teil.* Ed. Ernst Behler. Kritische Ausgabe vol. 18. Zürich: Thomas Verlag, 1963.

Schmidt, Paul. "Introduction." *Three Sisters.* By Anton Chekhov. New York: Theatre Communications Group, 1992.

_____. *Racine's "Phèdre. "* Ts., 1993.

_____. *Phèdre. Theater* 30.1 (2000): 102-127.

Schmidt, Paul, ed. *Meyerhold at Work.* New York: Applause Books, 1996 [1980].

Schröter, Klaus. *Thomas Mann in Selbstzeugnissen und Bilddokumenten.* Reinbeck bei Hamburg: Rowohlt, 1964.

Seabrook, John. *Nobrow: The Culture of Marketing, the Marketing of Culture.* New York: Knopf, 2000.

Segal, Charles. *Dionysiac Poetics and Euripides' Bacchae.* Expanded Edition. Princeton: Princeton UP, 1997.

Seidensticker, Bernd. "Comic Elements in Euripides' *Bacchae.*" *American Journal of Philology* 99 (1978): 303-20.

Shaw, George Bernard. *Major Critical Essays*. Harmondsworth: Penguin, 1986 [1891, 1895].

Shewey, Don. "Not Either/Or But And: Fragmentation and Consolidation in the Post-modern Theatre of Peter Sellars." *Contemporary American Theatre*. Ed. Bruce King. London: Macmillan, 1991. 263-282.

Siegmund, Gerald. "Das Phantasma des Kastraten." *Kontingenz und Ord*. Ed. Bernhard Greiner and Maria Moog-Grünewald. Heidelberg: Carl Winter Verlag, 2000. 117-131.

Silvermann, Kaja. *The Acoustic Mirror. The Female Voice in Psychoanalysis and Cinema*. Bloomington: Indiana UP, 1988.

Simpson, Charles R. *SoHo: The Artists in the City*. Chicago: Chicago UP, 1981.

Sinfield, Alan. *The Wilde Century*. London: Cassell, 1994.

Smith, Susan Harris. *American Drama: The Bastard Art*. Cambridge: Cambridge UP, 1997.

Solis, René. "Double secousse US à Bordeaux. " *Libération* 14-15 Nov. 1992.

_____. "Croisière en loufoquerie." *Libération* 16 Nov. 2001.

Solis, René, and Marie-Christine Vernay. "Créteil, états d'Amérique." *Libération* 4 May 1994.

Soloski, Alexis. "Garage Music." *Village Voice* 14-20 July 1999.

Sotinel, Thomas. "Willem Dafoe en son garage." *Le Monde, Supplément Festival d'Automne* 15 Sept. 2001.

Stasio, Marilyn. "*North Atlantic* Armed with Lots of Serviceable Laughs." *New York Post* 22 Febr.1984.

Steele, Mike. "Combination of Stein, soft porn is beguiling." *Star Tribune* 22 Nov. 1997.

Stein, Gertrude. "Plays." *Last Operas and Plays*. Ed. Carl Van Vechten, intro. Bonnie Marranca. Baltimore: Johns Hopkins UP, 1995 [1949]. xxix-lii.

Stoppard, Tom. *Arcadia*. London: Faber and Faber, 1993.

Stratton, Jim. *Pioneering in the Urban Wilderness*. New York: Urizon, 1977.

Thomson, Robert. "Way Back." *City Live* 6 June-5 Aug. 2000.

Turner, Darwin T. *Black Drama in America: An Anthology*. Greenwich: Fawcett Publications, 1971.

Usmiani, Renate. *Second Stage: The Alternative Theatre Movement in Canada*. Vancouver: British Columbia UP, 1983.

Vacche, Angela Dalle. *Cinema and Painting: How Art Is Used in Film*. London: Athlone, 1997.

Vanden Heuvel, Michael. "'Mais je dis le chaos positif': Leaky Texts, Parasited Performances, and Maxwellian Academons." Harding 2000: 130-153.

_____. "Waking the Text: Disorderly Order in the Wooster Group's *Route 1 & 9 (The Last Act)*." *Journal for Dramatic Theory and Criticism* 10.1 (Fall 1995): 59-76.

_____. "The Politics of the Paradigm: A Case Study in Chaos Theory." *New Theatre Quarterly* 9.35 (1993): 255-66.

_____. *Performing Drama/ Dramatizing Performance: Alternative Theater and the Dramatic Text.* Ann Arbor: Michigan UP, 1991.

Virilio, Paul, and Sylvère Lotringer. *Pure War.* New York: Semiotext(e), 1983.

von Becker, Peter. "Faust Fiction: Theater und Video in Zürich: *Imperial Motel*, eine transatlantische Goethe-Phantasie." *Die Zeit* 1 Nov. 1996.

Wehle, Philippa. "Rich Maxwell: Dramatizing the Mundane." *TheatreForum* 18 (2001): 75-80.

Wilshire, Bruce. *Role Playing and Identity.* Bloomington: Indiana UP, 1982.

Wooster Group, The. *Frank Dell's The Temptation of St. Antony. Plays for the End of the Century.* Ed. and intro. Bonnie Marranca. Baltimore: Johns Hopkins UP, 1996. 261-314.

_____. *Point Judith. Zone* 7 (1980): 14-27.

Yates, Frances. *The Art of Memory.* London: Routledge and Kegan Paul, 1966.

Zimmerman, Mark. "Some Sort of Awakening." *Performing Arts Journal* 20.2 (1998): 40-48.

Zutkin, Sharon. *Loft Living: Culture and Capital in Urban Change.* Baltimore: Johns Hopkins UP, 1982.

Notes on Contributors

Philip AUSLANDER is Professor in the School of Literature, Communication,and Culture of the Georgia Institute of Technology. His books include *Presence and Resistance: Postmodernism and Cultural Politics in Contemporary American Performance* (Michigan UP, 1992), *From Acting to Performance: Essays in Modernism and Postmodernism* (Routledge, 1997), and *Liveness: Performance in a Mediatized Culture* (Routledge, 1999). He also edited the four-volume collection on performance for Routledge's Critical Concepts in Literary and Cultural Studies Series of reference works (2003). In addition to his work on performance, Prof. Auslander writes art criticism for *ArtForum* and other publications.

Roger BECHTEL, Assistant Professor in the School of Theatre Arts at Illinois Wesleyan University, received his PhD in Dramatic Theory and Criticism from Cornell University and his MFA in Acting from the Yale School of Drama. He has directed and acted Off-Broadway and in a number of regional theatres, and served as Artistic Director for the Zeitgeist Café Theatre in New York. He has published articles and reviews in *The Journal of Dramatic Theory and Criticism*, *Contemporary Literary Criticism*, and *Theatre Journal*, among others, and has just finished a book manuscript titled *Making History: American Theatre and the Historical Imagination*. Dr. Bechtel also holds a JD from the New York University School of Law and wrote *Two Strikes*, a play dealing with contemporary labor issues.

Julie BLEHA is a New York City-based director, dramaturg, and educator. She has worked with numerous downtown NYC companies, most recently Target Margin Theater; she has also worked with London's Shared Experience Theatre and the Gate Theatre. She has taught at Columbia University, Fordham University, and the New School. She holds graduate degrees from King's College, London/Royal Academy of Dramatic Arts, and Columbia University.

Johan CALLENS teaches at the Vrije Universiteit Brussel. He is the author of *Double Binds: Existentialist Inspiration and Generic Experimentation in the Early Work of Jack Richardson* (Rodopi, 1993), *Acte(s) de Présence* (VUB Press, 1996), and *From Middleton and Rowley's "Changeling" to Sam Shepard's "Bodyguard": A Contemporary Appropriation of a Renaissance Drama* (Edwin Mellen, 1997). He has also edited two volumes of *Contemporary Theatre Review* on

Sam Shepard (Routledge, 1998) and a special issue of the journal
Degrés on intermediality (2000).

Ehren FORDYCE teaches directing and contemporary performance in
the Drama Department at Stanford University. Previously he has published work on Samuel Beckett, American avant-garde director and
author Reza Abdoh, and late 20th-century American experimental
drama. Currently he is writing on late 20th-century experimental staging practices.

Greg GIESEKAM is Senior Lecturer in Theatre Studies at the University
of Glasgow. He has published on a wide range of subjects including
community theatre, live art, writers as diverse as Sophocles, Osborne
and Pinter, and companies such as the Wooster Group, Forkbeard
Fantasy, and Glasgow's Citizens Theatre. He is currently writing a
study on the use of film and video in theatre, to be published by Pal-
grave Macmillan in 2005.

Branislav JAKOVLJEVIĆ specializes in modernist theatre and the avant-
garde. He completed his undergraduate studies in Belgrade, Yugoslavia, and his graduate studies in the Department of Performance Studies, NYU, where he also taught in the Drama Department. He is an
Assistant Professor in the Department of Theatre Arts and Dance, at
the University of Minnesota, Minneapolis. His articles have been published in the United States (*The Drama Review*, *PAJ*, *Theater*) and
abroad (Yugoslavia, Spain, England). His current research is focused
on the event in relation to performance.

Simon JONES is Reader in Performance within the Department of
Drama, Theatre, Film and Television at Bristol University. His re-
search interests include rhetoric and poststructuralist theory; pragmat-
ics of creativity in theatre; modern British theatre; Elizabethan and
Jacobean drama; and performance theory and work. He writes for and
directs *Bodies in Flight* theatre company. Productions of his include
Constants: A Future Perfect (1998), documented in *Performance Re-
search: On Memory* 5.3 (Winter 2000), and *Double Happiness: A
Transport* (2000), a multi-media performance with accompanying
Website *www.doublehappines2.com*, showcased in Singapore, Bristol,
Nottingham, Manchester, and Loughborough.

Ric KNOWLES is Professor of Drama at the University of Guelph, and
Editor of the journals *Modern Drama* and *Canadian Theatre Review*.
He has also edited *Theatre in Atlantic Canada* (Mount Allison, 1988)
and co-edited *Staging Coyote's Dream* (with Monique Mojica, Playwrights Canada, 2003) and *Modern Drama: Defining the Field* (with
Joanne Tompkins and W.B. Worthen, Toronto UP, 2003). He is the
author of *The Theatre of Form and the Production of Meaning* (ECW,

1999), *Shakespeare and Canada* (P.I.E.-Peter Lang, 2004), and *Reading the Material Theatre* (Cambridge UP, 2004).

Bonnie MARRANCA is the editor of *PAJ: A Journal of Performance and Art* and author of *American Playwrights: A Critical Survey* (1981, with Guatam Dasgupta), *Theatre Writings* (1984), and *Ecologies of Theater* (1996). She also edited *The Theater of Images* (1978, rpt. 1995), *American Dreams: The Imagination of Sam Shepard* (1981), *American Garden Writing: An Anthology* (1988, 2003), *Hudson Valley Lives* (1992, rpt. as *Hudson Valley Reader*, 1995), *Plays for the End of the Century* (1996), and *A Slice of Life: Writing on Food* (2003). With Gautam Dasgupta she co-edited *Theatre of the Ridiculous* (revised 1979 & 1997), Lee Breuer's *Animations: A Trilogy for Mabou Mines* (1979), Stein's *Last Operas and Plays* (1994), *Geographical History of America or the Relation of Human Nature to Human Mind* (1995), and *Conversations on Art and Performance* (1999).

Frédéric MAURIN is professor in the Theatre Department, Université du Québec à Montréal. He has published a book on Robert Wilson, *Le temps pour voir, l'espace pour écouter* (Actes Sud, 1998), edited a book on Peter Sellars (CNRS Editions, 2003) and written a number of articles for collections as well as journals such as *Théâtre/Public*, *Contemporary Theatre Review*, *art press*; *Cahiers de théâtre JEU*.

Daniel MUFSON is a writer living in Berlin. He has taught theatre at Yale University and Brooklyn College-CUNY, and his essays and interviews have appeared in *Theater*, *The Drama Review*, *Theatre Journal*, *American Theatre*, *Village Voice*, and Germany's *Theater Heute*, among others. He edited the anthology, *Reza Abdoh*, for Performing Arts Journal Publications, under its Johns Hopkins University Press imprint.

Jennifer PARKER-STARBUCK is a lecturer in Theatre and Performance Studies at the Scarborough School of Arts at the University of Hull, England. She received her PhD from the City University of New York, Graduate Center. Her current book project, entitled *Cyborg Theatre: Corporeal/Technological Intersections in Multimedia*, investigates multimedia performance and contemporary subjectivity. Her essays and reviews have appeared in *Theatre Journal*, *PAJ*, *The Journal of Dramatic Theory and Criticism*, *Western European Stages*, *Didaskalia*, and *Slavic and East European Performance*, for which she acted as managing editor (1996-2000).

David SAVRAN holds the newly established Vera Mowry Roberts Chair in American Theatre at the City University of New York, Graduate Center. Savran's major publications include: *Breaking the Rules: The Wooster Group* (1988), *In Their Own Words: Contemporary American Playwrights* (1988), *Communists, Cowboys, and Queers: The Politics* *of Masculinity in the Work of Arthur Miller and Tennessee Williams* (1992), *Taking It Like a Man: White Masculinity, Masochism, and Contemporary American Culture* (1998), *The Playwright's Voice: American Dramatists on Memory, Writing, and the Politics of Culture* (1999), and *A Queer Sort of Materialism: Recontextualizing American Theatre* (2003). He is the editor of the *Journal of American Drama and Theatre* and associate editor of *Theatre Journal*.

Gerald SIEGMUND studied Theatre, English and French Literature at the Johann Wolfgang Goethe-Universität Frankfurt/Main. Completed in 1994, his PhD thesis on "Theatre as Memory" linked the theatrical experience to concepts of memory derived from Freudian psycho-analysis. In 1998 he joined the staff of the Department of Applied Theatre Studies at the Justus-Liebig-Universität, Giessen, where he is still teaching. Since 1995 he has been working as a free lance dance and performance critic for *Frankfurter Allgemeine Zeitung, Ballettanz* and *Dance Europe*. He has published widely on contemporary dance and theatre performance, and edited and introduced the richly illus-trated *William Forsythe: Denken in Bewegung* (Henschel Verlag, 2004).

Michael VANDEN HEUVEL is Professor and Chair of the Department of Theatre and Drama at the University of Wisconsin-Madison. His es-says on the Wooster Group have appeared in his book *Performing Drama/Dramatizing Performance: Alternative Theater and the Dra-matic Text* and in periodicals such as *New Theatre Quarterly* and *The Journal of Dramatic Theory and Criticism*. He is currently at work on a study of theatre and complexity tentatively entitled "'Congregations Rich with Entropy': Theatre and the Emergence of Complexity," as well as an introduction to theatre theory for Blackwell Publishers.

Markus WESSENDORF is an Assistant Professor at the Department of Theatre and Dance at the University of Hawai'i at Manoa. His publica-tions include a monograph on Richard Foreman's Ontological-Hysteric Theatre, *Die Bühne als Szene des Denkens* (Alexander Ver-lag, 1998), as well as numerous essays on Bertolt Brecht, Richard Maxwell, the Wooster Group, Ron Athey, and contemporary drama in Hawai'i.

Dramaturgies

Texts, Cultures and Performances

This series presents innovative research work in the field of twentieth-Century dramaturgy, primarily in the anglophone and francophone worlds. Its main purpose is to re-assess the complex relationship between textual studies, cultural and/or performance aspects at the dawn of this new multicultural millennium. The series offers discussions of the link between drama and multiculturalism (studies of minority playwrights – ethnic, aboriginal, gay and lesbian), reconsiderations of established playwrights in the light of contemporary critical theories, studies of the interface between theatre practice and textual analysis, studies of marginalized theatrical practices (circus, vaudeville, etc.), explorations of the emerging postcolonial drama, research into new modes of dramatic expressions and comparative or theoretical drama studies.

The Series Editor, **Marc MAUFORT**, is Professor of English literature and drama at the Université Libre de Bruxelles.

Series Titles

No.13– Johan CALLENS (ed.), *The Wooster Group and Its Traditions*, 2004, ISBN 90-5201-270-9

No.12– Malgorzata BARTULA & Stefan SCHROER, *On Improvisation. Nine Conversations with Roberto Ciulli*, 2003, ISBN 90-5201-185-0

No.11– Peter ECKERSALL, UCHINO Tadashi & MORIYAMA Naoto (eds.), *Alternatives. Debating Theatre Culture in the Age of Con-Fusion*, 2004, ISBN 90-5201-175-3

No.10– Rob BAUM, *Female Absence. Women, Theatre, and Other Metaphors*, 2003, ISBN 90-5201-172-9

No.9– Marc MAUFORT, *Transgressive Itineraries. Postcolonial Hybridizations of Dramatic Realism*, 2003 (second printing 2004), ISBN 90-5201-990-8

No.8– Ric KNOWLES, *Shakespeare and Canada: Essays on Production, Translation, and Adaptation*, 2004, ISBN 90-5201-989-4

No.7– Barbara OZIEBLO & Miriam LÓPEZ-RODRIGUEZ (eds.), *Staging a Cultural Paradigm. The Political and the Personal in American Drama*, 2002, ISBN 90-5201-990-8

No.6– Michael MANHEIM, *Vital Contradictions. Characterization in the Plays of Ibsen, Strindberg, Chekhov and O'Neill*, 2002, ISBN 90-5201-991-6

No.5– Bruce BARTON, *Changing Frames. Medium Matters in Selected Plays and Films of David Mamet* (provisional title) (forthcoming), ISBN 90-5201-988-6

No.4– Marc MAUFORT & Franca BELLARSI (eds.), *Crucible of Cultures. Anglophone Drama at the Dawn of a New Millennium*, 2002 (second printing 2003), ISBN 90-5201-982-7

No.3– Rupendra GUHA MAJUMDAR, *Central Man. The Paradox of Heroism in Modern American Drama*, 2003, ISBN 90-5201-978-9

No.2– Helena GREHAN, *Mapping Cultural Identity in Contemporary Australian Performance*, 2001, ISBN 90-5201-947-9

No.1– Marc MAUFORT & Franca BELLARSI (eds.), *Siting the Other. Re-visions of Marginality in Australian and English-Canadian Drama*, 2001, ISBN 90-5201-934-7